GO
WITH
GOD

JIM BISHOP

GO
WITH
GOD

McGRAW-HILL BOOK COMPANY, INC.

NEW YORK / TORONTO / LONDON

GO WITH GOD

Library of Congress Catalog Card Number: 58-13856

FIRST EDITION

P 1

"For the Freedom of Mankind" by Stephen Vincent Benét, from *We Stand United and Other Radio Scripts*, Rinehart & Company, Inc. Copyright, 1942, by Stephen Vincent Benét. By permission of Brandt & Brandt.

"Lenten Prayer" by Walter Russell Bowie, from *Lift Up Your Hearts*, Abingdon Press. Copyright © 1939, 1956 by Pierce & Washabaugh. By permission of Abingdon Press.

"O God of Earth and Altar," by G. K. Chesterton, from *The Revised Church Hymnary*, The Oxford University Press, London. Words copyright. By permission of the publisher.

"Chorus (of Women of Canterbury)" by T. S. Eliot, from *Murder in the Cathedral*, Faber & Faber, Ltd. and Harcourt, Brace, and Company, Inc. Copyright, 1935, by Harcourt, Brace, and Company, Inc. By permission of the publishers.

"As Cherry Blossoms Fall," by Dr. Hachiroa Yuasa; "Like the Gallant Carp," by Dr. Hachiroa Yuasa; "As Mt. Fuji," by Dr. Hachiroa Yuasa; "A Teacher's Prayer," by Gabriela Mistral; "Bedtime Prayer for a Japanese Girl," by Dr. Hachiroa Yuasa; "Thanksgiving at Harvest"; "In Tune"; "Gilbert Islands Prayer"; "To the Good and Great Doctor"; "A Prayer for the Rising of the Nile" from the Coptic Liturgy; "The Sea of Thy Love," from the *Clementine Liturgy;* from *The World at One in Prayer* by Daniel J. Fleming, Harper & Brothers. Copyright, 1942, by Harper & Brothers. By permission of the publisher.

"For Those Who Struggle with Doubt" and "For Those Who Have Passed On" by John Hunter, from *Devotional Services*, E. P. Dutton & Co., Inc., and J. M. Dent & Sons, Ltd. By permission of the publishers.

"Nebuchadnezzar to Marduk" from *The Civilization of Babylonia and Assyria* by Morris Jastrow. Copyright 1915 by J. B. Lippincott Company. By permission of the publisher.

"Thou Hearest Our Cry" by Søren Kierkegaard, from *The Sickness unto Death*, translated by Walter Lowrie. Princeton University Press, 1944. By permission of the publisher.

"New Year's Day" by Søren Kierkegaard, from *Edifying Discourses*, translated by David F. Swenson and Lillian Marvin Swenson, Augsburg Publishing House. Copyright, 1943, by Augsburg Publishing House. By permission of the publisher.

"Let Me Not Be Discouraged" by Søren Kierkegaard, from *The Prayers of Kierkegaard* by Perry LeFevre; University of Chicago Press. Copyright © 1956 by University of Chicago. By permission of the publishers.

"Prayer of a Soldier in France" by Joyce Kilmer, from *Poems, Essays, and Letters,* Doubleday & Company, Inc. Copyright, 1918, by George H. Doran. By permission of Doubleday & Company, Inc.

"The Cross the Inspiration," "For Children," by Samuel McComb, from *A Book of Prayers*, Dodd, Mead & Co., Inc. By permission of the publisher.

"Restoration," "Good Friday," "The Strains of Life," "For the Transforming of Everyday Life," "In Sickness," "In Time of New Bereavement" by Peter Marshall, from *The Prayers of Peter Marshall*, McGraw-Hill Book Company, Inc. Copyright, 1949, 1950, 1951, 1954, by Catherine Marshall. By permission of the publisher and Catherine Marshall.

"Prayer for America" by Charles Wolcott Merriam (originally entitled "Prayer of Humility") from *Church Worship Book*, The Pilgrim Press. Copyright, 1931, The Pilgrim Press. Used by permission.

W I

"Collect for Ash Wednesday," "Collect for Palm Sunday," "Whitsunday," "Collect for First Sunday in Advent," "First Sunday after Christmas," "Canticle," "Benediction," "Morning Prayer," "In a Humble Sense," "We Confess," from *The Book of Common Prayer*, Oxford University Press, 1932. Reprinted by permission of Reverend John Wallace Suter, D.D., custodian of *The Book of Common Prayer*.

"Communion," "For Healing," "For Our Enemies" by Henry van Dyke, "For Brotherhood of Man," from *The Book of Common Worship*, The Westminster Press.

"Palm Sunday," "Good Friday" from *A Book of Worship for Free Churches*, The Board of Home Missions of the Congregational and Christian Churches. Copyright, 1948, by The Board of Home Missions of the Congregational and Christian Churches. All rights reserved. By permission of the publisher.

"The General Prayer" from *Common Service Book of the United Lutheran Church*, The United Lutheran Church in America. By permission of the publisher.

"An Intercession for the Churches of Christendom" from *Federal Council of Churches Bulletin*, 1940. By permission of the National Council of Churches of Christ.

"For the Sick and Sorrowing" from *The Ordinal and Service Book of the Church of Scotland*. By permission of the Church of Scotland Committee on Public Worship and Aids to Devotion.

"In the Sacrament of Motherhood" from *Prayers of Health and Healing*. The Student Christian Movement Press, Ltd. By permission of the publisher.

"Regina Coeli," "The Litany of the Most Holy Name of Jesus," "The Litany of the Blessed Virgin," "The Litany of the Sacred Heart of Jesus" from *The Raccolta*, compiled by Joseph P. Christopher, Charles E. Spence, and John F. Rowan, copyright on translation by Benziger Brothers, 1952. By permission of the publisher.

"Sukkoth," "Rock of Ages," "Purim," "Passover Prayer," "Shabuoth," "Sabbath Prayer." "Kiddush Services in the Home," "Introductory Prayer to the Kaddish," "Olenu" from *Union Prayer Book*. By permission of the Central Conference of American Rabbis.

"Hymn to Brahman" from *Upanishads*. Copyright by Vedanta Society of Southern California. Hardbound edition published by Vedanta Press, 1946, Vedanta Place, Hollywood, 28; paperback edition published by New American Library. Reprinted by permission of the Vedanta Society of Southern California.

"Abraham's Prayer" and "Praise Be to God" from *The Koran*, George Allen & Unwin, Ltd. By permission of the publisher.

"Bedtime Prayer" from *Prayers for Little Children* by Lucy W. Peabody, The Central Committee of the United Study of Foreign Missions.

"The Grandeur of the Holy Day" from *High Holyday Prayer Book*, translated by Philip Birnbaum; Hebrew Publishing Company. By permission of the publisher.

"Prayer" by John Galsworthy from *Moods, Songs, and Doggerels*. Charles Scribner's Sons and William Heinemann, Ltd. By permission of the publishers and of R. H. Sauter for the Estate of John Galsworthy.

"A Young Person's Prayer" and "Before a Surgical Operation" by John Underwood Stephens, from *Prayers of the Christian Life*. Copyright, 1952, by Oxford University Press. Reprinted by permission.

"Invocations of the Blessed Virgin," "To the Mother of God," "A Morning Hymn," "Prayer to Almighty God," "Easter Prayer," "Prayer for Divine Aid," "Invocations of the Immaculate Virgin to Achieve Purity," "Against Darkness of Mind," "For Compliance of God's Will," "In a Time of Desolations," "For the Divine Union," "An Act of Commiseration," "Prayer during Suffering" from *The Saints at Prayer*, edited by Raymond Ellsworth Larsson, Coward-McCann, Inc. Copyright, 1942, by Raymond E. F. Larsson. By permission of the publisher.

"Common and Proper Preface for Christmas" and "Sanctus" from the *Liturgy and Hymnal of the Lutheran Church*. By permission of the Permanent Commission on the Liturgy and Hymnal of the Lutheran Church in America.

"Hindu Prayer" and "Hindu Prayer to Buddha" from *Rig-Veda Brahmanas*, translated from the original Sanskrit by Arthur Berriedale Keith, 1920, Harvard Oriental Series, volume 25, Harvard University Press. By permission of the publisher.

"For the Fulfilment of God's Purpose for Our Lives" by John S. Hoyland, from *A Book of Prayers, Written for Use in an Indian College*, Society for Promoting Christian Knowledge. By permission of the publisher.

"Hymn to Osiris" from *An Anthology of World Poetry* by Mark van Doren, Harcourt, Brace and Company, Inc. By permission of the publisher.

"Prayer," suggested by a passage from *Arrowsmith* by Sinclair Lewis, Harcourt, Brace and Company, Inc. Copyright, 1925, by Harcourt, Brace and Company, Inc. Renewed by Michael Lewis. By permission of the publisher.

The author would like to acknowledge his thanks for the generous cooperation of the contributors to the "Prayers of Famous Contemporaries" section.

Dedicated
to our first grandchildren
the twins
Robin Frechette and Pamela Frechette

FOR THE RECORD

THE READER OF A BOOK like this is sometimes left with the feeling that the author is a holy man. I'm not. I disavow it because I do not want to add hypocrisy to my other sins. From where I sit writing this, there is a view across the Shrewsbury River and a steeple shows in the distance above the trees. This is Holy Cross Roman Catholic Church in Rumson, New Jersey. It is my church. The pastor, Father Joseph Sullivan, is my pastor.

I attend this church regularly. However, if one could peer into the heart of the pastor, my name would not be found among his better parishioners. I might be listed under the category "average." In no sense could I be called a pillar of my church. And yet I believe in my church and my God to the fullest and cannot imagine any greater catastrophe than falling away from them.

Once my mother thought that I might become a priest. It was a small, secret ambition of hers. I did not share it. Priests, I felt then, were austere instruments of God who could stare at one's eyes and see the blackness of the soul. I was afraid of them.

Years later, I wrote a book entitled *The Day Christ Died*. My father read part of it to my mother because she was then blind. She was snowy and small and prim. She listened to the words about the last hours of the Saviour's life and she smiled. "Jim would have made a good priest," she said quietly. It was the nicest, and most forlorn, thing she could have said.

We have always been a prayerful family. Prayer, like the payment of just debts, is a matter of good habit. We were taught to pray on arising, on retiring, and at such other times in the day as additional help was needed. If we were going on a picnic the next day, my mother would have the three children pray for good weather. If my father took a test for police lieutenant, we said prayers that he would be appointed. If monthly report cards were due at St. Patrick's School, all of us said a prayer that the marks would be good.

If a President was ill, we said a prayer for his recovery. If we read about a child who was ill and needed serum or some special medication, we prayed. If company was coming to the house and my mother was perspiring over a kitchen stove, she would tell us to "Say a prayer that this chicken turns out all right."

Prayer was never a special thing. It was as casual as breathing. If our prayers were not answered and we complained about it, my father said, "Are you trying to fly in the face of God? If He doesn't grant your prayer, He has a good reason for it." His mother, Mary Murphy Bishop, was probably the most truly religious person in our family.

I have never heard her boast about her faith or exhort others to go to her church, but I have heard her say, to her children and her grandchildren and her great-grandchildren, "You have a duty to God. You have a duty to your church. If you take care of both and do your best for your family, God will be good to you."

My mother's father—Alonzo Tier—was Protestant. His faith was deep. His wife and children were Roman Catholic. He had no objection to this, but he had strong feelings about people who did not keep up with their church duties. On Sunday mornings, when he came off duty as a policeman, he went through the house rapping on doors. "Come on," he would say. "It's time for church. Everybody up." He was a good cop, a good husband, a good father. So far as I know, his worst crime was going out with the boys on his day off. When he came home, at some hour of the night, it was often in an open barouche behind a lively horse and a driver. In his hands he would have a quart of vanilla ice cream with which to bribe my grandmother while he sneaked off to bed.

Prayer is still a daily part of our lives. My brother John lives by it. So does my sister Adele. My father—seventy-five years of age at this writing—drops to his knees every night. He concludes his prayers with three words addressed to my mother: "Good night, Jenny." My daughters, Virginia Lee and Gayle Peggy, also live by prayer. Like the others in our family, they pray not only for themselves but for all the people of the world. They pray also for the dead.

Still, if you spent some time among us you might not hear a reference to religion or prayer in a year. We are not publicly pious people. On the other hand, on your first visit you might find yourself in the middle of a lively discussion about which of the saints brings the quickest reply to a special-delivery prayer.

My mother believed so strongly in St. Anthony of Padua that she asked me to take his name at my confirmation. My father often addresses himself to the Blessed Mother of God. So did my wife, whose religious feelings, as you will find in a later section of the book, were fervent and unflagging. My father-in-law, Frank Dunning, never went to sleep without dropping to his knees (bones cracking loudly) to address a prayer to St. Joseph. My mother-in-law had such enormous faith in the rosary that, in her old age, when she watched television and saw her Dodgers losing a game, she brought out her beads and said them in hopes that her team would get a run or two.

These things are written to give you a fair perspective of the spiritual side of the author and the family from which he came. It is not over-painted. The portrait is a fair one. None of us were saints. We committed grievous sins from time to time, and we atoned. Always we strove to be slightly better Christians today than yesterday.

Sometimes our faith was naive and innocent. An example occurred when my daughter Gayle was eight. Ginny was fourteen. They were playing casino on Ginny's bed. The radio was on. The announcer said, "And now, this being the period of the high holy days, we will hear some Jewish scriptural music."

"Turn it off," Gayle said. "I don't like church music."

"We must listen," Ginny said. "Daddy says that it is good for us to know something about other religions."

"Okay," Gayle said with resignation. The first few bars of music sounded dull and sad to her. After a moment, she said, "Aw, turn it off."

Ginny, in superior wisdom, said, "Did it ever occur to you that Our Lord came from a Jewish family?"

Gayle slammed her hand down on the bedspread. "No!" she whispered. "Who converted Him?"

We were taught to respect people of other faiths, just as we were taught that people of other nations and other shades of skin are as close—or closer—to God as we. He, not we, would be the judge of their sincerity. A nun in St. Patrick's School once warned our class not to be surprised to find that the minister of a small dilapidated Protestant church up the street might precede us into Heaven. "I watched him from a convent window last Saturday," she said. "He not only preaches the word of God as he is given to see the word of God, but he is not too proud to climb up on the roof of his church with a mouth full of nails to hammer the shingles in place. This must be pleasing in the eyes of God."

A good measure of gratitude for the compiling of this book goes to Virginia Lee Frechette, who sent hundreds of letters to notables of many faiths around the world asking them to send their favorite prayers; to David Legerman, who conducted much of the research regarding prayers of the many sects; to Mrs. Ralph Walter, my secretary, who kept reminding me of deadlines; to Edward Kuhn, Jr., Executive Editor of McGraw-Hill, who saw it as a bigger and better book than I had in mind; to Herbert Mayes, editor of *Good Housekeeping* magazine, who saw it as a force for good long before the manuscript was ready; most of all to my wife Elinor, who was given exactly twenty-seven years and four months in which to make a better man of the one she married.

JIM BISHOP

Sea Bright, New Jersey

CONTENTS

GREAT PROTESTANT PRAYERS   161

GREAT CATHOLIC PRAYERS   195

GREAT JEWISH PRAYERS   217

*

PRAYERS FROM OTHER LANDS AND PEOPLES 327

PRAYERS FOR SPECIAL INTENTIONS   355

GO
WITH
GOD

DAY OF DESPAIR

WE WERE MARRIED *twenty-seven years. It was a good marriage, good enough to warrant saying, "If I had it to do over again, I would marry the same girl." This is not to say that it was an idyllic thing. Far from it. We disagreed—Elinor Dunning Bishop and I—on so many subjects that we spent considerable time in those twenty-seven years standing toe to toe and roaring defiance at each other.*

She was the most attractive and exciting woman I ever met. She was completely feminine, she loved to preen herself, and she enjoyed gay parties and gay people. She knew everything about children, and loved them. She knew very little about my career, but was understandably interested in the fruits thereof.

Her mother, Maggy Dunning, lived with us for twenty years. She and Elinor, with our two daughters, Virginia and Gayle, made our home a tiny matriarchy in which the male dog and I had rights of sufferance.

If Elinor was not a fan of my prose, then it must be said that I was not addicted to the things which were of interest to her: tie-back curtains, the price of beef, slip covers, babies, school,

3

measles, sheer stockings, small hats, the interplay of in-law politics, and putting up a spurious front for the neighbors.

Love, we found, was bigger than all of these things. In the early years, we were intensely jealous of each other. She had valid reason. I did not.

She was more religious than I and, when I tended to sag spiritually, it was Elinor who placed me back on the ecclesiastical rails. The following section concerns the days when prayer meant the most to me. It would be a worthless document if I did not make of it a highly personal account, including the turmoil of thought that occurs when a man appeals to God with his tongue trembling in desperation.

The *Giulio Cesare* walked slowly up her anchor chain. Her engines turned ahead and the big links clanked up through a chute onto the forepeak, wet and slimy. A hose tore the weedy growths from the black metal. And a petty officer leaning over the bows straightened, looked at the bridge, and waved both arms that the anchor was clear and the ship was moving on her own power. Out on the wing bridge, Captain Pinotti nodded and ordered all engines ahead one-third, course one-nine-four.

Behind the big ship the jade surface of the Mediterranean was broken by a dimple, then another. The stern swung slowly, majestically toward the rock called Gibraltar. A rusty little oiler, inbound, saluted the *Giulio Cesare*. There was no acknowledgment. On the reverse slope of Gibraltar, some English stood shading their eyes, watching the Italian liner leave for New York. An old Lancaster came in low and steady over the ship, heading for the military airport behind the anchorage. The southerly breeze draped a white cloud across the face of Gibraltar and pulled the edges toward the back, like a filmy scarf.

"All ahead standard," the captain said in Italian. The order was repeated twice. Pinotti, a small man with molasses skin

and a big nose, a man with the eyes of a Genovese gamin sup-
pressing laughter, moved onto the bridge and stood looking
out the port windows. Soon his ship was showing 18.7 knots. It
would be like this all the way unless, of course, there were
storms and headwinds and force five seas or better.

The *Giulio Cesare* was built for the South American run. The
Andrea Doria had foundered off Massachusetts, and the
Cesare was selected to honor the *Doria's* commitments. She was
five years old, and had a single green-striped funnel and the
bull horn of a true motor ship. She had the clean curving lines
of a yacht, but I had no joy of her.

I was in a hurry to get home. The *Cesare* and her thousand
merry-makers liked to wander. I had boarded the ship at
Cannes on the 3d and now, at 2 P.M. on the 7th, she was just
clearing Gibraltar. She had first sailed southeast to Naples, then
west to Barcelona, then on to The Rock, pausing at each port
for a few hours or a day.

At each dock, the Americans had poured ashore as though
there were a prize for the first one to land. They argued about
lire, pesetas, shillings, and dollars. Armed with cameras and
sensible shoes, they saw as much of each city as possible, and
hurried back to the ship laden with perfumes, bracelets, rosa-
ries, earrings, and castanets. They were uniformly flushed of
countenance and happy. On board they slept in the mornings
and read, deep in deck chairs, in the afternoons. And in the
evenings, when the motion picture was ended, they danced to
the music of the ship's orchestra and drank and made jokes
and wore paper hats and slapped at falling balloons. Most of
the passengers were Americans. The next largest group were
Italians of the diplomatic corps and industry. There were some
Canadians, a few French. In age, the first-class passengers
averaged about fifty; the second-class group, which engaged
in mass athletics on the stern every day, were about thirty
years of age; the tourist class attracted the very young and the
very old.

Pinotti conned his ship carefully. She had made her big

turn and was now on course two-seven-eight. Within the hour
she would breast the straits, leaving the jade Mediterranean
for the blue Atlantic. On her starboard beam the tawny hills
of Spain rose from the sea like soft taffy. To port, two Moroccan
dhows beat their way downwind toward the Atlas Mountains
of Morocco, standing like craggy blue glaciers nine miles off.

The captain left the bridge and, behind it, watched his navigator plot a course. They conversed softly in musical Italian,
the captain watching the slide rule, the retractors, the pencil,
and the line which took shape on the chart. It moved on the
axis of a small curve which cut south of the Azores by ninety
miles. The big ship would follow this curve like a slack-wire
walker. The captain patted the sides of his lean waist and
raised himself on the balls of his feet. He was pleased. The
final voyage on the *Cesare* had started well. When he got back
to Genoa, Pinotti would be on vacation for three months. After
that, he would resume command of the *Cristoforo Columbo*.

He understood that ship. She never kept a secret from
Pinotti. Not that the *Cesare* did. But when a captain moves up
to the line's biggest and fastest vessel, the ship seduces him.
Pinotti admired the *Cesare*, but he loved the *Columbo*.

The navigator rolled his chart and the captain went forward
to the bridge. He remained there until the broad Atlantic
Ocean showed up under his bows, blue and spangled with a
brassy sun. There was a slow tanker dead ahead, wallowing in
a starboard wind. Pinotti gave orders to the bridge officer to
pass her on the port side. He nodded to the big helmsman,
went to his cabin, and dropped on a couch, pulling a blue
blanket up under his chin.

I had been in Europe a month. It was my second trip, and
there had been little joy in it. It was like rocking a champagne
bottle to and fro until the cork popped, and then finding that
the bottle was empty. There was an odor of excitement, but no
substance. I knew what was missing from this trip, just as I
knew what was lacking in all the others.

There was a self-imposed loneliness in what I was doing. The word, perhaps, should be sulkiness. I was alone because she didn't want to come along . . . because I didn't want her to come . . . because she had assumed the role of housekeeper rather than wife. We were possessively in love with each other, but when her mother had moved into our house twenty years before, the angry silent competition between mother-in-law and son-in-law had begun. The son-in-law, who had never won and could not stand to lose, now had found a lonely dignity in turning away from his wife. *If I love you and you fail me, I will fail you again and again. If you hurt me I will run from you, and I will run far and hold my hands against my ears so that I cannot hear your cries. You are torn between your mother and your husband, and in their love they will shred you.*

It was like that. And yet there are shadings and ameliorations and dilutions of meaning which cannot be encompassed in words. I did not want to go away alone. For years I had wanted my wife to go with me on these trips—to go freely and whole-heartedly because she wanted to be with me.

"Will you go?"

She would look up from the deep chair and smile. I knew the answer. She knew that I knew. She understood the humiliation to me and she had no desire to humble me. But her fear of leaving her mother was greater. An only child is like one shoe.

"I don't think so," she said. "Can I think about it?"

"No."

"Momma isn't feeling well."

"The trip is important." Then I would describe where I had to go, what I had to do. A special series in Washington. Feature stuff from San Francisco. Or Europe, perhaps; Paris and the Riviera . . .

The smile deepened. The face was moonlike and wore a tiny fat nose and dark brown eyes too big for the other features. The hair was blue-black and straight. This was a proud woman. It was not only the seams of her stockings which had to be straight, but also the seams of her mind and her soul.

"You know me better than anybody else. The whole trip I would be worried. It isn't only Momma. How about the children?"

"Oh, please."

"Okay. Don't start."

"I'm not starting anything. I just asked a question." I sat and lit two cigarettes. She took hers and puffed and stared at me through the little blue pillow of smoke. "The kids are no problem. Ginny is a married woman. She and Charlie could come down here for a month."

Elinor shrugged. "Jimmy," she said with restrained asperity. "Think. Try to think for a minute. Virginia Lee happens to be twenty years old. A child. Married or not. Gayle Peggy is thirteen. Suppose Momma had a heart attack or something. You're not reasonable."

"My mother is sick and blind and diabetic and—"

"She has your father."

"Then you don't want to go?"

"Don't put it on that plane. You always manage to make yourself such a little tin hero."

"You do want to go?"

She laughed. When humor hit her suddenly, the head always went far back, the hand held the chest, the eyes squinted shut. She laughed so hard that I laughed with her. I walked across the room, pulled the cigarette from her mouth, and kissed her.

"You're terrible," she said.

"Am I?"

"No. But you maneuver and maneuver and I always wind up on the defensive. Listen. Suppose my mother didn't live with us. Suppose we had no children. I still wouldn't want to go to Europe." She made a wrinkled expression as though she smelled bad fish. "Who cares about Europe? Big deal. I'm too nervous to travel."

It was like that. *I'm off to Omaha—want to go? I have to write a story in Hollywood—how about it? I'm flying to Guatemala City Monday—would you care . . . ?* In all the years, she said yes twice. Once to Mexico City; once to San Francisco. On both occasions it was sweet and refreshing to work by day (while she shopped) and to see the city by night and not have to ask the headwaiter for a table for one.

Elinor Dunning Bishop was a complex and beautiful woman. She had as many sides as a good diamond.

At 6:30 P.M. the passengers began to fall into their evening patterns. The women were dressed in low necklines and high perfume; the men wore black ties and slick hair. At this hour, they came up on the ship's elevator to the boat deck. The afternoon motion picture was over, and the children were now in the cabins with governesses or ship's stewards.

A dozen of the adults crowded the little bar, where they ordered drinks and café espressos, and the babble of conversation was swift and light over the tinkle of ice and laughter. In the big lounge around the corner, white-jacketed stewards moved among the fat settees with trays of hors d'ouevres, bowing low over the white shirtfronts and bare shoulders as the ship's orchestra played Italian and American operettas.

The orchestra sat in a shell. The men wore fixed smiles as they sawed and scraped through such Americanisms as the scores of *My Fair Lady* and *Oklahoma!* The sun had set, and a burnt-orange glow rimmed the horizon in the windows behind the orchestra. A fresh wind from the north carried white feathers of spray across the ship and, as it creaked to port or starboard, the cellist and his chair slid a foot or two to the left, then to the right. The cello remained impaled on its point. The musician seemed to play his instrument only as he touched it *en passant.*

I sat in the lounge, where a jolly group had collected. An Italian countess of indeterminate years, speaking in precise English, was telling a joke. The stories became gayer, the laughter louder. Ship passengers require two days in which to sort themselves, but the screening is almost always perfect. In that time, the drinkers find each other; those with academic pursuits

gravitate toward each other; the golfers, the proud grand-
mothers, the readers, the deck athletes, the card players, the
romantic prowlers—by magnetic impulse they join their brethren in cliques.

The drinkers are always the warmest, the friendliest. They
radiate ruddy cheer even on the gray mornings. They need
friendship quickly, and they offer it at once. Almost all the
drinkers aboard the *Cesare* were pleasant tipplers who, in the
course of extending their hearts to each other, gave home addresses as well and admonished each other to "come down and
see us."

There was a manufacturer from Kentucky, a handsome graying man of fifty-five, who spent much of the voyage at the bar
with his tiny wife. He owned a bank and his wife owned him.
The countess was a tense butterfly, but she was under control
at all times and her primary interest was flirtation. A loud forty-
ish woman from New York, a lady of coarse voice and conversation, assumed the role of romantic aggressor in Genoa and
never relinquished it. There was a young Canadian gentleman
with square jaw and a big puff of yellow hair who was lionized
by the ladies and who tried, as adroitly as possible, to tell his
secret: he was going home to be married.

A Dutchwoman with a leonine face was cast as the bleeding
heart of the ship. Many of the women and some of the men
came to her with their problems. She had real sympathy to offer
and, in spite of her lack of beauty, was the only person to inspire lasting friendships. A dark and sadly attractive young
Italian woman struggled with English words and two babies.
She was en route to Fort Leavenworth, Kansas, to join her husband. He was a lieutenant in the Italian army, an exchange officer on duty in the United States.

Mrs. Daphne was the most attractive young woman in the
crowd. She had dark hair and eyes and creamy skin and a good
figure. She was, by ship reputation, very rich, and she drank too
much. On the boat deck she had a suite of rooms and a govern-
ess for her little girl.

The Italian countess said that Mrs. Daphne had been in Europe for a year to decide whether she wanted to continue with her marriage or not. Now she was bound for New York to meet her husband and had not come to a decision.

No one ever saw her daughter. In the predawn hours, she phoned the Dutchwoman or the Italian countess or the Canadian boy and begged them to come to her suite right away because she was sick and could not sleep. The ship doctor gave her pills. She was happy until the passengers retired. Then she sat in her drawing room and a carousel of thoughts began their monotonous rounds in her mind. She became terrified, always picked up the phone and pleaded with shipboard friends to dress and come up at once. She passed trembling fingers over a perspiring brow and breathed the phrase, "Please help me" over and over.

One evening Mrs. Daphne looked my way, laughed and said, "You're always thinking. What do you find to think about?" I smiled. My head shook slowly from side to side. "Nothing," I said.

"Nothing," she said. "He's probably writing a book about us." Everyone laughed. "Make me the gay one," she said, "like I really am." Her hand fluttered vaguely around the little room. "The rest of you can be heavies in Mr. Bishop's book. Me, I get the prince in the end."

It was near dinner time. What I had been thinking about was a matter of dreams. I seldom dream. At least I seldom remember dreaming. When I do, it is usually the same dream: two men are chasing me down a dark alley. Too late I see that the end of the alley is blocked. The men always catch me. I always fight. My arms feel weighted and I cannot seem to lift them. The strangers beat me to the ground and I awaken. It is a cowardly, helpless dream and I have been dreaming it for many years.

In London, I had a new one, a dream of Elinor. I awakened at the Savoy and sat with a cigarette for a few moments before I could decide whether it had been a dream or had actually

happened. There was nothing amorous about this dream, nor
the ones which followed. We were newlyweds and we were
playing miniature golf in Jersey City.

She was nineteen. I was twenty-two. We were happy and we
argued about whether to count her tee shot as a stroke because
it had missed a rain barrel and bounded off into the street. She
wore a huge Milan straw hat of chartreuse. To see where her
shots went, she had to lift the floppy brim. In the dream, it did
not occur to me that these things happened in 1930. There was
a "nowness" to them and, on awakening, I shuffled to the bathroom and was shocked to look at the man in the mirror. He was
approaching fifty, his hair was gray and tousled, and the lines
on his cheeks and under his nose looked like inverted V's.

A dream of Elinor occurred again in Paris. Dawn was coming
through the deep-cut windows of the Crillon Hotel when I
turned over in the big bed, awakened, and sat up. We had been
sitting up in bed discussing a book. Elinor claimed that she had
never learned how to read; that is, to read on two levels at the
same time. She read for plot. Nothing else. She paid no attention to the brush strokes of the author in painting a scene, or in
the devices of characterization.

So, early in our married life, we spent a little time in the late
hours reading aloud to each other. I was a cub reporter on the
New York Daily Mirror and I was anxious to learn. She was my
bride and she was anxious to learn something about her husband's work. Again I awakened feeling like Dr. Faust.

The third time I dreamed of Elinor was at the Carleton Hotel
in Cannes. I had a room on the second floor overlooking the
harbor. I had come home late after an evening at the roulette
tables with Mr. Otto Preminger. When sleep finally came, it
had come quickly, like the passing of an express train that starts
out as a dark speck down the track.

In this dream, she said nothing. She was young and beautiful
and she winked at me and beckoned with her finger. I followed,
and said nothing. We walked down strange streets, she a step in
front. When we reached a shadowed place, she turned and

cupped her hands behind my neck and held her lips up. The kiss was long and sweet and somehow saddening. I awakened and felt chilled.

The three dreams worried me. I couldn't understand why, but it seemed puzzling, after twenty-seven years of marriage, to find oneself beset with dreams of early marriage. I couldn't return to sleep. The harbor at Cannes was quiet. From the bed, I could see a flasher buoy far out. Every few seconds, it threw a long slash of red crayon across the onyx water, then erased it.

I looked at my watch. 4:30 A.M. Back home in Sea Bright, New Jersey, it would be 11:30 P.M. and Elinor would be watching the late show on television. In a few hours, she would be in the big Hollywood bed off the living room, a thin, frightened figure curled like a kitten against the meanness of reality.

Another two hours and she would be up, an emaciated woman lost in a voluminous nightgown. She would light a cigarette in the dark and then patter barefooted to the bathroom. She would open the medicine chest and take two white Miltowns from a bottle. Then a half glass of water. First a pill, then a sip. Then a pill, then a sip. Afterward, she would find her way to the front porch.

There she would sit alone, staring at the sea wall across the front lawn, hearing the thunder of the surf. In her loneliness, she would not disturb anyone in the house. In the dark, no one could see the stringy unwaved hair with the streaks of gray; no one could see the indented lips; no one, even she, would miss the upper denture. The red paint on her fingernails was cracked and chipped.

Only the eyes remained as big, as luminous, as dark as they once were. Now they wore a slanting ridge of flesh along the upper lids, and this gave her a slightly defensive expression. Her thoughts were always terrifying, and she seldom discussed them. When she did, Elinor was always apologetic and shrugging. "I don't know what to say," she would say. "I think of old age and death, mostly."

"And you wonder where your youth has gone?"

"It went so fast." She would lace her fingers together and twist them, and she would rub her bony knees rhythmically. "It went so very fast. It almost seems as though I was busy doing something, and when I turned around, it was gone."

"You're only forty-seven."

"Only? For goodness' sake, don't even mention it."

"I'm almost fifty."

"Better you than me, Jimmy Bishop. I thought I was old when we hit thirty. But forty-seven! Where did it all go?"

"We'll be grandparents next year and I know a lot of people who have lived through that."

"You think there will be anybody happier than I? Don't you think I want to live to see that baby?"

"Sure. As long as they don't call you grandma."

She had laughed. "You got it, kid. You got it. Let me be a grandma and let me hold the baby, but don't use the word 'grandma.'" Then, in a serious tone, "Oh, I don't know what's the matter with me. I'm all mixed up. I'm afraid to travel. I'm afraid to stay home without you. I'm afraid when the front doorbell rings. I'm afraid when the phone rings. I'm afraid of Momma. I pray for your mother and everybody." Tears would stand shimmering on the lower lids and sometimes, if she lost control momentarily, the features would distort and she would rub her knees faster and then wipe her eyes with the back of her hand. "I don't know what's the matter with me. Honest I don't. I wish I knew."

It was at this point that I lost patience. Not once. Every time. "Why," I would ask, "won't you please go to a doctor and find out? Why? They have doctors for nervous women. Holy smokes, you can't live on Miltown forever."

"Okay. Okay. Please don't start on me. Just give me until next week. If I'm not better by Monday or Tuesday at the latest, we'll go to a doctor and find out what the trouble is. You'll see. I'll be okay by next week."

The ship's lounge began to empty at eight. I went up to the boat deck on the lee side and stood in a sheltered spot to watch the dark sea. No light showed on the horizon. Where the top of the ocean meets the bottom of the sky there was a thin ribbon of luminescence. The *Giulio Cesare* held her head high for a moment, then plunged downward in a crosswind. She creaked and the heavy bow wave showed white, even in darkness. The ship began to lift, higher and higher until the bow jackstaff stood against the sky.

The wind from the north split with a dying moan against the radio antenna. Thin diffused gray smoke poured out of the funnel sideways and hugged the rim of the dark sea as it disappeared to port. The deck was wet. Behind the ship, a fat moon had climbed a half hour above the horizon. It caught the edges of scudding clouds and gave them shape against the tall masts.

I went below. Dinner aboard was always a series of elegant surprises. There were shrimps and soups and wines in such teasing styles that the diner patted his belly and said, "The heck with the diet. I may never come this way again." I do not drink but I enjoyed my table companions as they enhanced the discernment of their taste buds with sips of vintage wines and exclaimed in minor ecstasy at each new dish brought by the impeccable steward.

There were steaks and rib roasts and lamb in so many styles that at our table we used to order all the different specialties, so that all of us could see, smell, and swap tastes of each delicacy.

Ours was a good table. On my left was the young Canadian named Pete, whose popularity with the lady passengers was overwhelming. On his right sat the McPhersons, young Canadians en route home after spending three years in Switzerland and Germany. Mr. McPherson was a gentle scholar from McGill. His wife had long wire-straight black hair done in Spanish style at the nape of the neck.

On McPherson's right, halfway around the table from me, sat the Dutchwoman. She was big and homely, with mustard yellow hair and a warm, sympathetic disposition. She was jolly and had traveled much, but she never joined the game of tell-

ing about oneself, except to say that the Nazis forced her to
leave home and flee to Switzerland. After she got there, they
sent word that her mother was dying and refused permission
for her to go home for a day to bid her mother farewell.

To the Dutchwoman's right sat the Wax Flower. She was
tiny and blond. Her accent was an admixture of New York and
Galician and she alternated between feeling happy and feeling
affronted through each meal. If she liked turtle soup and rec-
ommended it to one of the others and they failed to order it,
she lapsed into silence.

She said that she did not know how to tell a joke, but she
told them. When someone else told a joke, she seldom joined
in the laughter, but preferred to lean toward the teller and say,
"Just a minute. Excuse me. Everybody is laughing but what is
funny?" There was a brittle attractiveness about her and, while
the rest of us were careless in our camaraderie, we were cau-
tious in our remarks to the Wax Flower.

I was listening to McPherson relate stories about Swiss
schools, while addressing part of my attention to a plate of beef
Stroganoff, when a very young bellboy came to the table.

"Mr. Bishop," he said. "You are wanted on the telephone."

"The telephone?" I said dumbly.

"Two decks up and forward to the bridge," he said. "It is in
the radio shack."

"The telephone?" I said again. "Who would want me on the
telephone?" The others stopped eating. They were looking at
me.

"It is New York," the boy said patiently. "Come, I will show
you."

My world dipped like the ship. Who would be calling me
from New York? I looked at my watch. The time was 9:35. It
would be 4:35 P.M. in New York. I followed the boy, turning
around to excuse myself, and I tried to look self-assured. New
York? Who? Sea Bright, New Jersey, perhaps. I could understand Sea Bright. That was home.

I followed the boy up the long interior corridor, across the ship to the elevator, up the elevator to the boat deck, around the corner to the back of the bridge, up a curving stairway, then to the left and into the radio shack.

Two men worked there. Both were gallant Italians, bowing, smiling, overly agreeable. One was thirtyish and wore his officer's cap rakishly, permitting a peep of gray to point a romantic feather in the direction of his dark-eyed gaze. The other was older, a man with a broad, broken face and a mist of old sorrow over the eyes.

They nodded to me, twirled dials, and yelled, " 'Ello New York?" " 'Ello New York?" " 'Ello New York?" and the sound of it dropped a nameless terror into the pit of my stomach. What was I afraid of? I do not know. I do not know. No one would call me if everything was all right. Something had to be wrong. Something had to be very wrong.

All at once, I knew what it was. It was Gayle. She had been riding her bike to school and had been hit. Gayle was thirteen, half boy, half girl. She was more at home in dungarees than in dresses. She was slender and swift afoot and in mind, got poor marks in school, and laughed behind her hand at her elders.

It had to be Gayle. It couldn't be Elinor. She had passed two physical examinations in the past three months. It couldn't be Ginny. She was the epitome of intelligent care in all things. It couldn't be Charlie. He was the only young man I knew who drove a car slowly and never took an unnecessary risk. He was husky, healthy, and twenty-one.

" 'Ello New York? 'Ello New York? We have the party, Meester Beeshop now. We have the party, New York." He nodded to me to go into a little alcove. There was a shelf and a phone. I lifted the phone. When I am worried, I sit on my emotions. I become deep-voiced and coldly calm.

"Hello," I said. There were whistles in the phone. From far away, I heard a voice in mid-sentence. Then it burst in clearly.

"Daddy? This is Ginny." The tone sounded worried. My intestines began to loop and tighten.

"Yes, honey?"

"I'm down at Sea Bright, Daddy. Mommy was operated on this morning."

"Mommy was what?"

"Operated on. Operated on. Can you hear me?" The whistles started again. They were shrill little things and they glided up and down the scale in discord.

I shouted. "I can hear you, honey. Mommy was operated on. Yes. What for?"

"What did you say, Daddy?"

"What for? What for? What's the matter with Mommy?"

"The doctor says peritonitis. It was this morning at ten o'clock."

The brain works swiftly when it is confused and frightened. Peritonitis? Elinor? Ridiculous. There must be some mistake. Peritonitis comes from a ruptured appendix. Or doesn't it? Peritonitis. What did I read about it? Penicillin? Yes, penicillin arrests the infective stage of peritonitis.

I didn't know whether I was relieved to know that Gayle had not been hit by an automobile or distressed to learn that Elinor was in a hospital.

"Where is she?"

"Monmouth Memorial."

"What does the doctor say?"

"She's doing all right, Daddy. Can you hear me?"

"Clearly. You're excited. You're talking too fast. Was it her appendix?"

"Was it what?"

"Mommy's appendix."

"Mommy had no appendicitis. She was throwing up at night."

"That could signify appendicitis."

"No. She was getting nauseated every night. We begged her to see the doctor. On Thursday—"

"What?"

"Last Thursday night at two in the morning she felt so sick that she awakened Gayle."

"Gayle?"

"They were sleeping together in the big bedroom. Mommy woke her up and said to please call the doctor, that she felt very sick. Gayle woke me up. I phoned him and he said to get Mommy in the hospital. He made the arrangements."

"Speak louder, honey."

"Daddy, I can't hear you."

"Tell me what broke."

"Broke?"

"What broke? What caused the peritonitis?"

"I don't know, Daddy. They wanted to let Mommy come home Sunday, but she had bad stomach pains Saturday and a fever. There was an emergency operation this morning."

A sickness and a weakness spread through me. The news was as unreal as my old nightmare dreams. And as frightening. Elinor was always well physically. She liked to act ill in recent years; at bedtime she always doled out two aspirin for herself and two for her mother. She complained of headaches before cooking dinner, or before getting dressed to go out. At meal-time, one cross word from anyone caused her to stop chewing and to say warningly, "I'm eating."

But she was seldom a sick girl. The only real illness in the twenty-seven years of marriage was a sudden hyperthyroid condition when Gayle was born. Her weight fell off and she never regained it. The fullness of figure was lost. For a time, she was gray and weak. Then her strength returned, and her appe-tite, but not the weight.

"What do the doctors say?"

"The doctors? She's responding, whatever that means. No, not responding. Reacting is the word."

"I feel so sorry for you kids."

"We're worried about you. Please don't worry. Mommy is going to be all right. Charlie and I stopped in and lit candles."

"Call me, honey. Call me with any news. Don't keep me waiting."

"I won't."

"Give my love to Gayle and Charlie. Tell Mommy I'll try to

get off this ship. I don't know how, but I'll try to get off. When she's out of the ether, tell her I'm hurrying home to her. Tell her—tell her I love her dearly. . . ."

Cabin 138 was small. It wasn't more than nine by six, with a bunk against the right wall and a door leading to a shower on the left. It had no porthole on the sea and, sitting on the bunk, the room became smaller and more stuffy. The only sound in it was the hum of an air conditioner.

I got on my knees to pray, and prayer would not come. I was riding a scenic railway of thoughts, and as I made the climbs and dips in my little mental car I felt myself being pulled and twisted in many directions. I thought of God but could not feel His presence. I pray at least twice each day—on arising, on retiring—and I do not use formal prayers. My petitions, my thanks, are addressed to Him in everyday language. Elinor was the only truly religious person in our house. I thought of her, and of Ginny, leading us in prayer so many many times.

Prayer, on this particular evening, became difficult. One of the thoughts which kept racing through my mind was that it was hypocritical to ask for a favor when, in fairness, I could not remember having done one for Him. The second thought was my repeated admonition to Elinor, "Stop complaining. We've had so much good luck that I'm sure we're due for something bad."

It was easy to say the words of my prayer, but it was a recitation of emptiness. I could not concentrate on what the words meant for more than a few seconds. The intent of sincerity was derailed and I found myself thinking of Elinor in a hospital bed, scared numb, even with the children at her side, praying silently for me to hurry to her. She had faith in me. She believed in her heart that, no matter what happened, I was the only person who could explain it to her and get her out of it.

Such faith is almost always misplaced. Still, I tried to foster it and live up to it. Somehow, I had to get off this ship at once and get to the hospital. The distance was about 3,300 miles, and

there was no land between the ship and New York Harbor, but
I had to. . . .

Prayer came suddenly. The words were not consciously con-
trived. They came into my mind and off my tongue easily.
"Please God, don't let anything bad happen to her. Let her
live. I need her more than You do. She's a girl who has always
been afraid of the dark, so please give her a break. I'll make it
up to You somehow."

There was more to it and it sounded spuriously pathetic to
me, but, I hoped, not to Him. How does one ask for the life
of a wife? Do you say, "We've been married twenty-seven years
and life is going to be very dull and useless without her"? Do
you say, "Oh, we've had our battles, of course, but my heart
slows and my feet drag when we are apart only six weeks, so
please don't take her away forever"? Or do you say, "If one of
us must go, let it be me"?

The manner in which it is said, I feel certain, is unimpor-
tant. No matter what words come out, no matter the eloquence
or awkwardness, it must be assumed that God knows what is in
the heart and that He will read it there.

Many of my prayers during these days of despair were addressed to the Virgin of Guadalupe. This is ironic because until
a few years ago I had no faith in her and did not believe that
she existed. She was, I thought, a Mexican superstition. The
legend said that she had appeared to an Indian about 400 years
ago and, in effect, promised protection to the people of the
Americas. My reaction was that the Indian was deranged or
intoxicated.

In the matter of miracles and apparitions, I am a doubter.
I would like to believe without question, but the Thomasonian
quality has its compensation. When doubt is erased, faith becomes rocklike. I am not impressed by crutches hanging in grot-
tos or by stigmata on the hands and feet of the holy. I believe
that miracles occur daily, but I am not wise enough to separate

the supernatural from the mystical and the psychological, and it is easier to reject all of them.

Some years ago, I accepted an assignment from a magazine editor to go to Mexico City and investigate the Guadalupe story. Staying at the Del Prado Hotel, I examined dusty records, probed, interviewed, and went over the terrain where the Mother of God was alleged to have appeared to the Indian. In ten days, I became convinced that the apparition had occurred, exactly as related.

This was a shock rather than a pleasant experience, because it upset a preconceived judgment. One night in the Del Prado I reexamined all the notes I had written about *da Virgen de Guadalupe* and found that the weight of evidence was in favor of the apparition. Such material as had to be accepted on faith alone I dismissed. What was left was convincing.

The apparition occurred in December of the year 1531. This was thirty-nine years after Columbus discovered the New World. Cortes and his Spanish soldiers were in Mexico City. He brought Franciscans from Spain to convert the Indians; but the natives, who had a right to regard the oppressors as infidels, did not convert easily. Some became Catholics. Not many.

Don Fray Juan de Zumárraga was the first bishop of Mexico. He was a lean ascetic and, unhappily, practical. His work was to convert as many of the city's 200,000 Indians as possible. He did not regard himself as an historical figure—the first Roman Catholic bishop in a new world. He did not dwell upon the possibility that soon the Spanish soldiers would begin to marry Indian girls and that a whole new subrace would begin to spread over the hills and across the lush jungles. He was concerned only with his daily work.

This was ninety years before the Pilgrims landed.

There was a hill behind Mexico City called Tepeyac. It was, and is, barren, and its surface composition is alkaline. The converted Indians used the Tepeyac trail to walk to the city. One was Juan Diego. He was fifty-five years old, sad, lonesome, a man of gentle resignation, a widower. Originally his name had been Cuautitlan, but with Christianity and baptism came the new name.

Juan wore a tilma, a loose-fitting outer garment made of white hemp. On his way into the city one morning, while crossing below the ridge of Tepeyac, he heard music. He stopped and noted that the sun was coming up in the east, but that the hill behind him was bathed in gold light. A voice called, "Juanito. Juan Diegito!"

He was not frightened. The Spanish priests had told Juan so much that was unusual that the Indian would not have been alarmed to find God standing before him. Juan turned toward the voice and, halfway up the Tepeyac hill, saw a lady. She seemed to him to be standing in front of the sun, because bars of light radiated from her blue garment.

She spoke to him in Spanish and said, "Juanito, the least of my sons, where art thou going?" Juan Diego nodded, as though this were a sensible question from a credible lady, and he said, "My lady, I must go to the church at Tlaltelolco to study divine mysteries, which are taught to us by our priests, the emissaries of our Lord and Saviour."

The wonder of this situation, to the Indian, was that for the rest of his life he could quote her next statement without hesitation, and he proved it many times. "Know and take heed, thou," she said, "the least of my sons, that I am holy Mary, ever Virgin, Mother of the true God for whom we live, the Creator of all the world, Maker of heaven and earth. I urgently desire that a temple should be built to me here, to bear witness to my love, my compassion, my succor and protection. For I am a merciful mother to thee and to all thy fellow people on this earth who love me and trust me and invoke my help.

"I listen to their lamentations and solace all their sorrows and their suffering. Therefore, to realize all that my clemency claims, go to the palace of the bishop of Mexico, and say that I sent thee to make manifest to him my great desire, namely that here in the valley a temple should be built to me. *Tell him word for word* all that thou hast seen and heard and admired.

Be assured that I shall be grateful and that I will reward thee, for I will make thy life happy and cause thee to become worthy of the labor thou hast taken and the trouble thou performest to do that which I enjoin thee. Now thou hast heard all my bidding, least of my sons. Go and do thy utmost."

The remarkable part of this speech was that Diego could say it without fully understanding it. He decided to remember his manners. "Lady," he said, "I go to do your bidding. As your humble servant, I take my leave of you." He was, if one can trust the chronicle of Antonio Valeriano, Juan's contemporary, only slightly impressed. The Indian's mind was centered on a more important matter: his uncle, Juan Bernardino, was gravely ill.

The messenger was admitted to the office of the bishop. His Excellency was vaguely attentive. Juan told the entire story and was astonished at the perfection of his memory. The bishop dismissed him with a wave of the hand. "You must come again sometime, my son," he said, "when I can hear you more at my leisure."

The bishop was a practical man. He had met religious crackpots at home in Spain, and he had met them here in this wilderness. They heard things. They saw things. They dreamed things. They were pests, but they too were his children and he could not be abrupt.

Juan Diego was not surprised, not offended. All the records show that he expected no one to believe him. He himself had doubted when he first saw the Lady, and his words were, "Have I ceased to sleep?" He was en route home to the sick uncle when he saw the Lady on the hill again. He removed his big straw hat and whispered, "Niña mía." He told her the bishop's reaction and he wondered why, if she were the Mother of God, she didn't appear before the bishop and demand the church. It did not occur to him that the churchman should not have needed a sign from heaven.

"So I beg you most earnestly, my lady," he said, "to send someone of importance, well known, respected."

He turned his eyes down to the chalky dust under his rope sandals and waited. The Lady told him that she had many messengers, but "it is altogether necessary that thou thyself shouldst undertake this entreaty and that through thy own mediation and assistance my purpose should be accomplished."

Juan Diego promised to try again. On Sunday, after Mass, he was at the door of the bishop's residence. The priests and house servants remembered. One said that the bishop was busy. Another said that he had retired to pray. Another said that the bishop was in conference with his counsellors. Juan Diego, in the rough white tilma, said that he would wait.

It was a long wait. When it was obvious that this man was too ignorant to be discouraged, he was admitted to the bishop. Juan had begun to tell about the grand lady and her wish for a temple to be built at Tepeyac, when he broke down and sobbed. He looked at the bishop through tear-rimmed eyes and said, "God grant that this may be so."

His excellency said that tears would avail Juan nothing. He must answer questions. Some priests were called in, and these took turns firing probing, mean little questions at the Indian. What did the Blessed Mother look like? What was she wearing? What was her voice like? What was it that she had said the first morning? What had she said in the afternoon? Why did she want a church built out in Tepeyac? Was anyone with her? Tell us again the words that she used.

The bishop became convinced that this Indian was neither insane nor a faker nor intoxicated. He had apparently absorbed too much religion in too short a period of time and now suffered from mild delusions. He sent Juan Diego away and suggested that, if he saw the Lady again, to please ask for some sign to prove that Juan represented her.

The Indian left. He wished heartily that he had not become involved in this question of a church, because his uncle was now dying and he would rather spend time with the old man. On the hill, he must have been hurt to see the Lady again and to realize that only he saw her and that no one would believe him. He stood in the high white sun of noon, his black hair glistening, and he told the Lady what had happened.

"So be it, my son," she said. "Return here tomorrow in order that thou mayest secure for the Bishop the sign for which he has asked. When this is in thy possession, he will believe thee...."

Juan Diego did not want to meet the Lady again. He was sick with fear for his uncle's life and, the following day, when he hurried to Mexico City to get a priest, the Indian did not take the Tepeyac trail. He followed one to the east of the older one. He was on the outskirts of the city when, to his embarrassment, he saw the Lady walking down a hillside toward him.

She did not appear to be angry with him. "What is the matter, least of my sons?" she said. "Where art thou going?"

"God grant that you may be content with me," said Señor Diego. "I am going to cause you grief. I must tell you that a poor servant of yours, my uncle, is seriously ill. He has the plague and is about to die."

Perhaps the Lady saw this as an opportunity to protect the people of the New World before they were ready to give her the church she asked. She said, "Do not fear this illness nor any other illness nor affliction. Am I not here beside thee, I, thy merciful mother? Let nothing distress or harass thee. As to the illness of thy uncle, he will not die of it. Indeed, I ask thee to accept as a certainty my assurance that he is already cured."

The Indian weighed the words. This, for him, was the moment of truth. Should he continue his journey to fetch a priest for the dying, or should he accept the orders of the Lady of promises? He told her that he would do her bidding.

"Go," she said, "to the summit of the hill where thou didst see me before and where I gave thee thy first orders. There thou wilt find flowers. Gather them and assemble them. Then fetch them thither."

He went. He crossed to the west and climbed Tepeyac. There he found roses growing. Juan Diego was perhaps more surprised at this than at the vision of the Lady. All Indians knew that roses did not grow in December. Besides, nothing could grow on the chalky alkali of Tepeyac, except a little mesquite and prickly pear.

Diego crooked his arm under the tilma, made a makeshift apron, and dropped the roses in it. Dutifully, he brought them back to the Blessed Mother. She said nothing. She took the roses and rearranged them.

"Least of my sons," she said, "this cluster of roses is the sign which you are to take to the bishop. You are to tell him, in my name, that he will recognize my will and that he must fulfill it. I enjoin you that only in the presence of the bishop shall you unfold your mantle and disclose that which you carry."

The Indian folded the tilma up over his chest, so that the roses were hidden. He walked down the trail toward Mexico City and, at the palace, he announced that he would like to see the bishop. The priests pretended that they did not hear him. He stood in the tile foyer, head down, tilma folded upward.

The palace personnel teased the Indian. They asked what he was concealing. He did not answer. A few decided that his silence amounted to insolence, and they threatened to throw him out into the street. One pulled at the tilma and saw a flower. A few others tried to snatch one from him.

They knew that such roses did not grow in the area in December. One looked upon Juan Diego in awe and ran to tell the bishop. His Excellency came into the room and stood frowning. Politely, the Indian reminded the bishop that he had asked for a sign.

"Behold and receive them," said Juan Diego, and he dropped his arm. The roses cascaded to the tile floor. The bishop took a look, gasped, and fell to his knees. His lips moved in prayer; his eyes were tearful with remorse. The priests and servants in the room fell to their knees. The messenger had expected them to understand the sign, but he had not expected abasement. Juan Diego looked down. There, on the front of the tilma, was the image of the Lady exactly as he had seen her. Even the bands of gold radiation flowed out from behind her blue gown. It was this, not the roses, which had caused the bishop to drop to his knees and weep.

The church was built and was called the Basilica Santa Maria de Guadalupe Siempre Virgen. Uncle Juan Bernardino recovered and said that he had seen the Lady in his hut. The bishop, who was still practical, called in European art experts to examine the tilma and the portrait. Each one said that the twine was too lumpy to be used as a surface for painting; besides, there was no artist, European or Indian, who painted in the style of this portrait.

One of the disturbing factors, to the bishop—who now believed, but could not understand the meaning of the apparition —was why the complexion of the Lady had a bluish ashen cast. It was not until ten years later that the first generation of children born of Spanish fathers and Indian mothers began to grow up. All of them had a bluish cast to their complexions, and it was as though the Lady had foretold that the first mixing of European blood and native blood in the New World would be distinguished by the hue with which man has endowed her for centuries.

No other generation except the first had this cast of skin.

The tilma hangs now in a glass case behind the high altar at the Basilica of Guadalupe. On it the portrait of the Lady is bright and fresh. In the upper right-hand corner is a dark stain. This was made by art experts who came from Europe early in the twentieth century to examine the tilma. They used corrosive acid on the upper corner in an effort to find out why this ordinary tilma, which should have disintegrated into bits of lint in 200 years, was still intact after 400 years.

I examined the tilma and the records, and I found myself believing. Like Don Fray Juan de Zumárraga, I was finally convinced. However, my belief was based almost entirely on negation. If the matter had been faked, then the bishop, the priests, Juan Diego, and his uncle would have to have been parties to it. The bishop, as chief plotter, would have been at the mercy of an ignorant Indian. If this were so, Don Fray would hardly have portrayed himself as a doubter.

The group would need a fine painter, one who would know, ten years in advance of the fact, that the offspring of Spaniards and Indians would have bluish-gray complexions. The painter would also have to paint in a style unknown to anyone in the wilderness of the new continent and unknown to any of the recognized masters of Europe. He would also have to paint his portrait on woven twine—something which cannot be done today, even after the fabric has been sized and coated.

On my return from Mexico, a small gold statue of Our Lady of Guadalupe was given to me by Father Paul Bussard, publisher of *Catholic Digest*. The Lady became the friend of the twentieth-century doubter—me. It was my habit to pray to her, usually once a day, and ask her to protect my wife and children and parents spiritually, mentally, and physically from all harm.

At 11 P.M. I was back in the radio room with an idea. The information I got from Ginny was meager. She too was sick with fear and probably remembered only a part of what the doctors told her. If I radioed a plea to Mr. Edward Mahar, city editor of the *New York Journal-American,* he would help. He belonged to a special clan of men who believe in a true fraternity of friendship.

SS GIULIO CESARE CHATHAMRADIO VIA RCA 7 2145
EDMAHAR CITYDESK JOURNAL AMERICAN

NYK

IM ABOARD GIULIOCESARE HEARD MY WIFE OPERATED ON AT LONG BRANCH MEMORIAL HOSPITAL IN NEW JERSEY CONDITION GRAVE CAN YOU RADIO CAUSE AND HER CHANCES MY HEART IS WITH HER.

JIM BISHOP

Somehow, this made me feel better. Ed would do more than inquire. He would also determine whether everything was being done to help her to recover. He would speak to the doctor directly and without equivocation; and if a consultation with specialists was necessary, he would tell the doctor to order it. He would also give my daughters the assurance of outside interest and help.

The hopelessness of being imprisoned on a gay cruise ship left me for a while. I stopped in to see the chief purser, a stout, graying Italian who can say no in the most polite Latin tradition. I told him that my wife was ill and explained the circumstances. He permitted his friendly smile to die, and he pursed his lips and clucked with sympathy.

"Is there any land between us and New York?" I said.

The smile. The shrug. "None except the Azores. They are to the north."

"How far?"

The shrug. No smile. "Maybe a hundred miles. The bridge would know exactly."

"Is there an airbase there?"

"I do not know. The ship, I am sure, could not deviate from its course. You worry too much, Mr. Bishop. Your wife, she will be fine."

"When will we pass the Azores?"

"Today is Monday? Wednesday then. Wednesday for sure. But they will be out of sight to the north. We do not pass close."

"Do you know if a seaplane can be chartered?"

"Mr. Bishop, this is impossible. Merely to slow this ship down costs much money."

My nerve ends were beginning to fray. "I understand. But you have many ships. I have one wife."

"Excuse me. You think it would help better if you were with her?"

"It would help me."

"Ah." He nodded vacantly. "You may speak to the captain, but I assure you that nothing can be done. You could have left the ship this afternoon at Gibraltar—"

"I didn't know until tonight."

He stood. This, I knew, was the end of the interview. "If there is anything I can do, Mr. Bishop. . . ."

My morale began to sag. For an hour, I felt that everything would be all right and I felt good. She had been operated on; the worst was over. Lots of people recovered from peritonitis. Then the stainless-steel clamps of fear began to tighten around my chest and the moisture collected on my palms. What to do? Where to go?

I tried standing on the boat deck in the cool breeze of darkness, but again my mind wandered and I was looking along the narrow pathway of moonbeams on the sea and wondering whether we would ever again watch it together.

A bed is no good to the sleepless. However, I tried it. The stout steward, Luigi, brought me a pot of tea and an apple and a knife. I sipped the tea, said the prayer again, the one to the Virgin of Guadalupe, and went to sleep. It was a deep untroubled sleep, and I felt that I had just dropped off when I heard a knock on the door of 138.

"Come in," I said. It was a young bellhop. He had a radiogram. I looked for a quarter in U.S. currency. "What time is it?" I said. He said eight o'clock. I had to sit up a moment, blinking at him stupidly, to understand where I was and what had happened the night before.

"Then it was not a dream," I said. He looked at me and smiled. I gave him the tip and he left. The message said:

ELINOR OPERATED ON PERITONITIS TODAY. CONDITION SATIS-FACTORY THIS STAGE DOCTOR SAYS. CABLE FURTHER TO-MORROW.

EDDIE MAHAR

At once I was in a new world. I was thankful and hungry and happy. I rang for Luigi and ordered a breakfast. In slow and simple English, I told him the story and of how worried I felt last night and of how her condition was satisfactory and what a great day this was and how, someday soon, he would be meeting Mrs. Bishop on this ship eastbound to the Riviera. That was one trip she would make: an autumn honeymoon.

The steward did not understand all of it. He summoned Marie, the little maid in black. He told her, in Italian, what he understood. Over the hot cereal and toast, I could almost follow his story by her changing expressions. At the end, she smiled and looked at me.

"Your wife, signor. She is better?"

I tapped Mahar's cable. "Much. The word satisfactory is the best I've heard in a long time." There was a ship's newspaper. I read it and knelt and said a prayer of fervent thanks and asked that Elinor's condition remain satisfactory. And then, when I got home and she got home, we would start all over again.

The warm soapy shower rinsed old sorrows from the skin. Under it I made a list of vows. No more arguments, ever. No more making fun of how stupid women can be. No more derogatory mentions of Momma. No more worrying about the children to the neglect of our own lives. A couple of books were selling pretty well, and Elinor and I could afford to travel. Trips around the world on the *Caronia* started at about $3,500, and we would make this one alone. A little bit more compromise on both sides, a little bit more thinking of the other, and we would have a dream existence.

The quality and beauty of a summery dream—many of the 9,945 days we had been together had had it. Before anything else we were sentimentalists, savers of old theater programs, fading heart-shaped boxes which once held candy, old ticket stubs which read "Tulane vs. Colgate, Yankee Stadium" or "Cornell vs. Princeton, Palmer Stadium," albums of yellowed pictures, old tarnished gifts now reposing in bureau drawers, gift cards with the dates on them and "To Baby, from Baby."

I was in the ballroom off the forward lounge when the little bellhop peeked in and grinned. My shipboard friends stopped talking and the several expressions froze as I tipped the boy and ripped the envelope. I read it and swallowed.

"Good news," I said. "It says 'Off critical list holding her own love Ginny.' That's my married daughter." All of them knew. The word had spread in the night and they had exercised one of two options, to mention Mrs. Bishop's health discreetly and hopefully or not to mention it.

I beamed and looked at my shoes. Someone said, "This calls for a drink if I ever heard a call." I looked up and said that this one was on me. A tall man named Ben Williamson said nothing doing, that I was merely the next of kin and had no proprietary rights on salutes to my wife.

In a few minutes, the little bar was gay and the passengers who had been shy about discussing my misfortune now asked many questions about Elinor and the children and the little town of Sea Bright, New Jersey, and how one writes for a living and would Mrs. Bishop still be in the hospital when I got home and how old were the children, and most of the questions were sweet and complimentary.

On the port side, weather was making up. A medium heavy sea was riding down from the north with feathers. The *Giulio Cesare* wallowed in the troughs and lifted her thick steel bows, and spray flew topside and across the anchor gear. Passengers moving in the long corridors used the hand rails. Two women were getting permanents in the beauty salon and three sat waiting. A group of passengers lounged under robes on the promenade deck chairs and two teen-age boys played ping-pong on the enclosed deck.

A few hardy ones shivered at the edge of the outdoor swimming pool. Overhead, low gray clouds crossed the ship's masts heading for warmth to the south. There was sporadic gunfire on the starboard side. These were the hardy trapshooters, having their morning go at being men among men.

The day, for me, moved slowly. It dragged its feet along the minute hand. Elinor was recovering, but now I wanted no more of this ship. I wanted to be home right now. I wanted to be in the hospital. I wanted to talk to the doctors and, most of all, now that the danger was past, I wanted to know what had caused peritonitis.

At 2:30 P.M. I took a nap.

For this day, I could not conjure up Elinor's face. I could remember the individual features, but I could not make myself see the whole face, nor could I make myself hear her speak. I sat in 138 and tried hard to recall her, but she kept slipping away. This induces a form of emotional panic, and so I reached harder for the face and the voice and the harder I reached, the more she retreated into the mists.

It is a ridiculous and cruel thing not to remember a woman who has been everything in twenty-seven of a man's forty-nine years of life. I had spent more years with her than with my mother and father, and their faces and voices came easily. Gayle, thirteen, with the jaded, left-handed smile of the wise innocent, was clear. Ginny, beautiful and intelligent and a worse sentimentalist than her parents, could be conjured on the bulkhead wall. Charlie, big and broad, a kid with red hair and the manners of an old Southern Colonel, was a cinch to recall.

Why not Elinor? I had to go all the way back to when we met to bring her back to me. It was a blind date. She was sitting in a lobby. I said hello. She acted suspicious. She challenged almost every nice thing I said. Before the evening was over, it developed that she was supposed to be a date for my friend Al Porter; I was supposed to be the escort for the other girl.

This led to an argument in which my friend Al invited me out in an alley to continue the discussion privately. It was a fine start. At 1 A.M., with dried blood on my nose, I escorted her home. She was angry and uncommunicative and, on the front porch, I was trying to apologize and say goodnight when I heard a voice from behind a living room screen. "This is a fine time to be bringing a decent girl home."

Her mother. This was the first meeting. I tried to explain to the voice behind the screen but the window slammed and a shade fell. Elinor must have felt sorry for me because, at this point, she said, "Are your ancestors Irish"?

"On all sides," I said.

"So are mine," she said. "Forget tonight. Call me if you are so disposed, and don't bring your friend Al."

We were engaged three months later, married in nine. The things I could recall about the wedding were St. John's Roman Catholic Church in Jersey City; the best man, John Dundas, walking at my side out of the sacristy and whispering, "Take it easy. This isn't a race"; the reception on the roof of the Elk's Club with some old cousin of the bride's reading a long poem to the newlyweds; Fred Grimsey lending us his car with signs and tin cans on it; the apartment my mother-in-law picked out for us at $70 a month rent.

Elinor worked as a broker's secretary in Wall Street and earned $30 a week. I worked as a cub reporter on the *New York Daily Mirror*. Salary, $25 a week. We had no money and everything was bought on the time-payment plan. Once a week we invited our friends to the apartment to show off a new rug, a new radio, a new kitchen set, or a pair of end tables. We danced and ate and had a gay time and sometimes awakened in the morning to find the lights on and the marks of dead cigarettes burned into the rug or the settee.

We always attended Mass at St. Aloysius Church on Sunday, because the bride gave the bridegroom no peace until he stirred, got up growling, bathed and shaved, tried to sip orange juice, dressed, and left on time. My faith in God and in my church was always firm but hers was stronger by far, and she had forebodings of all kinds if we did not get to Mass or say our daily prayers or go to confession and communion regularly.

She wanted babies at once. Hers was a special built-in yearning for little ones; and when pregnancy did not ensue promptly, Elinor made special visits to church to light candles and to ask the Blessed Mother to help her. Other girls might have gone to a doctor. But babies were a special mark of favor from God and His Holy Mother, and Elinor knew to whom to appeal.

There was a depression and the brokers cut down on secretaries. At twenty, Elinor was one of the juniors. Besides, she had a husband. When the time came to cut the payroll, Mrs. Bishop was one of the first to be dropped. Overnight, our economic situation became impossible. I addressed myself to Émile Gauvreau, the managing editor. He said that he liked my work and would raise my salary. He did. The salary jumped ten dollars in the next week, and four weeks later it jumped fifteen more. Six weeks after that there was an additional ten-dollar raise.

Mrs. Bishop stopped looking for a job. She became pregnant. When she was in her third week, she was on the phone telling her girl friends how tight her waistline was and how sick she felt in the morning. We were in debt and went deeper into debt. We bought bassinettes and bathinettes and a baby carriage and diapers and layettes and things in pink and things in blue. We even bought a little pink and white dresser to hold most of the items. She wanted a girl.

She talked babies and read about babies and had no more knowledge of her own anatomy or the anatomy of pregnancy than a fifteen-year-old girl who gets her information from girl friends. Twice, I found her standing outside local shops looking into strange baby carriages and cooing at the infants.

The baby was born dead. It was a little girl and she never had a chance. Elinor blamed herself and I said no, it was my fault. She cried. I couldn't. The doctor said that there was nothing wrong with either of us and, if we would be patient, we could in time become parents. He left, taking the little girl with him. All I could think of was that my wife wanted this live doll and it had been denied her.

The shock of failure was with Elinor a long time. This was owing to her feeling, throughout the pregnancy, that she was going to have a baby and that all women had babies and, except for minor discomfort, nothing unhappy could occur. Still, she had courage. She told our doctor—Arthur Trewhella—that she wanted to become pregnant at once and that I was opposed to it. The doctor had a talk with me. He said that Elinor had a lot of built-in fears and that it would be good for her to have a baby. I asked him if he could guarantee that the next baby would be born alive. No, he said, he couldn't, but he was willing to bet that it would.

We, who knew everything, learned slowly. The moment we agreed to try again to have a family, it became impossible. Four years went by before Elinor—now stout at 145 pounds and twenty-five years of age—could announce smugly and with lowered lids, "Don't look now, but I think I'm preg."

She was. This time, Doctor Trewhella called in a consultant and, from their conversation I understood that Mrs. Bishop was prone, in some mysterious way, to tear the edge of the placenta, thus robbing the unborn infant of food. Happily, she understood none of it. Precautions were taken, and my wife was put into the hospital a month ahead of time for rest. She prayed again for a girl.

The baby was a little girl. She lived four hours. The shock was so bad and so enduring that, two years later, when Virginia Lee was born at 8 pounds and a few ounces, Elinor lay gray and despairing in her bed and refused to believe that she had a live baby girl.

After that, we entered the happy period. She gave Ginny oil baths and dressed and undressed her and changed her and nipped at the infant's neck and talked to her and tried to train the scanty yellow strands into curls. Six years later she had Gayle, who was born prematurely and with fat threshing legs. Elinor's cup was filled.

I invited her mother, a widow, to come to live with us. Maggy was a stout, slow-witted Irishwoman of great charm. Her size was 52. She was one of the most generous women I've ever known. She baby-sat, and got into all of our quarrels, and spoiled the children, and refused to go to bed if we were

entertaining, and knew how to cook delicious food out of a
nearly empty refrigerator.

She liked baseball and had her radio on at all hours if the
Dodgers were playing. On occasion, when they were a run
behind, she brought out her rosary and prayed to God for a
run or two. When I suggested that God might possibly be a
Giant fan, she looked horrified and said, "That's blasphemy.
God forgive you."

When she was at a christening or a wedding she enjoyed the
refreshments, and her face got red and perspiration plastered
her hair against her forehead. And she would say loudly, "Have
fun. You're only young once." She was only old once, but she
tried to have as much fun as possible. She would never look at
another man.

"My Frank," she would say, panting for breath, "let me tell
you. My Frank was the best there is. I wouldn't look at the best
one left."

She lived with us for twenty years. She was hypersensitive
and would permit no one to contradict her on any subject.
Tears were always close to the lids. Elinor was her only child,
and she would not leave a house, enter one, put on a dress,
buy a gift card, get herself a drink of water, or turn her radio
on without the assistance of her daughter.

If Maggy leaned hard on Elinor, Elinor wanted her to lean.
I called them "the Corporation" because they thought alike on
everything. If there was a call from upstairs, "Elinor-r-r-r!" my
wife dropped everything and ran. Often, it developed that her
mother had just thought of something that happened a long
time ago, or she was wondering whose birthday was May 8,
or perhaps she wanted some cubes of ice in a glass of water.
Whatever it was, Elinor ran.

"Why?" I said a thousand times.

"Why?" she would say. "I'll tell you why. Because if anything
ever happens to my mother, I don't want it on my conscience
that I didn't do everything for her. That's why."

Maggy had old-fashioned courage. If you believed in God and attended to your church duties and your family, you were right in everything you did. Once she became your protagonist, you could rob a bank and she would testify that somebody goaded you into doing it. In the same ratio, if she was opposed, Maggy was a long-time hater. And if the name of someone on her despised list came up, she could not mention the person without squinting her eyes almost shut and hissing as she talked.

When matters went poorly for my brand of writing, Elinor and I were troubled. Not Maggy. "Listen," she would say. "Now listen to me. I don't know much about writing and half the time I don't even know the words I read, but you can write good; and if them editors is that dumb not to buy what you write, then we are all going to have to sit and wait until they wake up."

She was a remarkable woman.

We were always reckless, economically. We spent as lavishly of money that we did not have as we spent of emotions which we did not understand. Few couples could stare at new crisp pull-back window curtains with such relish. We loved them. We loved what they did for our home. She knew so much about decoration and I so little that I was content always—or almost always—to follow her lead in color, in design, in symmetry.

Elinor had an inordinate pride in her home, as she had in her children. Each had to be the best dressed. As a writer, I was never more than average, and I needed luck to add to my income. Luck smiled agreeably, and I moved from newspaper work to magazine editing to writing books, and except for three years of poor free-lance writing, we did well.

It was not enough. We owed money to furniture houses, to banks, to butchers, to grocers. We paid and paid and paid. A check for $1,000 from an editor could arrive in the morning and, after deposit, it would be dissipated in a confetti of small checks by the following morning. We had a credo: "Debts? Who would be without them?"

A few years ago, I paused to meditate on our marriage and our lives. I had the shocking feeling that we had been running at top speed for twenty years and had not moved an inch. My career was like dozens of others—no better, no worse. The stonecutter's lines appeared deeply under my eyes and the hair was gray. A second chin and a second stomach came as the dividends of time.

Elinor still looked pretty when she was made up and well dressed. She had the smart sweet air of a matron who lives in Westchester or La Jolla or any of ten thousand towns between. The roundness of face had gone and the lips had thinned. The figure was flat and thin, the legs which once had modeled stockings looked as though they had been taken from a window mannequin. In an evening dress, the shoulders were little lemon-colored doorknobs. She had a slowly increasing nervousness, a feeling of impending doom with no knowledge of what form it would take.

"It is like," she said sadly, "a perpetual hangover. It is as though I had been drinking and I was afraid to look at my hands for fear that they were shaking. It's as though"—the face would contort and tears would come to dampen the wretchedness of the features—"Oh Jimmy, I don't know. I don't know."

She demanded more and more obedience and evidence of love from her daughters, from me. The slightest criticism, or even lack of enthusiasm, was an affront. She devoted herself more and more to Maggy, and now Maggy needed the devotion because she was deep in the seventies and suffered increasing attacks of what she called "the blues." Maggy was five feet tall and weighed 180 pounds. At seventy-four, the effort to rise from a chair, without assistance, was almost futile.

More and more, the old lady took to her room, alternating between playing soap operas on her radio, fingering her rosary, and looking out of her little bedroom window obliquely toward the street. The children helped her to the bathroom, helped her back, put her slippers and stockings on, took them off. When they helped her, Maggy's self-deprecation was instantaneous: "Lovey, I can't do nothing no more. I'm just old."

For five years, we had had few visitors. The children and I were gregarious. Although not a word was said against having visitors, we stopped inviting people to our house. The children sometimes asked their schoolmates to wait outside for them. If a man or woman got inside the door, he was cordially greeted by Elinor and her mother, both of whom smiled and made apologies for their appearance. And Elinor always shook the bottles to see if there was enough to offer a scotch or a bourbon to the company. Both sat smiling and twisting and untwisting their hands and making little sallies and asking questions about family, children, mutual friends. When the visitor left, they looked at each other. Elinor drew a long breath, and Maggy looked toward Heaven and shook her head.

Now and then they would decide to make the effort to go to someone else's home, if invited. On those occasions, the tensions drew strings around all our throats, because if any of the rest of us uttered a word out of proper context, Elinor would storm into her mother's room half dressed and say, "I'm not going, Momma. You go."

It required pleading and apologies and coaxing to reorient the situation. And then, when the visit was over, Elinor and her mother would relax in the car and tell each other how glad they were that they got dressed and went out.

"Does you good," Maggy would say.

"I enjoyed myself," Elinor said. "Of course, even in front of people my husband never has a kind word for me, but he's a good boy underneath. I understand him."

The frightening thing, to me, was the inexorability of this long walk downhill. These women were becoming recluses. They did not want to go out; they wanted no one to come in. Later, when the doorbell rang, they disappeared and would not answer it. And, after more time, they did not want to answer the telephone either.

Still, there were remissions. Each time they occurred, Ginny and Gayle and I—in solemn secret conference—assured each other that the ladies had taken a turn for the better. In retrospect, it seems to me that Maggy took the lead in these sporadic decisions to live with the rest of the world.

One of these was the Republican Convention in San Francisco in 1956. Elinor decided to go. For years, I had been accustomed to making these assignments alone; for years, I accepted dinner invitations alone. In recent times, hostesses had become accustomed to addressing invitations solely to "Mr." Sometimes they asked politely why my wife never accompanied me to the theater or to dinner and I always said that she was not well.

The trip to San Francisco turned out to be the loveliest, most memorable of them all; a trip in which all the early history of happy days came alive in musical echoes. We dined everywhere, saw everything, tried everything, bought everything, because we now had the money.

We made fun of each other and laughed and took The Owl down to Los Angeles. We stayed at the Beverly Hills Hotel, and the manager sent flowers. We went to the motion picture studios and the newspaper offices, and Elinor met Bob Hope and Alexis Smith and William Randolph Hearst and Cecil B. deMille. On the train coming home, she was momentarily saddened leaving Chicago, sorry to see it end.

Still, she missed her mother and she missed Gayle and Ginny. For a little while, back home, she sounded like a happy extrovert as she recounted the trip.

"Did you meet Pat O'Brien?" Maggy said.

"No, Momma. We didn't."

"Too bad. Jimmy should have introduced you to him. A fine man, that Pat O'Brien."

There was a difference in Maggy now. At times, her face appeared to be as yellow as the harvest moon. She, who enjoyed eating, used her fork to push the food from one side of the plate to the other. Overnight, she had surrendered. She was seventy-seven years of age and she was so tired that she was beyond sleep.

Overnight, the old nervousness returned to Elinor, except that it was enhanced beyond anything she had suffered before. She smoked cigarettes swiftly. She did not want to dress or wash. She did not want to work around the house. And the thought of cooking was enough to drive her to bed. She lit a cigarette, found one already burning in an ash tray, and chuckled at herself, saying, "Who's nervous?"

She sat on a bed beside her mother and, with eloquent eyes, begged Maggy to live. Momma was afraid of doctors; so was daughter. They wanted to be treated by telephone. Dr. Bernard Krull managed to visit both, and he came away shaking his head. Maggy was in heart failure. He watched her go upstairs to her room by climbing the stairs on her hands and knees.

Elinor sat in a housecoat looking at her hands. They shook all the time. She and her mother prayed as hard and as fervently as anyone can, but neither one had the strength to go to church. "If I go," Elinor said, "the walls start coming in on me. I guess that's claustrophobia, isn't it?" I said I guessed it was. Her hair was stringy, and if the doctor said to take two tablets of Miltown per day, my wife took six.

Sometimes, she sat in a stupor, looking up and grinning out of half-closed eyes, the hands held on the lap turned in toward each other like claws. Ginny, who was now married, came to the house as often as possible to cook. When dinner was ready, Maggy said that she didn't feel like eating. Elinor said that she wasn't hungry. Later, when the dishes were done, Elinor would stand at the drain board, pour herself a glass of cold milk, slap a sandwich together, and gulp it down as though someone might catch her at it.

I bought her a mink coat, and when she opened the big box and saw a shimmer of light run down the fur, she wept. "Every

woman wants a fur coat," she said to our daughters, "and I'm
the luckiest. But I won't wear it. I know I won't." She showed
it off about six times.

She went to bed at nine or nine-thirty every night. And she
was up at 2 A.M., sitting at a window, puffing on a cigarette,
and praying for daylight. In the next room, Maggy sat in a
nightgown, her bare feet on the floor, rubbing her knees and
looking out of the little window at a street light across the
street. Her mouth moved in prayer, stopping momentarily
when a late car passed by.

Time dragged its feet. Again, there were remissions. We
went to our summer place in Sea Bright (where we planned to
live all year around) and late one morning Elinor came out
of the bedroom all dressed up and made up and Gayle was so
happy that she almost wept.

"Holy smokes!" she said. "Get a load of Mommy."

Mommy looked pretty. She did not look forty-seven. She
was bright and cheerful and she wanted Gayle to take her
across the street to our beach pavilion. She sat near the thunder of the surf and she told me that she was going to treat
herself to a new deal. "I'm all right now," she said. "I'm going
to stop worrying about Momma and I'm going to think of us.
It should have been us all along—and it really was us—but
Momma had nobody but me and I felt that I should do everything I could for her."

I asked her if she knew what her deepest fear was. She
shrugged, as though I was prying into something too personal
even for a husband. "I don't know," she murmured shyly.
"Death, I guess. It's all silly, I know. You don't have to tell
me. The best way I can describe it is that it seems like I was
very busy and I turned around and suddenly found myself
old."

"You're not old."

What really happened, I felt, was that I had failed her at the
worst time. In recent months, I had lost patience. I no longer
pleaded with her to go to a doctor, or to a psychiatrist, or to

talk to a priest. I gave up. I kissed her on the cheek when I got home and I kissed her good-by when I left. I did not bother with the niceties of inquiring about her health or advising her what to do about a headache, an earache, or a pain in the back. I no longer said, "Please get dressed. A man is coming to see me." I just said, "I'm having dinner at The Colony. I'll be home later."

Continued treatment of this kind must have led her to the despairing feeling that she was going to lose not only her mother but her husband too. This aggravated her condition. Once, sitting with Ginny, she said, "You have Charlie. Gayle's got Daddy. Who have I got?"

After the morning she got dressed and walked across the street to the beach, Elinor began to try hard to do the things we wanted her to do. She did not want to do them, but she was determined, at great loss of pride, to win our love back. We had a maid to cook, but Elinor wanted to help. She polished mirrors and dusted tables and, although she feared boats almost beyond reason, she gulped and got aboard our cabin cruiser and pretended to enjoy the ride. Her favorite word became "relax."

"I want to relax" . . . "If only I could relax a little" . . . "I feel relaxed here. It's so nice and cool" . . . "Ask your mother and father to come down for a weekend. It will relax them."

One morning in July we were having breakfast. Maggy was too sick to get out of bed. She called "Elinor-r-r-r!" My wife tapped her mouth with a napkin, looked at me with stricken eyes (as though the call forboded some dire news), and went upstairs. Maggy wanted assistance to go to the bathroom. The old lady could barely walk. Elinor performed the service as she had so many times before.

She closed the door on her mother and waited, standing at the top of the stairs. We continued to eat. After awhile, my wife whispered down the stairs, "Jimmy, do you think she's all right in there?" I thought for a moment, half asleep, half awake. "Certainly," I said. "She's okay." Elinor waited a little while longer and then began to call softly to her mother through the closed door. "Momma? You all right, Momma? I don't want to bother you, Momma. I just want to make sure—." She opened the door. She peeked inside. Maggy's head lolled back, the eyes wide open and staring at the ceiling. Elinor's hands began to shake and she came downstairs quickly and quietly and said in pleading tones, "I wish you'd go upstairs and have a look at Momma. I think she's fainted."

Maggy was dead. A guest helped me to drag her back to bed. I phoned the doctor and whispered the news. He said he'd be right over. I phoned Father Joseph Sullivan at Holy Cross Church in Rumson. He said he'd come at once. Elinor sat at the kitchen table. The eyes were pleading again.

"She's all right, isn't she? Just a little faint? Maybe I better go up there and sit with her until the doctor comes." I said no, and the tone was tired. I said that Momma was very sick. It would not be good to hold out any hope for her. Very sick, I said again. She's very old and very tired. The kindest, and cruelest thing I could say was, "Maybe you'd better pray that God takes her." What I was trying to say was that she had better brace herself and I wanted to lead her into thinking of her mother's passing in stages. I could not bring myself to say that Momma had gone. And yet, when I would not permit Elinor to go up and sit with her mother and she saw that I did not go back up, she must have known.

She was weeping when the doctor arrived and shortly after him the priest. After all the years of service, after all the lavish love, she did not give way to hysterics. The hands twisted, the tears flowed, the head was bowed. And as the priest consoled her, all she could murmur was, "Poor Momma. Poor, poor Momma."

After the funeral, Elinor needed more tranquilizers. This was understandable. The children and I knew that she was probing her conscience at all hours of the day and night, asking herself over and over if there was anything she could have done for Maggy in all those years that she had not done. There were feelings of guilt too, feelings that if she had done this or that or had paid closer attention to her mother's minor ills Maggy would be alive today.

Prayer, I believe, was what kept Elinor from cracking. After six weeks, she began to think again of getting out. It wasn't much, but it gave her a change of scenery. At night she knelt at the foot of the bed in her nightgown, praying hard and tapping her chest with her fist.

In bed, she went to sleep at once. Her happiest moments were in unconsciousness, and she often dreaded to awaken. Sometimes, if a doorbell or the sound of breakfast from the kitchen brought her back to reality, she squinted her eyes and hoped hard that she could get back to sleep. The pills were taken two at a time, and the children hid them from her and doled them out sparingly into the thin trembling palms.

I asked her if she wanted to go to Europe with me in September and she thought about it a moment, smiled, and said no, thanks. But later, she said when I got back I was going to be surprised at how well she was. Again, I showed the cruel lack of patience.

"How can you talk about getting better when you can't even go upstairs in your own house because Momma died up there? How can you recover when you won't even see your doctor? How can you even mention recovery when you keep yourself drugged on these lousy pills and you sit in a chair hours on end half awake and half asleep? Who are you kidding?"

It was a bad beating, but I couldn't think of anything else. I was approaching a stage where I began to feel sorry for myself. This was a bad thing and the antidote was to be callous. The antidote was to have no feelings. The antidote was to point out the flaws in her thinking and let her devise ways of combatting them. The antidote was to stop caring.

I sat in Cabin 138 and this was the only portrait I could summon. The hurt mute look as she sat on the red couch. Her knowledge that what I said was true but that saying it would not help her, would only confirm her own fears that she would never get well. I could not conjure a vision of her as young and beautiful and happy. All I could see was the pinched tired face and the big eyes unblinking under the lashes.

Thinking hurt. I went up to the top deck to send a radiogram.

ELINOR BISHOP
MONMOUTH MEMORIAL HOSPITAL LONG BRANCH NJER
EVERY MINUTE BRINGS ME CLOSER TO YOU MY HEART IS AL-
READY THERE LOVE YOU DEARLY CHIN UP

                                                              BABY

I hesitated before signing it. My impulse was to write "Jim." She would have detected a chill in that. "Baby" had been the term of special endearment between us for so long that I decided to use it, no matter how hard the Italian radio operator stared at it and me.

The exultation that came with the knowledge that my wife was recovering began to wear off. Morale sagged and I wasn't good company for my table companions or at the little bar. A growing despondency is not easy to rationalize. Within the space of time between lunch and dinner, I felt spent and discouraged. I was sliding down a spiral chute.

There was a momentary lift when Mahar's next radio arrived:

DOCTOR REPORTS ELINOR RESPONDING BETTER CONDITION
STILL SATISFACTORY OUTLOOK BRIGHTER AND ELINOR GETTING
BEST CARE MEDICAL ATTENTION WILL KEEP WATCH RADIO TO-
MORROW

                                                              MAHAR

At 10 P.M. the ship's orchestra was playing American jazz. Passengers in daring gowns and black ties sat around the disc of dance floor chatting and drinking. The despondency died in me. I listened to the jokes and I laughed; and my foot began to tap with the music. The bellhop threaded his way through the tables. I saw him. The foot stopped. He was looking around the sea of faces and it was possible that he was looking for any one of a thousand passengers.

He saw me and smiled. "De telephone, Meester Beeshop." I followed. What was it now? A turn for the worse? It could not be a turn for the better because she had been improving for twenty-four hours. It had to be bad news. How bad? It could be Ginny to tell me that my wife had gone.

I did not speak to my friendly little executioner. I was busy praying all the way up to the top of the ship. When I got in the radio room there were the same faces—the smart looking little Romeo with the gray hair, the man with the broken face—they smiled like old friends. They twirled dials and called "'Ello New York? 'Ello New York?" and I said to myself, I'll be hearing this for many years to come.

They nodded to the little alcove. I sat. I swallowed. I said hello. It was Eddie Mahar, whose warm friendly voice always opens conversations with the same signature: "How the hell are you? Listen . . ." He had a lot to say and every bit of it was succinct and important.

He had been in steady touch with the doctor, the Italian Line, the Air Force in Washington. The situation was this: Elinor now had pneumonia. It was a complication, but not necessarily a fatal one. It was one more hurdle for my wife to jump. The doctor still felt optimistic. Eddie pointed out that he and the doctor could have lulled me with lies, but they figured that I wanted to know the truth and there it was.

The *Journal-American* had been in touch with the Italian Line and the Air Force. All hands agreed to try to get me off the *Giulio Cesare* and fly me home.

I listened. The voice was strong, then fading, then strong again. Eddie was confident. It was contagious. "Stop worrying. This has been a serious matter. She's rallying. Ginny tells me she was asking for you this morning. She asked Ginny if she had been operated on and the kid said yes. Then she asked how long it would take for you to get to the hospital and Ginny said that you were trying to make it as fast as possible.

"Now Jim, the plot is this. The Air Force has a base on an island in the Azores called Terceira. You'll be passing somewhere near it tomorrow. We're going to try to send a crash boat out to meet the *Giulio Cesare* if your captain will come close enough. This is a thing you have to ask him. The Italian Line here is willing, but the captain is still the captain.

"If he will do it the crash boat will take you off, and there is a regular night flight out of Terceira for Maguire."

"That's near Trenton."

"Near Trenton. Right, Jim. That flight will get in here Thursday morning about eight o'clock. How far is it from Trenton to the hospital?"

"An hour's drive."

"How far?"

"An hour. About forty miles, Ed."

"O.K. You should be with your gal at 9 A.M. Thursday. Now listen. We'll be doing everything we can on this end. Guy Richards and Dick Graf and George Carroll are doing everything they can. It's up to you to ask the captain to swing off course. If he says yes, let me know at once. We'll take care of the rest."

I said thanks. This is a weak word and, across 3,000 miles of seaway, it is weaker. Captain Pinotti was in his cabin behind the bridge. Up close, the captain is a small gracious person with shrewd laughing eyes, a long nose, and a deep romantic voice.

He listened to the story. He sat at his desk, a shielded light throwing a saffron diffusion over his face. A small pen on the blotter kept in faithful swing with the ship, rolling first to one side, then the other. The captain asked a few questions about Mrs. Bishop's present condition. He asked more questions about Gayle and Ginny.

"You are certain of the—the—the cooperation from the Air Force?"

I said yes. I explained that in the United States I had a syndicated column and that the city editor of one of the newspapers, the *Journal-American,* had contacted the Air Force and made arrangements.

He nodded. He sat looking at his clasped hands under the desk light. Then he shrugged.

"It is a difficult thing," he said. "To do this, I must take the ship north—which I can do now; it is easier now than later— and we will lose an hour. I must contact the Italian Line in New York." He expanded his hands, palm up. "If they say yes, Mr. Bishop, then we will pass Terceira in the evening."

"What day?"

"Tomorrow."

"Oh, tomorrow."

He beckoned me to follow him to the navigator's depart- ment. The two spoke in Italian. The navigator looked at me, listened to the captain, and nodded with comprehension. Then he shook his head. "I am so sorry for you," he said. He bent over his big artist's desk and worked with pencil, ruler, re- tractors, and clock.

"At six o'clock," he said, "Greenwich time, we can be one mile south of Terceira light." The captain excused himself. "I have much to do," he said. His operator put in a call for New York, even though it must have been an hour before dawn in the metropolis. Later, the captain found me in the ballroom and said that the big ship was now headed for Terceira.

"The Air Force will have a small boat to take you off?" he said. I nodded. "Yes sir." He studied me for a moment, and then he smiled and permitted himself a small intimacy. He patted my shoulder. "Your good wife will be all right. You take my word. For the children who are alone with her, I will do this thing."

Tomorrow would be Wednesday. If I got off the ship in the evening, and the Air Force had a night flight to Maguire, I should be at Elinor's side on Thursday morning. By that time, she should be feeling a little better. I knew what she would do when I walked in. She would cry.

By this time the radio shack had become a source of dread for me, and I could not think of it or go in it without feeling damp and chilled.

A message went out to Ed Mahar telling him that the ship would pass one mile south of Terceira at 6 P.M. Greenwich Mean Time and to have a crash boat out to take me off the leeward side. I thanked him and his city desk men who had done so much for me. I understood the amount of work, the phone calls to Washington, the memos flying back and forth, the contacts that were necessary to make all of this come true.

Cabin 138 looked brighter. The steward brought me some tea and I told him the story. He was so excited that he called Marie to hear the whole thing over again. They offered to help pack. No, I said, I would do it myself. All of the things I would not need tomorrow were slammed into valises which were squeezed shut.

In packing, some papers fell out of a briefcase. They were letters. The first was from Gayle, written the day I sailed on the *United States,* and mailed to England.

Dear Dad,

How was it? Everything here is fine. Mommy did great coming home in the car. Its ten o'clock now and we are getting ready for bed. I fixed her two aspirins and she is fine. *Don't worry about a thing.* Rocky is fine. As you know, I start school Monday. Mrs. Walter was great.

Mommy never stopped talking coming down in the car. That is about all. We went over to the beach today, and Aunt Agnes was there. So they talked and talked and talked. Nothing else is new except *we miss you.* Rocky got a good whack today for trying to eat the towels off the clothesline.

Love and Kisses,
Gayle Peggy

Another one was dated the next day.

Dear Dad,

Nothing is new here.

Mommy did not sleep so good. Aunt Agnes called. Nothing is new with her. She wanted to know how everything is. It is crumby here. It looks like rain.

Don't worry about a thing. Rocky's dog tag came today.

Love and Kisses,
Gayle Peggy

There was one from Ginny, and it took on more meaning now than when it was received at Cannes.

Dear Daddy:

I'm really sorry I haven't written sooner, but I wanted to wait until I had really good news about Mommy, and now I have. Tonight we arrived from Westwood [Ginny's home] and as soon as we got in the door, she announced that she was going upstairs [to her mother's room for the first time since her death]. Probably because you had mentioned it in the letter we just finished reading.

She asked me to go up and turn the lights on and to please stay with her, which I did. She cried a lot, but she did it and so far has been up three more times tonight. She says she can probably go up any time from now on. So that's one big hurdle she has finally gotten over.

Mommy has really been doing well. Gayle and she came up Tuesday night for Claire's shower. The trip up was fine; she was just a little nervous, but not as bad as usual. She was the belle of the ball at the shower, and she was certainly a help to me. She made the punch, fixed the salads, set the table, washed dishes and really kept busy. She must like my cooking, because she's even eating well. Honestly, she has been trying. She started several letters to you, but her hands shake, so she never completed them.

Now she says she wants to buy a "smart outfit" and have me give her a permanent wave so she'll be a living doll when you come home. . . . We all send lots of love and kisses and we miss you terribly and wish you would hurry home to us all. Our prayers are always with you and we hope you have a good trip home. We'll see you soon.

All our love,
Ginny

I went back to the sickening radio room and sent another radiogram to Elinor. It said I LOVE YOU—and between the lines, "Hold on, hold on."

Later in the night there was a Marconigram from Mahar saying that everything was being arranged, and to be prepared to leave the ship at Terceira. My worries evaporated. Everything was turning out fine. With such friends, how could I lose?

The worries were gone, but sleep would not come. It was like the night before a vacation trip when I was a child. I saw the Air Force boat, the little island, the trip to shore, meeting the officers, packing the gear aboard a DC-6, the long runway, the night hours sitting with the crew in the glow of an instrument panel, smoking cigarettes and drinking coffee and swapping flying stories, and then the long let-down in the morning at Trenton, the customs clearance, the good-bys and the thank yous, and a cab rocking forty miles to Long Branch.

I flew it again and again. I could see Elinor propped up, the pink bed jacket, the flowers, the tears, the relatives who would not have the discretion to leave the room for a moment. It was like this all night. Before dawn, I slept.

At lunch, I was the wit of the table. The time was 1:30 P.M., Wednesday. In a few hours I would be off this ship and speeding home. My table companions asked about Elinor and I told them that she had rallied and was doing well. I ate everything that was offered, including a fattening dessert. Everyone wanted to know what caused the peritonitis and I said I did not know. I reminded myself to ask Ginny the next time she was on the phone.

We were sipping coffee when the little cabin boy came into the dining room. I looked at him and looked away. This time he must be looking for someone else. Out of a thousand passengers. . . .

"Meester Beeshop," he said. He didn't have to say any more. I arose, excused myself, and followed him. By this time, the other passengers had begun to give me a stricken glance whenever I was summoned. I put on the reassuring smile.

There was the long corridor, the elevator, the long walk up behind the bridge, and the smiling, bowing men in the radio room.

"It is New York," the one with the broken face said. "New York calling you emergency." I died a little. He and his assistant turned dials and switched switches and nothing happened. They kept yelling " 'Ello New York. 'Ello New York," until I didn't want to listen. They got New York and there was an additional wait. The New York operator returned and, as Broken Face held the earphones slightly apart from his ears, I could hear the garbled voice, sounding like thick suds falling down a sink drain.

"She say," he said carefully, "eet is John Bishop call you emergency. Now John Bishop is not home." I began to breathe. It meant that my father had heard the news about Elinor and was worried about me. It was not something to get excited about.

I called Mahar while I was in the room. He was not available. Guy Richards of the *Journal-American* got on. He said that the U.S. Air Force Base at Terceira had been alerted. The commanding officer, he said, was Brigadier General Smith. A crash boat would be waiting south of Terceira Light. He asked what the weather was like and I said that we had a pretty good running sea with a wind out of the north. It was sunny, and if the ship could get in close on the south side of the island, the little boat would have no trouble. Everything was in order, I said. I would be waiting and would he please get word to Elinor that I'd be home in the morning. He said he sure would. I asked how she was doing and he said that he had no new reports, which was good.

Later in the afternoon, Captain Pinotti asked me to join him in the radio room. He had his first officer and chief purser with him. They tried to contact Terceira by voice. They called the word until it sounded like a monotonous litany. Between calls, they spoke to each other in English so that I would understand. The captain said that he should have received a message from General Smith by now. The amenities of the situation were that the general should contact the ship and inquire about last-minute instructions.

I said that none were needed, really. The time would be 6 P.M. and the place would be one mile south of Terceira Light. The captain smiled. Yes, he said patiently, but if the general were bringing a big ship in this close, I would contact him anyway to find out about weather and to see if there was a time change—at least to acknowledge the existence of the other party to this thing.

He was right. The operator said that Terceira could call us but we could not call Terceira. The reason was that it was a Portuguese station and they would not answer unless addressed in Portuguese. Besides, they were closed down much of the time. Broken Face called Pan American two hundred miles south and, for a moment, he had them. "Please," said Broken Face, "use your facilities to call General Smith at Terceira. What? U.S. Air Force please. Tell him you are in touch with *Giulio Cesare* and the captain would—" The circuit winked out.

Broken Face said that he would be happy to call the Air Force direct, but he did not know the military call letters and most such establishments will not answer a civilian call unless it is an emergency. "Tell them," I said, "that this is an emergency." He smiled. It was four o'clock. I sat at a desk and sent a radiogram to General Smith asking his help at 6 P.M. Captain Pinotti felt that the Air Force was snubbing him and did not want to do anything further except to be at the proper place at the proper time. Finally, however, he looked at me again and said, "I will send a Marconigram direct to the general." He did.

"I will tell him," said the captain in that precise, schoolteacher English, "that de sheep will be one, one and a half mile south of Contendes Point at eighteen hundred fifteen. This will be 6 P.M. ship's time. We will be there. The rest is up to them."

The good-looking radio assistant picked up the transmitter and tried his luck at calling Terceira. " 'Ello Angra Raddio. Angra Raddio 'ello. This is *Giulio Cesare* calling. 'Ello Angra Raddio. Angra Raddio 'ello."

My stomach began to knot again. There was no reason for it, but it knotted as though I were sitting in a room full of bad news and was helpless to get away from it. "This is *Giulio Cesare* calling. *Giulio Cesare* calling Angra Raddio. 'Ello."

At 4:29 P.M. contact was established. The roomful of officers was electrified into silence. "Angra Raddio. This is *Giulio Cesare* calling. Yes. I have been trying to get you, Angra. The captain of de sheep would like to talk to the general at the air base. Yes, please. What is that, sir? Yes, that is right. Please to hold the contact."

The contact was broken at 4:31 P.M. It was a squally, partly sunny afternoon on the boat deck. I kept looking ahead for Terceira. There was no island. Just white caps racing across the bows from the north. The ship lunged and reared. Some of the women passengers were distressed to find that when there is a blow the elevator service shuts down. A few men played gin rummy in the library and traded genial insults.

Everything of mine was packed. The stewards took it below to a hatchway and undogged the big doors on the port side. The purser gave me a visitor's permit to land at the Azores. Everybody wished Mrs. Bishop good luck and some told me that I would be sorry I wasted so much time worrying. I didn't agree, but I didn't say so.

I had spent a lot of time praying because there was no other way of helping her. It also helped me to know that I was doing something for her. I had had a feeling almost from the start that this one was a matter for God's intervention. She had never been seriously ill before, and I had a horrifying feeling that she might feel she was face to face with the thing she dreaded most: death. All normal persons fear death, but her fear was a soul-eating thing. She couldn't bear to think of the death of a friend, much less dwell upon her own. She had to work her nerve up for days merely to visit her father's grave, and he had been dead for a long time.

So most of my prayers had two petitions: one was to please anesthetize her against knowledge of the seriousness of her illness and the other, to please spare her more, for my sake. Still I could not shake my personal dread that the prayers were weak instruments, not worth listening to. There is a whispering frailty at a time like this; one must ask himself in honesty why God would want to bend an ear to me. What had I ever done for Him? Nothing, except to betray Him as infrequently as possible. This is hardly a point to stress in prayer. I would gulp several times before I could get myself to say, "Look, I could have hurt You more than I did. I might have been a worse sinner. Think back on the times I resisted temptation for Your sake. So please give Elinor a break. Please let her live."

I prattled through words and they sounded like neatly assorted phrases with less meaning than a baby's babble. Sometimes, in the solitude of 138, I tried saying them again and again so that the words would begin to assume a new shape and meaning. I prayed to the Virgin of Guadalupe and asked her to ask her Divine Son to will that my wife would recover. I had little faith in my prayers to Him, but I had tremendous faith in her prayers to Him. I knew that she would do it, no matter what she thought of me.

At 5:45 P.M. I was on the bridge. The sun was out, sitting red and dull above the port bow. The captain stood at one of the windows on the broad bridge. The helmsman held his wheel and kept staring at the compass in front of the wheel. He swung the wheel a few spokes to the right or to the left, but it didn't seem to turn the ship.

The captain had ordered all off-duty bridge officers to be on the bridge. He told them, in Italian, to disperse themselves all over the bridge and the outboard wings and to use their glasses to find a small crash boat. There were at least a dozen men on the bridge as Terceira came up like a brown stone out of the sea.

It came up suddenly and it grew swiftly. Pinotti studied the conformation in the late sun. Then he lowered his glasses and pointed to a tiny white spot over the bows. "Contendes," he said. He looked at his watch and grinned like a little boy who has just achieved 100 in arithmetic.

"We should be one mile off that point at six o'clock," he said. As we approached, I could see the cliffs, the little villages on the south side, the huge brown rocks standing up out of the sea.

"Half speed," the captain said, in Italian.

"Half speed," the officer of the watch said.

"Half speed," the helmsman said.

The ship seemed to move as before. It was driving straight for the little white lighthouse. Looking down from the wing bridge, the ship seemed to be creeping. There was a stone mole to the west of the point, and overhead a big silvery Air Force plane made its final swing around the *Giulio Cesare* before heading across to the other side of the island and down onto the landing strip.

"Do you think he sees us?" I said to the captain.

"Of course. He is only a thousand feet."

"Then he will report that we have arrived," I said hopefully.

"This," the captain said, "is not necessary. They know that we are here. We must find their boat." He went back to looking.

"Slow engines," he said.

"Slow engines," the officer of the watch said.

"Slow engines," the helmsman said.

In a minute, the *Giulio Cesare* seemed to be under bare headway. The captain looked back and said loudly, "Turn to port on a heading of one-seven-five." The order, in Italian, was repeated; and now the big bows, a city block ahead of the bridge, began a slow sensuous turn in the warm green seas. We hugged the lee of the island.

Passengers were up on deck and the word went from mouth to mouth that we were passing a beautiful island. On the sun deck cameras were clicking and spinning. People came out of their houses in the villages and watched the big ship creep by. They did not wave. They looked and shaded their eyes against the sun, and then they went indoors.

A dozen pairs of binoculars swept the horizon forward and aft. Two junior officers had nothing to do but look behind the ship to see if a crash boat came out after we had passed; others stared dead ahead; still others were out looking to port and starboard. The captain showed no anxiety. He walked back and forth, whispering a question, inclining his head to get the answer.

The ship moved along the edge of the island like a knife in slow motion along the rim of a pie. I looked. My anxiety began to mount. This was the island. Where was the boat? They could not have forgotten. No, they had not forgotten. The boat was somewhere along this serrated edge, keeping close to shore to stay out of the north wind.

Pinotti searched every cove. As the ship neared the westerly end of Terceira, he said to me, "I cannot go back. I am very sorry for you, but I cannot go back." I nodded. "I understand," I said. He shrugged. "They should be out here. It is now"—he looked up at the ship's clock—"six-thirteen. They should have been waiting for us."

"Certainly," I said. "It is not your fault."

"It is not a thing of fault, Mr. Bishop. Everyone can try. This is the situation. I must go back on my run. I cannot wait longer." I looked back at Terceira and there was a block in my throat so that I had to cough before I could speak.

"You have done your best, Captain," I said. "You certainly have. I appreciate it. You must get the ship back on course."

He looked at me solemnly. The great thing that he had done for the little ones had not worked out. There was no crash boat; there was no message from the Air Force; there was nothing but an island so close that I could have rowed ashore in fifteen minutes.

"I am sorry for you, Mr. Bishop." He waved to the helmsman. "All engines ahead full," he said. When this order had been properly repeated, he said, "Course one-six-eight." He and I stood on the wing bridge and watched Terceira diminish until, at 6:34, it was again a brown stone in the sea.

Below, I had to explain to Signor Lo Bianco that the little boat was not there. I had to explain it to my room steward. I had to explain it to my friends. Each one said, "But what happened?" as though I knew. I found a place alone and ordered a café espresso. Silently, I told Him that I didn't mind the disappointment or any other disappointment so long as she recovered. Nothing else was of consequence. Let her get well, and someday we would laugh about Terceira. Someday she and I might pass it in another ship and I would tell her about this day.

At 7:30 P.M. Wednesday I tried to phone Ginny. Contact could not be established. I kept thinking, "The kids expect me in the morning and I'm not going to be there." At 8:20 P.M. there was a moon up and I looked at it from the forward lounge. Suddenly everything began to turn to bitterness in my mouth. The trip, the illness, the operation, the Air Force, my own inadequacy—all of it was sickening. I didn't want to think of it but the little thoughts kept skipping through my mind. The ship was slow. The passengers were thoughtless. In another three hours this big moon would be coming up over the sea in front of Monmouth Memorial Hospital. Would she see it? Her room was no more than a half mile from the Atlantic Ocean. Would she see it? Would she wonder if I could see it? And what good would it do if both of us looked at it and made a wish? What good? None at all.

At 8:20 P.M. the little bellhop found me. "Eet is New York, Mr. Bishop." This time I had no guts left. This time I knew it was bad news before I got to the phone. The moisture was on my palms and forehead. I walked up to the radio room mechanically, not feeling the steps, not hoping for anything.

It was Guy Richards. I told him that the Air Force had failed to make the rendezvous. He couldn't believe it. Through the wild whistles of the distance, he groaned, "We worked all night on this." I asked if he had any news of Elinor. "She's doing well from what I hear," he said.

Broken Face was beckoning to me. There was a call coming in. I thanked Guy and got off. Then Ginny got on. "Daddy?" she said. "Daddy?" There was tension in her voice. I had known that sound from the time she had learned to talk. "Can you hear me?" I said yes, and how was Mommy.

"Mommy is very bad," she said. "She has pneumonia."

"Pneumonia?" I said stupidly. I couldn't absorb the meaning.

"The doctor says she hasn't much of a chance, Daddy." I tried to speak. I tried to say something sensible and pacifying. There are no such words.

"Please do everything you can for your mother," was what finally came out. "Think of what she would want you and Gayle to do, and then do it.

"I've prayed for her," I added helplessly.

"We do too, Daddy. All the time."

"They were going to take me off the ship, but the Air Force forgot to send a boat."

"Oh, you won't be getting home?"

"No, honey. No. I feel badly for you kids, but you are going to have to take care of things yourselves."

"Don't worry, Daddy. We'll do it. Charlie has been wonderful."

"I knew that all the time. Does the doctor say there's any hope?"

"I can't hear you."

"Hope. Hope. Is there any hope?"

"Not much. She was coming out of the peritonitis all right and now it's pneumonia."

"Is she conscious?"

"Sometimes. Sometimes she goes off and talks to someone and they are not in the room. Then she looks up at me and she asks if you're coming home and I tell her yes."

"Did she get the wire I sent?"

"Yes. She read it. Now she sleeps a lot and she shivers a lot as though she feels cold. I keep telling her that everything is going to be all right and you'll be at the hospital in the morning."

"Keep telling her that."

"What, Daddy?"

"Keep repeating it. Tell her that I'll be there in a few hours. O.K., Ginny?"

"Sure, Daddy."

"My heart goes out to you kids."

"We know."

"Good-by, honey."

"Please don't worry, Daddy."

I prayed in the cabin, outside the cabin, in the corridors, on the promenade deck—begging, pleading for something that would not be granted. I was in panic. I tried to get Ed Mahar to ask the Navy or the Coast Guard to take me off the ship in a flying boat. It did not occur to me that there are few of these giants left and that none would have the range, much less the inclination, to fly out 2,000 miles from New York to pick up a solitary man and fly him back to New York.

Another wireless message went to Elinor:

DEAR: NOW I WILL BE FLYING TO YOUR SIDE AS SOON AS NAVY PLANE PICKS ME UP AT SEA. I LOVE YOU AND ONLY YOU. THE NEXT HONEYMOON STARTS IN A FEW DAYS.

JIM

It was one more pointless gesture. She was in a coma most of the time and couldn't read it. If someone read it to her, it is doubtful if she would understand. She would probably have tried hard to concentrate, would have smiled faintly, and gone back to sleep. She was beyond the words of love, beyond hope or despair or fear. She was on her way to rejoin her mother.

Another message went to Mahar.

ELINOR DYING. I AM BEGGING FOR HELP IF HELP IS POSSIBLE.
NAVY HAS LONG RANGE FLYING BOATS. GIULIO CESARE WILL
BE AT 38 DEGREES 20 MINUTES NORTH 36 DEGREES 43 MIN-
UTES WEST AT 1730 GMT THURSDAY. PLANE COULD PICK ME
UP PROCEED TO AFB TERCEIRAS TO REFUEL. IF NAVY CAN DO
IT THEY MUST COMMUNICATE DIRECT WITH CAPT. PINOTTI
HERE. ASK GINNY IF I CAN SPEAK TO ELINOR IN HOSPITAL.

                                        JIM BISHOP

This was the product of a wandering mind. The flying-boat
idea was out of the question. So was the notion of speaking to
Elinor. I had some ridiculous thought that, by talking to her—
even if she couldn't answer—that I could rouse her out of her
lethargy and help her to live. Neither of the wild ideas in the
radiogram were worth discussion.

Mahar's reply came back fast.

IMPOSSIBLE ANY PLANE RENDEZVOUS YOUR POSITION 1730
GMT THURSDAY. DOCTOR REPORTS NO CHANCE TALK WITH
ELINOR NOW. MAYBE LATER. WE'RE TRYING ALL SOURCES
HELP YOU. WILL CONTACT LATER.

                                        MAHAR

Below, I found Monsignor Luigi Floran, the ship chaplain.
His English was limited. He asked me if I would join him in
prayers for my wife in the chapel. We walked aft. He turned
a corner and pulled a curtain back and there was a miniature
church, with altar, candles, pews. We knelt. Again I begged
for her life, although now I was certain that God had no intention of permitting her to live. All the signs pointed the other
way. The monsignor prayed in the serene manner of devout
men, and we lit candles. I tried to press an offering on him and
he shook his head no.

"In de morning at Mass I weel remember her again," he said.

Back on the promenade deck, some women passengers became solicitous. One urged me to sit in the Belvidere Lounge.
Another said that I should go right to the little bar and have

a double brandy. One said to eat. Get something in the stomach. A fourth said that if I listen to the ship's orchestra, all worries will fade from my mind. They asked me how old she was and I said forty-seven. They were shocked that one so young had to die.

They were nice, but they had the wrong man. None of their suggestions would work, and none of mine would either. The gay ship with its colored balloons and paper hats and laughter was now a prison. I could run but there was no place to go. Men and women who had not exchanged a bow of recognition with me now sought me to commiserate and to ask a multitude of questions that had the quality of an employment questionnaire.

I went to Cabin 138, undressed, got into bed, got out again, and tried another prayer. Back in bed, I thought that reading would help. I tried a few pages of a popular book, and nothing got through to my mind except a clock on a courthouse and someone's mother talking to her son. I closed the book and got up and dressed. The moon was high now and as bright as a polished half dollar. The ship moved through the night steadily, always heading toward the horizon and never getting there. No matter how fast it moved, it remained in the center of the same dark bowl.

There were some late drinkers at the little bar and I sat with them for a while, willing to talk about anything but Elinor. After an hour, I went back to the cabin. I might have asked the ship's doctor for a sedative, but it is another of the many things which did not come to mind.

Still, my thoughts were all somehow short circuited and I slept. Late in the morning, I got up and shaved and dressed. No little bellboy had come to the cabin and I was afraid to go up to the radio room. I did not want to see that little boy.

I went to the dining room alone and had some orange juice and coffee. The waiter was sympathetic. I crossed my fingers and held them up so that he could see. "Keep your fingers crossed," I said. Back in 138 I unpacked my clothes and took my time hanging things, because time was what was going to drive me crazy. I had so much of it and so little to do. She had so little of it and so much to do.

At 3:10 P.M. Thursday, Ginny phoned. I walked the long corridor and up the stairs to the radio room for the final time. Broken Face gave me a big smile. Those eyes of his with the old sorrows in them told me that they understood. I sat in the little alcove.

There was some chatter between operators. Then someone said, "Okay Sea Bright. Here's your party." There was a moment of quiet. Ginny's voice came on and she sounded as though all the storms of the seas were tearing at her. The voice came in full and then faded. It rose and fell. There were shrieks and whistles in the sky and she spoke to me through them all.

"Daddy? Daddy? I can't hear you. Mommy died. She died this morning."

"I am so sorry for you, honey."

"I can't hear you, Daddy. Mommy died. She's gone." Suddenly, I could hear the tears through the wild bedlam of storms and distance and time. "Ooh, Daddy. What are we ever going to do?"

Broken Face looked in. He shrugged. The connection was gone. I looked up at him. Thanks, I said. He said he would try later. I said sure. I got up and began to walk out. He asked me if everything was all right.

"Yes," I said. "God was good. He took her. She would have been more and more afraid."

He shook his head and smiled. "I am sorry for you, signor," he said.

I did not know how much he understood of my English. I held my hands up. "Her hands would have been shaking more and more. She was becoming our little baby. God was good. He knew.

"Thy Will Be Done," I said.

PRAYERS OF FAMOUS
CONTEMPORARIES

Eʟɪɴᴏʀ ᴡᴀѕ ɢᴏɴᴇ. *My prayer had been denied. To the children, to me, this was the heartbreaking event of our lives. We were going to have to learn to live with this fact. In spite of the emotional numbness, Ginny and Gayle at once fell into the habit of receiving communion regularly for the repose of the soul of their mother. I arranged a series of monthly Masses for my wife, my mother, and my mother-in-law. The three ladies had died within eighty-four days.*

The more I thought about these things, the more firmly convinced I became that God listens to all prayers. In His infinite wisdom, He denies many petitions, grants many others. At home, I had been working on a book to be called My Favorite Prayers. *This was to have been the selected prayers of famous people of many faiths.*

I revised the idea to include a veritable treasury of prayers, modern and historic, embracing as many religions as possible. This book is the result of that work.

The section which follows deals with the favorite prayers of well-known people in many walks of life. It is largely Ginny's work, because she typed the many hundreds of letters which elicited these few prayers. One of our contributors, Ramón Magsaysay, died shortly after penning a prayer in which these words occur: ". . . and no famine, sickness or death can torment us long. . . ."

In this book, you will find that prayer follows many beautiful paths. All of them lead to the same inn.

Dwight David Eisenhower

Dwight David Eisenhower was Commander in Chief of the Allied Forces in Western Europe in World War II. He was elected thirty-fourth President of the United States in 1952 and reelected in 1956. This prayer is excerpted from the one prepared by President Eisenhower for his first inauguration.

Give us, we pray, the power to discern clearly right from wrong, and allow all our words and actions to be governed thereby and by the laws of this land. Especially, we pray that our concern shall be for all the people, regardless of station, race or calling.

May cooperation be permitted and be the mutual aim of those who, under the concepts of our constitution, hold to differing political faiths: so that all may work for the good of our beloved country, and Thy glory. *Amen.*

Daniel A. Poling

Dr. Daniel A. Poling, clergyman, editor, and author, is one of the best-known and most widely read (and quoted) members of the Protestant clergy in America. He is editor of *The Christian Herald*.

I do not ask, O Lord
A life all free from pain;
I do not seek to be
In this vast world of need
Without my load of care.
For this I know, the cross
Is my eternal gain,
And he who struggles on
At last shall enter in,
And be victorious there.

So, Lord, just keep me fit within,
And give me strength to fight,
And I will follow through the din,
From darkness up to light.
Amen.

Admiral Arthur Radford

Arthur William Radford was born in Chicago on February 27, 1896. He was graduated from the United States Naval Academy in 1916 and advanced to the rank of admiral, seeing duty in both World War I and II. He was Chairman of the Joint Chiefs of Staff from 1953 to 1957, retiring to private life as a banking consultant.

Heavenly Father, I come before Thee in all humility seeking strength for the duties entrusted to me by our nation. Grant that whatever abilities I may possess shall always be used in the interest of peace and shall be devoted to war only when freedom and honor so dictate. Keep the people of our nation strong in the power of Thy might, alert but calm in the face of danger, humble and charitable in the hour of triumph, and always conscious of Thy sway in the affairs of men and nations.

Give unto me the wisdom, judgement and the courage to do that which needs to be done in order that I may worthily be numbered among those who will help shape a better life for the people of tomorrow. Grant, O Lord, that I and all the military leaders of the free people of this world may perform our tasks so well that, with Thy blessing, ours may be vanishing positions and future generations will have no need of the particular services we must now render to our country and to the world. Unite our country in an eternal purpose to preserve and bear aloft the torch of nations who love Thee and keep Thy commandments. Without Thee our best efforts must be in vain. With Thy help we cannot fail. *Amen.*

Franklin Clark Fry

Franklin Clark Fry, president of the United Lutheran Church in America, was ordained to the Lutheran ministry in 1925. He did a great deal of relief work in Korea and was made an honorary citizen of that country in 1953. He became head of the Lutheran World Federation in 1957. The following prayer is taken from the Gelasian Sacramentary, a collection of liturgical forms dating from at least the seventh century.

O God, from Whom all holy desires, all good counsels, and all just works do proceed: Give unto Thy servants that peace which the world cannot give; that our hearts may be set to obey Thy commandments, and also that by Thee, we, being defended from the fear of our enemies, may pass our time in rest and quietness; through the merits of Jesus Christ Our Saviour, Who liveth and reigneth with Thee, and the Holy Ghost, ever One God, world without end.

Harold Russell

Harold Russell saw service in World War II as a parachutist, lost both his hands in combat, and was National Commander of Amvets from 1949–1951. He appeared in the film *The Best Years of Our Lives,* winning a Motion Picture Academy Award in 1946. He died in 1956. Here is his favorite prayer, which was composed by Rabbi Weinburg, Brookline, Massachusetts.

Almighty God and Father, unto Thee do we pour out our hearts in thanksgiving for the freedom we enjoy and for the heritage of liberty and human dignity which our forefathers have bequeathed to us as our birthright. We thank Thee for the United States of America and for the spirit which inspires us here to strive to break down the barriers that separate man from his fellow man. Help us, O Father, to direct our efforts to the end that within the borders of our blessed land there may always be heard the glorious strains of a symphony of humanity united together in brotherhood under Thy Divine Fatherhood.

We thank Thee too, for the memory of our tragic comradeship in time of war. Grant that we may never forget the purposes and goals for which we suffered and for which so many of our comrades died. May we remain united in the search for peace and brotherhood even as we were once united in the struggle to overcome tyranny on the battle field.

Sanctify our memories and cause them to serve as an unfailing inspiration to us to bring closer the day when each man shall sit under his vine and under his fig tree with none to make him afraid.

Speed the day when nations shall beat their swords into plowshares and their spears into pruning hooks, when a divine peace shall be made to reign in the hearts of all Thy children. *Amen.*

Archbishop Michael

His Eminence the Archbishop Michael of North and South America was born in Greece in 1892. He was ordained to the Greek Orthodox priesthood in 1919 and has been Archbishop of the Americas since 1949. He is the author of many books on religion.

O Lord, forgive them that hate and injure us. Do good to them that do good to us. To our brethren and kinfolk grant their desires for salvation and eternal life. Visit them that are in sickness and heal them. Guide them that are on the sea. Journey with the travelers.

To them that minister and are beneficent unto us, grant forgiveness of sins. According to Thy great mercy, have mercy upon them that have desired us, unworthy ones, to pray for them.

Remember, O Lord, our fathers and brethren that have fallen asleep before us, and give them rest where the light of Thy countenance shineth. Remember, O Lord, our brethren that are in captivity, and deliver them from all their bonds.

Remember, O Lord, them that bring forth fruit and do good works in Thy holy churches, and grant them their desires for salvation and eternal life.

Remember us also, O Lord, Thine humble, sinful and unworthy servants; and enlighten our minds with the light of Thy knowledge, and guide us in the way of Thy commandments.

Through the prayers of our most holy Lady, the ever-virgin Mary, and of all Thy saints; for Thou art blessed to ages of ages. *Amen.*

Harry S. Truman

Harry S. Truman was born in Lamar, Missouri, in 1884. He became thirty-third President of the United States upon the death of Franklin Delano Roosevelt and was reelected for a second term in 1948. In 1952 he retired to his family home at Independence, Missouri.

Oh, Almighty and everlasting God, creator of
Heaven, Earth and the Universe:—
Help me to be, to think to a *T* what is right;
make me truthful, honest and honorable in all
things; make me intellectually honest for the
sake of right and honor and without thought
of reward to me.
Give me the ability to be charitable, forgiving
and patient with my fellow men—help me to understand
their motives and their shortcomings—even as
Thou understandeth mine! *Amen, amen, amen.*

Francis Cardinal Spellman

Francis Joseph Spellman was born in Whitman, Massachusetts, in 1889. He was ordained in Rome in 1916 and appointed cardinal in 1946. He is one of the most widely known and best-loved Catholic clergymen in America and is the author of several books, including *Cardinal Spellman's Prayer Book* and *What America Means to Me, and Other Poems and Prayers*. Here is his "Prayer for Children."

How strange seems Christmas in the frame of war!
How feebly, through our dreadful night, the star
Of Bethlehem its deathless radiance shows!
How blasphemous the roar of guns and planes
Upon the silence of this sacred eve
Which Christian faith makes consecrate to Him
Who came to be the Prince of Peace, and gain,
Not by brute force, but by the might of love,

The kingdom of men's souls, with sacrifice
Divine! Well we believe there is no hope
For men, save in His gift of Self for them;
Nor is there love surpassing Love enshrined
In Bethlehem. For only God, Who was
Himself a Child, can light the road to peace.

We do not sense the toll of war, the price
Man pays for putting faith in force of arms,
Till we have seen war's children and their woe,
The innocent who reap of Herod's wrath.
It is the children; they are lambs of God,
They are our generation's sacrifice
For immolation on the altars raised
Not to the loving fatherhood of God
But to the cold and cruel cult of Mars.
Dear Christ, some of the altars we have built,
With all the skill that science could command,
With all the speed our genius could beget,
Have graven golden images enshrined.
Blind hatreds fog the Tablets of the Law.
Dragon's teeth are seed for children, sired
For War's brute reaping. Cycle without end!
Once more, it is the innocent who die!
Oh, wilt not Thou, Who wast Thyself a Babe,
Implant in deadened souls Thy mercy's grace,
That we may labor in this darksome hour
To save Thy children for a better day,
And thus ourselves be found unworthy less
Than now, of mercy at Thy Judgment seat!
Thy Spirit wrote, "A little child shall lead them";
And now the day is here for Thee, a Child,
To lead us stricken peoples back to peace,
To pour within America's great soul
Desire both strong and pregnant with resolve
To save, from out the ruins of our hatred,

Our children, innocent of wrong. 'Tis late,
Yet this most precious gift we beg of Thee!

Somewhere—the place it matters not—somewhere
I saw a child, hungry and thin of face,
Eyes in whose pools life's joy no longer stirred,
Lips that were dead to laughter's eager kiss,
Yet parted fiercely to a crust of bread;
And since that time I walk in ceaseless fear,
Fear that the child I saw, and all the hosts
Of children in a world at play with death,
May die; or, living, live in bitterness.
Thy love, Thy Blood alone, can quell man's wrath,
Thy Spirit, only, feed men's famished souls.
O Christ, have pity on Thy little ones!
From out a million broken homes they cry
To Thee, the Friend of Children, and their God.
They truly, even as Thou, how long ago,
For sins that others wrought, are sentenced now.
O God, today, above the cries of war,
Hear Thou Thy children's prayer, and grant to us
Thy peace, God's peace—and bread for starving children!

Arthur Hays Sulzberger

Arthur Hays Sulzberger entered the newspaper business in 1919, became
chairman of the board of *The New York Times* in 1957. His favorite is
this prayer suggested by a passage from *Arrowsmith* by Sinclair Lewis.

God give me clear eyes and freedom from haste!
God give me anger against all pretence!
God keep me looking for my own mistakes!
God keep me at it till my results are proven!
God give me strength not to trust to God!

G. Bromley Oxnam

Garfield Bromley Oxnam was born in California in 1891. He was ordained to the Methodist Episcopal ministry in 1916 and elected a bishop in 1936. He has also had a distinguished career as author, educator, and lecturer. This prayer was first offered at the Senate of the state of Maryland.

It was Thy Son, O God, who taught us to address Thee as Our Father. We repeat the precious words with reverence and with love—Our Father. When we say Our Father we know that the Eternal, who keeps the stars in their courses, notes the sparrow's fall, and knows each one of us by name; When we say Our Father we know that nothing can separate us from the love of God, nothing. We know that in all matters affecting our eternal welfare, we are beyond the reach of any human dictator; we are not dependent upon any human institution. For these assurances, O God, we bow in humble gratitude.

We thank Thee for our country and its freedom; for fathers who knew that men were sons of God and of infinite worth, endowed with inalienable rights. We are sustained by their insight. The state does not confer these rights, it merely confirms them. They belong to us because we are men, and we are grateful.

We thank Thee for our rich heritage in faith and in freedom. We humbly declare that for most of us, our faith and our freedom will cost us nothing. We have never been stoned, or imprisoned, or persecuted. But the fathers risked their lives, their fortunes and their sacred honor. The early Christians suffered. O God, may we be worthy of them, and in an hour when faith and freedom are in peril, grant us the wisdom, the courage and the devotion, so to think, so to plan, so to serve, so to live and if needs be so to die, that our children and our children's children may live as free men, in the free society, free to search for the truth that frees. Bless the representatives of the people here assembled, the Governor, the President of these United States, we ask in the name of our Blessed Lord. *Amen.*

Mary Pickford

Mary Pickford had a long and distinguished career in the era of silent films and was known as "America's Sweetheart." She is the author of *Why Not Try God*.

I know that You alone have created me—created me spiritually in Your own image and likeness. I know that You guide and protect me every second. It is I who have wandered from your love and care and, at times, "forgetteth what manner of man I am"—seeing but dimly in the mirror.

I sincerely desire to see clearly my shortcomings, my faults, my sins. I earnestly pray to be humble, obedient and loving in order that I may inherit here and now and forever my divine sonship, to be worthy to walk with Thee. *Amen.*

Pierre van Paassen

Pierre van Paassen was born in The Netherlands in 1895. He came to the United States in 1923 and is a Doctor of Hebrew Letters as well as a world-renowned author. He is perhaps best known for his widely read book, *Days of Our Years*. He was ordained as a Unitarian minister in 1946 and has been active in humanitarian causes all his life.

Blessed be Thou, O Lord our God, Father of Jesus Christ and also our Father. May Thy Name be hallowed in all the earth. Praise, glory and thanksgiving be unto Thee in this day and in the age to come.

Keep Thou and bless, we pray, all who confess Thy Name. Comfort and strengthen all men and women and children who are sick or in sorrow or in poverty. Be with them who are troubled in spirit and whose soul is in distress. Be gracious, we pray Thee, to those who do not enter into Thy House, who reject Thy Word and the witness of Thy saints and sages. Look down with loving-kindness, especially upon the people of Russia. Lighten their darkness, we beseech Thee, O Lord. Take from them all ignorance, hardness of heart and contempt of Thy Word. Fetch them home, Blessed Lord, to Thy flock. For Thou art the Good Shepherd and the Great Physician of souls and the yoke of Thy Law is gentle and true.

We pray Thee for the lonely ones in our midst and for all those who are made to suffer physical pain or revilement and persecution for Thy Name's sake and for conscience's sake and for truth's sake, those in prisons and slave camps and dungeons. Show the beauty and loveliness of Thy Face before the closing eyes of them, wherever they may be, who in this day or in this night must fight the last fight with death. And give our beloved dead Thy peace.

We commit ourselves to Thee with all our joys and sorrows and disquietudes, with all that we lack and all we desire. Sanctify us through Thy service in love, in righteousness and in justice, so that we may at the last gain the highest and everlasting good and dwell forever more in the holiness of Thy presence.

We place our country and its destiny in Thy hands. Deal not with us, O God of Mercy, according to our transgressions. Blot out our national sin of pride and vain boasting. Create a new heart within us, O Lord, and cleanse our hands of blood guiltiness. Forgive us for the murder of Thy children in Hiroshima!

O, that Thou wouldst rend the heavens; O, that Thou wouldst come down! Let the world see that Thou alone makest all things new. Make a new covenant with us.

O Lord, make a new Pentecost! Pour of Thy Spirit upon Thy people in America that they may have the courage to stand forth in the face of the Molochs and Mammons of our time to testify and witness for peace. For Thou workest with the hands of all of us, and Thou runnest with the feet of every one of Thy servants. Make us doers of the Word and not mere empty, idle and arrogant phrases. Make us aware that the glorification of violence leads to lovelessness and bitterness and ashes and death.

Endow us with the will to build higher and higher the
of Thy Kingdom, so that they may yet, in this hour of h
ity's extremity, rise above and dominate the rivers of hatred
and blood now coursing in the universe. May the day speedily
dawn that we shall neither know nor teach war and the preparation for war anymore. Let us at last be done with the world's
game of guilt and blood, and learn to follow Thy path and Thy
way. For it is not through might, nor through strength, but
with Thy Spirit that it shall come to pass. Our God and God of
our fathers, our hope is in Thee; Thou art our Rock and our
Redeemer. Through Jesus Christ, Thy Son, our brother. *Amen.*

Harry A. Bullis

Harry Amos Bullis was born in Hastings, Nebraska, in 1890. While attend-
ing college, he became a wholesale dealer in sewing machines and followed a business career, becoming chairman of General Mills in 1948. He
is also renowned as a philanthropist and public-minded citizen, and has
served in numerous organizations for the betterment of mankind.

Oh God, I ask not for easier tasks. I ask for stronger aptitudes
and greater talents to meet any tasks which may come my way.
Help me to help others so that their lives may be made easier
and happier. Strengthen my confidence in my fellow men in
spite of what they may do or say.

Give me strength to live according to the Golden Rule,
enthusiasm to inspire those around me, sympathy to help
lighten the burdens of those who suffer, and a spirit of joy and
gladness to share with others.

Help me to make a worth-while contribution in the world.
Give me courage and confidence to meet adversity with a smile
and wisdom to see the good in all things. Renew in me the
resolve to do Thy will honestly and fearlessly and grant to me
a peaceful mind.

Clare Boothe Luce

Clare Boothe Luce, author and playwright, was United States Ambassador to Italy 1953 to 1957. This prayer was originally given by Lord Astley before the Battle of Edgehill.

> Lord, Thou knowest
> I shall be verie busie
> this day.
> I may forget Thee. Do not
> Thou forget me.

Norman Vincent Peale

Norman Vincent Peale was born in 1898 and ordained a minister of the Methodist Episcopal Church in 1922. He is the author of the famous book, *The Power of Positive Thinking*, which has influenced millions of Americans. One of his favorite prayers is this one composed by George Washington and delivered at his first inauguration.

ALMIGHTY GOD, we make our earnest prayer that Thou wilt keep the United States in Thy holy protection; that Thou wilt incline the hearts of the citizens to cultivate a spirit of subordination and obedience to Government; and entertain a brotherly affection and love for one another and for their fellow citizens of the United States at large. And finally that Thou wilt most graciously be pleased to dispose us all to do justice, to love mercy and to demean ourselves with that charity, humility and pacific temper of mind which were the characteristics of the Divine Author of our blessed religion, and without a humble imitation of Whose example in these things we can never hope to be a happy nation. Grant our supplication, we beseech Thee, through Jesus Christ Our Lord.

Mel Allen

Mel Allen, born in Birmingham, Alabama, in 1913, is one of the nation's foremost sports broadcasters. This anonymous prayer was read on a telecast of Ed Murrow's *Person to Person* show, and thousands of viewers wrote to the Columbia Broadcasting System requesting copies. It is called "The Prayer of a Game Guy."

Dear God, help me to be a sport in this little game of life. I don't ask for any easy place in the line-up; play me anywhere You need me. I only ask for the stuff to give You one hundred per cent of what I've got. If all the hard drives seem to come my way, I thank You for the compliment.

Help me to remember that You won't ever let anything come my way that You and I together can't handle. And help me to take the bad breaks as part of the game.

Help me to understand that the game is full of knots and knocks and trouble and make me thankful for them. Help me to get so the harder they come the better I like it.

And, O God, help me to always play on the square. No matter what the other players do, help me to come clean. Help me to study the Book so that I'll know the rules, and to study great players. If they found out that the best part of the game was helping other guys who were out of luck, help me to find it out too. Help me to be a regular fellow with the other players.

Finally, O God, if fate seems to uppercut me with both hands and I'm laid on the shelf in sickness or old age or something, help me to take that as part of the game too. Help me not to whimper or squeal that the game was a frameup or that I had a raw deal.

When in the falling dusk, I get the final bell, I ask for no lying complimentary stones. I'd only like to know that You feel that I've been a good, game guy. *Amen.*

General Mark Clark

Mark Wayne Clark was born at an army post in New York in 1896. He was graduated from the United States Military Academy in 1917, saw duty in both World Wars, and was commander of United Nations forces in the Far East during the Korean War. When he retired from active duty, he became president of The Citadel Military College of South Carolina. This anonymous prayer from *Daily Word* is a favorite of his.

Father, in Thy name I pray,
Let me know Thy will today.
With Thee I am unafraid,
For on Thee my mind is stayed.
Though a thousand foes surround,
Safe in Thee I shall be found.

I have faith that Thou wilt always
Be guarding and directing me.
In the air, on sea or land,
Thy sure protection is at hand.
Momently Thy love I share,
Thy grace and Thy protecting care.

Spirit of the Lord Most High,
Gracious spirit that is I,
In Thy word my needs are filled,
In Thy love my fears are stilled.
In Thee I am stanch and strong,
Thou art with me all day long
Showing me the way to go,
Helping me always to know
Thou art justice, peace and life
Healer of the nations' strife.

General Douglas A. MacArthur

General Douglas A. MacArthur was born in Little Rock, Arkansas, in 1880. He had a brilliant military career and became Allied Supreme Commander in the Southwest Pacific during World War II, also commanding the occupation forces in Japan after V-J Day. After serving in the Korean War, he entered private life to head Remington-Rand as chairman of the board. General MacArthur has one son, and this prayer is called "A Father's Prayer."

Build me a son, O Lord, who will be strong enough to know when he is weak, and brave enough to face himself when he is afraid; one who will be proud and unbending in honest defeat, and humble and gentle in victory.

Build me a son whose wishbone will not be where his backbone should be; a son who will know Thee—and that to know himself is the foundation stone of knowledge.

Lead him, I pray, not in the path of ease and comfort, but under the stress and spur of difficulties and challenge. Here, let him learn to stand up in the storm; here, let him learn compassion for those who fail.

Build me a son whose heart will be clear, whose goal will be high; a son who will master himself before he seeks to master other men; one who will learn to laugh, yet never forget how to weep; one who will reach into the future, yet never forget the past.

And after all these things are his, add, I pray, enough of a sense of humor, so that he may always be serious, yet never take himself too seriously. Give him humility, so that he may always remember the simplicity of true greatness, the open mind of true wisdom, the meekness of true strength. Then I, his father, will dare to whisper: "I have not lived in vain."

Henry Knox Sherrill

Henry Knox Sherrill was born in Brooklyn in 1890. He became an Episcopalian minister in 1915 and has been Presiding Bishop since 1947. He was also president of the National Council of the Churches of Christ in America (1950) and of the World Council of Churches (1954). He is one of America's best-known Protestant clergymen.

O Almighty God, who alone canst order the unruly wills and affections of sinful men; grant unto Thy people, that they may love the thing which Thou commandest, and desire that which Thou dost promise; that so, among the sundry and manifold changes of the world, our hearts may surely there be fixed where true joys are to be found; through Jesus Christ Our Lord. *Amen.*

Rabbi David de Sola Pool

David de Sola Pool was born in London, England, in 1885. In 1907 he became minister of the Spanish and Portuguese Synagogue, Shearith Israel, in New York City. He became president of the Union of Sephardic Congregations in 1929 and is one of the best-known and highly respected members of his faith.

Lord God, give me understanding of the mind so that I may come to know what is right and what is wrong, and may mine be the strength of moral will to choose the right.

Give me also understanding of the heart so that I may count my days and attain a heart of wisdom as I try the more understandingly to fulfill Thy will and Thy commandments of life. Yea, open my heart that I may the better understand the heart of my fellow men and thereby come to love my neighbor as myself.

Give me also wisdom of the soul so that I may face life with reverent spirit and ever feel that I am in Thy presence.

Then, as I open my mind, my heart and my soul to Thee, I shall know peace within my own being, and shall further peace on earth among Thy children.

May all Thy children be strengthened to know Thee and harken to Thee so that darkness may be lifted from the earth and all may walk through life with mind, with heart and with soul uplifted towards the light and the peace that come from Thee. For then shall we truly feel the blessing of Thy love through all our days of life on earth.

J. C. Penney

James Cash Penney was born in Hamilton, Missouri, in 1875. Founder and chairman of the board of a company operating over 1,700 retail stores in the United States and Canada, he is a living exponent of the Golden Rule and has been tremendously active in the movement for community improvement in America. A leading Christian layman, he is winner of a Horatio Alger award.

Oh Lord, Father of us all, help me to do justly in all my dealings with Thee and with my fellow men. Give me the understanding to recognize my need to forgive others, that I may receive forgiveness from Thee. Give me the courage to do justly even if it costs something dear to me. I thank Thee for what Thou hast already taught me in Thine infinite justice.

Help me to love mercy, to go beyond what is acceptable in earthly society, to do more than is expected. Grant that I may grow in love and compassion so that through me Thou canst give hope, faith and love to others. I thank Thee for all that Thou hast already given me in Thy great mercy.

Lead me to walk with Thee in true humility. Let me learn to let Thy Holy Spirit within be my Companion so that I do all things for the love of Thee. I thank Thee for Thy love.

Guide me in all these things this day. May I so follow the example of the Carpenter of Nazareth in my work that it may be pleasing in Thy sight; in my contacts with my associates and all with whom I meet, that others may be helped to know Thy way. In the name and spirit of Jesus Christ. *Amen.*

Walter P. Reuther

Walter P. Reuther was born in Wheeling, West Virginia, in 1907. He began as an apprentice tool- and diemaker in a steel mill and rose to become president of the United Auto Workers. He is one of America's greatest labor leaders, and has worked constantly for the betterment of the worker's lot.

Almighty and Eternal God, to whose bounty we owe all that we have and all that we are, we thank Thee for the unlimited resources Thou hast bestowed on our beloved country. To these resources and to Thy goodness we rightfully attribute release from painful sufferings and our own happiness and prosperity.

We thank Thee for the opportunity which is ours of alleviating the sufferings of others, and we humbly petition the guidance of Thy Holy Spirit that we may ever use Thy gifts in accord with the dictates of Thy Divine will.

As we offer all our goods during this time of world crisis and consecrate all our efforts of body and mind to Thy service and to the welfare of our fellow men, we humbly pray for our leaders, civic and religious, that, guided by the light of Thy Divine wisdom, they may lead the world out of darkness and chaos to the light of a just and lasting peace.

Bless this assemblage, we beseech Thee, and reward the members of this organization for their efforts in bringing about a greater recognition, on the part of all, of the nobility of the labor of man. Their history is evidence of their consciousness of the dignity and merit of the individual man, regardless of his racial or national origin. Grant that we may profit by the example they have set us. May we all be united in the bonds of charity and may the peace of Christ dwell in our hearts.

—Spoken originally by Monsignor R. B. Navin, 1951

Thomas J. Watson

Thomas J. Watson was born in upstate New York in 1874. At his death he was chairman of the board of International Business Machines Corp., which he founded. He was an officer of numerous philanthropic, patriotic, religious, and cultural organizations and was decorated by many foreign governments for his philanthropic work.

Heavenly Father:
    I thank You for the blessings of another day.
    Keep me mindful of the needs of others,
    And guide us in our efforts for world peace . . .
    In Jesus' Name! *Amen.*

Henry R. Luce

Henry R. Luce was born of American parentage in Shantung Province, China, in 1898. He is renowned as a publisher and editor-in-chief of *Time, Fortune,* and *Life* magazines, among others. The following verses are from *Psalm* 19, verses 1–3, 7–9, 13, and 14.

The heavens declare the glory of God; and the firmament sheweth his handywork.

Day unto day uttereth speech, and night unto night sheweth knowledge.

There is no speech nor language, where their voice is not heard.

The law of the Lord is perfect, converting the soul: the testimony of the Lord is sure, making wise the simple.

The statutes of the Lord are right, rejoicing the heart: the commandment of the Lord is pure, enlightening the eyes.

The fear of the Lord is clean, enduring for ever: the judgments of the Lord are true and righteous altogether.

Keep back thy servant also from presumptuous sins; let them not have dominion over me; then shall I be upright, and I shall be innocent from the great transgression.

Let the words of my mouth, and the meditation of my heart, be acceptable in thy sight, O Lord, my strength, and my redeemer.

Rear Admiral Samuel E. Morison, Ret.

Samuel E. Morison was born in Boston, Massachusetts, in 1897. He entered his naval career via the field of scholarship, first having been a professor of history at Harvard. He was appointed historian of U.S. naval operations in World War II and has written many famous books.

> Dear Lord, give us a safe issue from
> all our present difficulties, and keep
> us mindful that we must resolve our problems
> in accordance with the teachings of Thy
> Blessed Son, Jesus Christ.

Rabbi Louis Finkelstein

Louis Finkelstein is the chancellor of the Jewish Theological Seminary of America. Among his favorite prayers is this traditional Jewish prayer said when the scrolls of Jewish law are taken from the Ark.

Master of the universe, fulfill the wishes of my heart for good; grant my request, even that of Thy servant, the son of Thy maid-servant, and my children, and grandchildren, to do Thy will with a perfect heart. Save me from evil desire. Make the Torah our portion, and do Thou grant us the merit that Thy Divine Presence may be with us; bestow upon us the spirit of wisdom, of understanding, of counsel and strength, of the spirit of knowledge and the fear of the Lord.

May it also be Thy will, O Lord our God and God of our fathers, that I may be granted the opportunity to perform deeds of righteousness in Thine eyes, and to walk in the ways which are upright before Thee. Sanctify us through Thy commandments, so that we may attain the good and long life of the Future World; and protect us from evil deeds and the evil hours which afflict this world. As for him who trusteth in God, let loving kindness surround him.

Amen, selah.

Rabbi Israel Goldstein

Israel Goldstein was born in Philadelphia, Pennsylvania, in 1896 and became a rabbi in 1918. He has served as leader of many Jewish organizations and became chairman of the World Jewish Congress in 1950. He is one of the acknowledged leaders of the Jewish people in America. Here is his "Prayer for a New Year."

Lord and Creator:

Thou whose miracle of creation is renewed every day, help us to approach the new year in our lives with a new heart and a new spirit. May we make of the new year a new opportunity to deepen the bonds of family devotion. May we be cleansed of the old hatreds and prejudices, look upon our fellow man of whatever race, creed or color, with new eyes, seeing him as one of Thy children and therefore one of our brothers. May we, fortified with new hope, strive to lend such strength and influence as we possess to the forces which work for world peace in our time.

Create in us a pure heart and a right spirit renew Thou within us. If one sincere resolve stir within our hearts, do Thou, O Lord, strengthen it. If one fervent prayer tremble upon our lips, do Thou accept it. Our days pass away like a shadow, and Thou art from everlasting to everlasting. We are transient like the dust, but Thou art eternal. We are prone to error and sin, and Thou art pure Spirit. Help us, as we open a new chapter in the volume of life, to draw more nigh unto Thee and thus become more true to our God-given destiny. May we, as we grow older in years, grow deeper in understanding and broader in charity.

May the new year be a year of peace, near and far—inner peace of soul to those who seek Thee, and a cessation of strife among men. *Amen.*

Louis Bromfield

Louis Bromfield, distinguished American novelist, was born in 1896. He wrote many best-selling books, including *Early Autumn*, winner of the Pulitzer Prize novel award in 1926, *The Rains Came*, and *Malabar Farm*. He died in 1957 at his famous Malabar Farm in Lucas, Ohio.

Oh, Lord. I thank you for the privilege and gift of living in a world filled with beauty and excitement and variety.

I thank you for the gift of loving and being loved, for the friendliness and understanding and beauty of the animals on the farm and in the forest and marshes, for the green of the trees, the sound of a waterfall, the darting beauty of the trout in the brook.

I thank you for the delights of music and children, of other men's thoughts and conversation and their books to read by the fireside or in bed with the rain falling on the roof or the snow blowing past outside the window.

I thank you for the beauties of the four seasons and of the churches and the houses built by fellow men that stand throughout the centuries as monuments to man's aspirations and sense of beauty.

I thank you for the powers of mind which find in the universe an endless and inexhaustible source of interest and fascination, for the understanding of so many elements which make life the most precious of gifts.

I thank you for all the senses you have bestowed upon me and for the delights which they bring me. I thank you for my body itself which is so wonderful and delightful a mechanism.

I thank you for the smile on the face of a woman, for the touch of a friend's hand, for the laughter of a child, the wagging tail of a dog and the touch of his cold nose against my face.

I thank you for all of these things and many more, and above all I thank you for people with all their goodness and understanding which so far outweigh their vices, their envy, their deceits.

Thank you, God, for life itself, without which the universe would have no meaning.

Eddie Cantor

Eddie Cantor was born in New York City in 1892. He is perhaps America's best-known comedian and the dean of show business. He is active in interfaith charities and has helped thousands of underprivileged boys through the Eddie Cantor Camp Committee, which he founded and supports.

Dear God . . .

Please help me to repay the debt I owe America, the land of the Free and the Home of the Brave. And make me able to help those who need help. *Amen.*

Ramón Magsaysay

Ramón Magsaysay, late President of the Philippines, was born in 1907 and died in an airplane crash in 1957. He was one of his country's greatest heroes and fought with the guerrilla forces against the Japanese all during World War II.

In Your service, Lord, we enlist ourselves: our farmer when plowing in Your land, our fisherman when on Your sea, our soldier in Your swamp with our boatman rowing him safely home after a righteous war to return to his nursing wife and children playing games peacefully; all of us simple folk, barefoot yet devout, who worship in Your household and welcome ourselves to live under Your roof so that not rain nor sun nor insects nor fire nor flood nor earthquakes nor any other blight can turn us out naked and homeless; and no famine, sickness or death can torment us long while we believe strongly in Thee, Our Father, and so into Your care we humbly put ourselves, we who govern mere islands, for You are the wisest governor and Yours the perfect law in the government of the universe and out of which, night and day, we draw stern example and merciful spirit in our littlest gestures to our far-reaching acts affecting the life and fate of our nation. Bless us, and receive into Your grace our labors, our acts and our eternal love in honor of Thee. *Amen.*

Cecil B. deMille

Cecil Blount deMille was born in Ashfield, Massachusetts, in 1881 and has been identified with motion pictures since 1913. He is famous for many great films which he has produced, including his early *King of Kings* and, more recently, *The Ten Commandments*.

Lord, teach me to pray
Not for myself alone, but for all who need You
Not with my lips alone, but with Your Mind in me
Seeking not only Your gifts, but, above all, You.
Not my will, but Yours,
Not my feverish pursuit of things, but Your Grace
Make the mind a channel for the Divine Mind—and
        let the spirit of truth speak through my lips.
Whether I work or play or eat or sleep or read or
        talk or whatever I do
Even when I forget You
Abide in me.
Use me
Always
Not for myself alone, but for all who need You.
Increase my faith.
Dear God—I thank You for Your Wonder and Your
        Glory,
I thank You that You hear our prayers.
So be it—always.

Margaret Culkin Banning

Mrs. Banning is a distinguished author of some twenty-five books, and an essayist on phases of American life and activities. She has selected the following prayer from the Ordinary of the Mass.

Set a watch, O Lord, before my mouth,
and a door around my lips, that my
heart may not incline to evil words, to
make excuses in sins.

Jackie Robinson

Jackie Robinson, born in 1919 in Cairo, Georgia, was the first Negro to enter big-league baseball. He was a star second baseman for the Brooklyn Dodgers from 1946 to 1956. The following prayer is from Psalm 23.

The Lord is my shepherd; I shall not want.

He maketh me to lie down in green pastures: he leadeth me beside the still waters;

He restoreth my soul: he leadeth me in the paths of righteousness for his name's sake.

Yea, though I walk through the valley of the shadow of death, I will fear no evil: for thou art with me; thy rod and thy staff they comfort me.

Thou preparest a table before me in the presence of mine enemies: thou anointest my head with oil; my cup runneth over.

Surely goodness and mercy shall follow me all the days of my life: and I will dwell in the house of the Lord for ever.

Loretta Young

Loretta Young is widely known as a motion-picture actress and TV star. Here is her favorite prayer.

Lord, Thy Will—not mine—be done.
Lord, give me patience, and then strike
hard. This suffering does not nourish
my heart—but by bearing it patiently
I may at least increase the fire of
Divine Love, by which alone life can
profit us anything.

Henry J. Kaiser

Henry J. Kaiser was chairman of the board of Kaiser Industries during World War II and built everything from ships to planes, including the famous "Jeep." He is also widely known for his participation in civic and philanthropic projects.

O God, help us find the spark of soul
Thou hast dropped in every human being.
Help us live each day by faith—
Faith in our fellow men and our highest aspirations,
Faith that brings us fellowship with Thee
And gives us eyes to see
God in everything.

John D. Rockefeller, Jr.

John D. Rockefeller, Jr., was born in 1874 and became associated with his famous father's business interests in 1897. Later, he devoted most of his time to philanthropic projects.

To Thee, Oh God, Father of mankind, we come in deep humility, asking forgiveness for our sins. We have too often been selfish, unkind and intolerant. May love for Thee and for our fellow men dominate and ennoble our lives! Give us to know the meaning of duty, the joy of service, the rewards of sacrifice. May even death have for us no fear so long as it be nobly met! And may we face the unknown, calm and unafraid, because of an abiding faith in Thee!

Sir Hubert Wilkins

Sir George Hubert Wilkins, explorer, scientist, and lecturer, was born in Australia in 1888. He has explored both the Arctic and Antarctic, made pioneer flights over both Poles. He was a member of the first submarine voyage under the Arctic ice.

> My Father, I beseech
> Support in my desire to worship,
> To enjoy privilege without abuse,
> To have liberty without license,
> To have power and refuse to use it for self-
>   aggrandizement,
> So that the experience of living will lead me and
>   my fellows to greater spiritual reality.

W. R. Matthews

The Very Reverend Walter Robert Matthews, who composed this "Prayer for Light," was born in 1881. He is Dean of St. Paul's Cathedral in London and is a renowned educator and author.

O God, Who clothest Thyself with light as with a garment, and makest the outgoings of the morning and evening to praise Thee, mercifully grant that, as by Thy created light we perceive the wonders of Thy universe, so by the uncreated light of Thy Spirit we may discern the adorable majesty of Thy Being, and that our hearts and minds being illuminated by His Presence, we may walk in Thy paths without stumbling, until at last all shadows flee away and in Thy Perfect Light we see light, Who with the Son and the Holy Spirit art God for everlasting. *Amen.*

Lewis L. Strauss

Lewis L. Strauss was born in 1896 in Charleston, West Virginia. He was secretary to Herbert Hoover during the First World War, and in 1953 was appointed by President Eisenhower as Chairman of the Atomic Energy Commission. He resigned this post in 1957. This prayer was selected by him from the prayers used in the Sabbath Liturgy in Jewish Temples.

May the time not be distant, oh God, when Thy Name shall be worshipped over all the earth, when unbelief shall disappear and error be no more. We fervently pray that the day may come upon which all men shall invoke Thy Name, when corruption and evil shall give way to purity and goodness; when superstition shall no longer enslave the minds, nor idolatry blind the eyes, when all inhabitants of the earth shall perceive that to Thee alone every knee must bend and every tongue give homage. Oh may all, created in Thine Image, recognize that they are brethren so that, one in spirit and one in fellowship, they may be forever united before Thee. Then shall Thy kingdom be established on earth, and the word of Thine ancient prophets be fulfilled: The Eternal alone shall rule forever and ever.

Oveta Culp Hobby

Oveta Culp Hobby became head of the WACs during World War II. She was appointed to President Eisenhower's Cabinet as Secretary of Health, Education and Welfare in 1953, serving until 1955.

Almighty God, make us to know the light of Thy spirit; lighten our darkness; defend us from all perils and danger; give unto Thy servants that peace which the world cannot give, that our hearts may be set to obey Thy commandments and express Thy love for all mankind.

GREAT PRAYERS

OF HISTORY

To MY WAY OF THINKING, *the single enduring fact of prayer is that men, no matter how great, become humble and honest when they address God. In sum, the words they mouth for the world are not related to the words they are moved to express toward their Maker. In this section, which contains some of the great prayers of all time, compare the words of the one who prays with his place in history.*

Savonarola, who was hanged in 1498, was a belligerent, vindictive man. Compare this belligerence with his final words: "I implore pardon for aught in which I have offended against this city and its people, whether in things spiritual or temporal, and for all things in which I have erred knowingly."

The humility and the wisdom of the words of prayer would lead one to believe that men and women, in the face of death, assess themselves and their spiritual wealth or poverty much more clearly than at any other time. Oliver Cromwell composed his deathbed prayer on the day of a terrible storm in England in August, 1658, and he began it with the confession: "Lord, though I am a miserable and wretched creature. . . ."

There is a prayer by George Washington in this section. I

do not think he prayed well. He prayed proud. The Sunday after the assassination of Abraham Lincoln a Negro, whose name is lost in the footnotes of history, opened his prayer with a rare figure of speech: "O Lord, we come to Thee holding up our souls as empty pitchers, to be filled from the fountains of Thy love." Who can but admire the same man's reference to Lincoln: ". . . when his work was done, you saw it was done, and took him up higher. . . ."

It is a pity—a real pity—that such a man's name should be lost.

Martin Luther's De Profundis

Martin Luther (1483–1546), the great religious reformer, was father of the Reformation in Germany. He became an Augustinian friar and was ordained a priest in 1507. He was excommunicated by Pope Leo X in 1520 and in 1522 began to organize the church which had been born out of his attack on the Catholic church. This prayer is from the Catherine Winkworth translation.

> Out of the depths I cry to thee,
>   Lord God! oh hear my prayer!
> Incline a gracious ear to me,
>   And bid me not despair:
> If thou rememberest each misdeed,
> If each should have its rightful meed,
>   Lord, who shall stand before thee?

> 'Tis through thy love alone we gain
>   The pardon of our sin;
> The strictest life is but in vain,
>   Our works can nothing win,

That none should boast himself of aught,
But own in fear thy grace hath wrought
    What in him seemeth righteous.

Wherefore my hope is in the Lord,
    My works I count but dust,
I build not there, but on his word,
    And in his goodness trust.
Up to his care myself I yield,
He is my tower, my rock, my shield,
    And for his help I tarry.

Though great our sins and sore our wounds,
    And deep dark our fall,
His helping mercy hath no bounds,
    His love surpasseth all.
Our truly loving Shepherd he,
Who shall at last set Israel free
    From all their sin and sorrow.

Last Prayer of Savonarola

Girolamo Savonarola, the Italian religious reformer, was hanged in 1498 at Florence, together with two of his disciples, for sedition and heresy. His fanaticism made enemies for him in the highest places of the Roman Catholic Church of his time.

My Lord, I know Thou art the Trinity, perfect, invisible, distinct in three persons, Father, Son and Holy Ghost.

I know Thou art that eternal Word that descended from heaven to this earth in the womb of the Virgin Mary, and ascended the wood of the cross to shed thy blood for us miserable sinners.

I beseech Thee, my Lord, I beseech Thee! Save me, I beseech Thee, my Comforter, that so much precious blood may not be shed for me in vain.

But let it be shed for the remission of my sins from the day I received the water of baptism until this hour, which I lay before you, and for which I crave your pardon.

I implore pardon for aught in which I have offended against this city and its people, whether in things spiritual or temporal, and for all things in which I have erred knowingly.

Martin Luther before the Diet of Worms

Martin Luther was summoned before the Diet of Worms, a brilliant assembly consisting of the Emperor and dignitaries of church and state. It was before this assembly, on April 18, 1521, that he made the famous declaration: "There I take my stand. I can do naught else. So help me God, Amen." The day before, Luther was seen to fall on his knees in prayer—the prayer quoted here—which was answered when the Emperor later issued a proclamation of religious toleration in Germany.

O, God, Almighty God everlasting! How dreadful is the world! behold how its mouth opens to swallow me up, and how small is my faith in Thee! .... O! the weakness of the flesh and the power of Satan! If I am to depend on any strength of this world—all is over. . . . The knell is struck. . . . Sentence is gone forth. . . . O God! O God! O Thou my God! help me against all the wisdom of this world. Do this, I beseech Thee; Thou shouldst do this . . . by Thy own mighty power. . . . The work is not mine, but Thine. I have no business here. . . . I have nothing to contend for with these great men of the world! I would gladly pass my days in happiness and peace. But the cause is Thine . . . and it is righteous and everlasting! O Lord! help me! O faithful and unchangeable God! I lean not upon man. It were vain! Whatever is of man is tottering, whatever proceeds from him must fail. My God! my God! dost Thou not hear? My God! art Thou no longer living? Nay, Thou canst not die! Thou dost but hide Thyself. Thou hast chosen me for this work. I know it! . . . Therefore, O God, accomplish Thine own

will! Forsake me not, for the sake of Thy well-beloved Son,
Jesus Christ, my defence, my buckler, and my stronghold.

"Lord—where art Thou? ... My God, where art Thou? ....
Come! I pray Thee, I am ready. ... Behold me prepared to lay
down my life for Thy truth ... suffering like a lamb. For the
cause is holy. It is Thine own! ... I will not let Thee go! no, nor
yet for all eternity! And though the world should be thronged
with devils—and this body which is the work of Thine hands
should be cast forth, trodden under foot, cut in pieces ... consumed to ashes ... my soul is Thine. Yes, I have Thine own
word to assure me of it. My soul belongs to Thee, and will
abide with Thee forever! *Amen!* O God send help! ... *Amen!*

Sir Thomas More Imprisoned in the Tower

Sir Thomas More (1478–1535), former Lord Chancellor, was executed
on Tower Hill in 1535 because he would not take an oath acknowledging
Henry VIII supreme head of the Church in England, which would mean
breaking with Rome. He was canonized in 1935.

Illumine, good Lord, my heart! Glorious God! Give me from
henceforth Thy Grace, so to set and fix firmly mine heart upon
Thee, that I may say with St. Paul, the world is crucified to me,
and I unto the world. Take from me all vainglorious minds,
and all appetites of mine own praise. Give me, good Lord, a
humble, lowly, quiet, peaceable, patient, charitable, kind,
tender and pitiful mind; and in all my works and words and
thoughts, to have a taste of Thy Holy Spirit. Give me a full
faith, a firm hope, a fervent charity, and a love to Thee incomparably above the love to myself. May I love nothing to Thy
displeasure, but everything in order to Thee! Give me a longing to be with Thee; not for avoiding the calamities of this
wicked world, nor so much the pains of purgatory, nor of hell;
nor so much for the attaining of the choice of heaven, in respect of mine own commodity, as even for a very love to Thee!

Lady Jane Grey in Her Last Imprisonment

Lady Jane Grey (1537–1554) was the innocent victim of a plot to seize the throne of England. The great-granddaughter of Henry VII and the wife of Lord Guilford Dudley, she was proclaimed queen in 1553. A few months later she was deposed, and the following year executed, together with her husband.

O Merciful God, be Thou unto me a strong tower of defence, I humbly entreat Thee. Give me grace to await Thy leisure and patiently to bear what Thou doest unto me; nothing doubting or mistrusting Thy goodness towards me; for Thou knowest what is good for me better than I do. Therefore do with me in all things what Thou wilt; only arm me, I beseech Thee, with thine armour, that I may stand fast; above all things, taking to me the shield of faith; praying always that I may refer myself wholly to Thy will, abiding Thy pleasure, and comforting myself in those troubles which it shall please Thee to send me, seeing such troubles are profitable for me; and I am assuredly persuaded that all Thou doest cannot but be well; and unto Thee be all honour and glory. *Amen.*

Last Prayer of Mary, Queen of Scots

Mary, Queen of Scots (1542–1587), a devout Catholic, was distrusted by the Scottish people because of her religious beliefs. Forced to flee to England, she was held prisoner by Queen Elizabeth, and beheaded February 8, 1587. This prayer was offered on the eve of her execution.

> O Lord my God, I have hoped in Thee,
> O dear Jesus, set me free.
> Though hard the chains that fasten me,
> And sore my lot, yet I long for Thee.
> I languish and groaning bend my knee,
> Adoring, imploring, O set me free.

Sir Francis Drake at Cádiz

When the Spanish Armada was being outfitted in the harbor of Cádiz for the projected conquest of England, Sir Francis Drake (about 1540–1596) sailed boldly into the harbor and, despite shore batteries, destroyed almost the entire Spanish fleet.

O Lord God, when thou givest to thy servants to endeavor any great matter, grant us also to know that it is not the beginning, but the continuing of the same until it be thoroughly finished which yieldeth the true glory; through him that for the finishing of thy work laid down his life. *Amen.*

Francis Bacon in Prison

Francis Bacon (1561–1626) was one of the most accomplished men of his time and one of the most erudite men of any age. He was a scholar, a judge, a statesman, and a philosopher. He became Lord High Chancellor of England under Queen Elizabeth, but fell into disgrace and was imprisoned after being convicted of accepting bribes in the administration of law. The following prayer was written in prison when he believed himself about to die.

Most gracious Lord God, my merciful Father, from my youth up, my Creator, my Redeemer, my Comforter. Thou (O Lord) soundest and searchest the depths and secrets of all hearts; Thou knowledgest the upright of heart, Thou judgest the hypocrite, Thou ponderest men's thoughts and doings as in a balance, Thou measurest their intentions as with a line; vanity and crooked ways cannot be hid from Thee.

Remember (O Lord) how thy servant hath walked before Thee; remember what I have first sought, and what hath been principal in mine intentions. I have loved thy assemblies, I have mourned for the divisions of thy Church, I have delighted in the brightness of thy sanctuary.

This vine which thy right hand hath planted in this nation, I have ever prayed unto Thee that it might stretch her branches to the seas and to the floods. The state and bread of the poor and oppressed have been precious in mine eyes; I have hated all cruelty and hardness of heart: I have (though in a despised weed) procured the good of all men. If any have been mine enemies, I thought not of them; neither hath the sun almost set upon my displeasure; but I have been as a dove, free from superfluity of maliciousness. Thy creatures have been my books, but thy Scriptures much more. I have sought therein the courts, fields and gardens, but I have found Thee in thy temples.

Thousand have been my sins, and ten thousand my transgressions; but thy sanctifications have remained with me, and my heart, through thy grace, hath been an unquenched coal upon thy altar. O Lord, my strength, I have since my youth met with Thee in all my ways, by thy fatherly compassions, by thy comfortable chastisements, and by thy most visible providence.

As thy favors have increased upon me, so have thy corrections; as Thou hast been alway near me, O Lord; and ever as my worldly blessings were exalted, so secret darts from Thee have pierced me; and when I have ascended before men, I have descended in humiliation before Thee.

And now, when I thought most of peace and honor, thy hand is heavy upon me, and hath humbled me, according to thy former loving kindness, keeping me still in thy fatherly school, not as bastard, but as a child. Just are thy judgments upon me for my sins, which are more in number than the sands of the sea, but have no proportion to thy mercies; for what are the sands of the sea to the sea, earth, heavens? and all these are nothing to thy mercies.

Besides my innumerable sins, I confess before Thee, that I am debtor to Thee for the gracious talent of thy gifts and graces, which I have neither put into a napkin, nor put it (as I ought) to exchangers, where it might have made best profit;

but misspent it in things for which I was least fit; so as I may truly say, my soul hath been a stranger in the course of my pilgrimage. Be merciful unto me (O Lord) for my Saviour's sake, and receive me into thy bosom, or guide me in thy ways. *Amen.*

Oliver Cromwell on His Deathbed

Oliver Cromwell (1599–1658) was Lord Protector of England during a time of great crisis. Although he declined the crown, he named Richard as his successor before he died and earnestly prayed for the English nation. This prayer was made as a dreadful storm—actually a hurricane—raged over London, August 30, 1658. It is a notable example of prayer by the head of a nation.

Lord, though I am a miserable and wretched creature, I am in covenant with Thee through grace. And I may, I will come to Thee for thy people.

Thou hast made me, though very unworthy, a mean instrument to do them some good, and Thee service; and many of them have set too high a value upon me, though others wish and would be glad of my death; Lord, however Thou do dispose of me, continue and go on to do good for them. Pardon thy foolish people! Forgive their sins, and do not forsake them, but love and bless them.

Give them consistency of judgment, one heart, and mutual love; and go on to deliver them, and with the work of reformation; and make the name of Christ glorious in the world. Teach those who look too much on thy instruments, to depend more on thyself. Pardon such as desire to trample upon the dust of a poor worm; for they are thy people, too. And pardon the folly of this short prayer. And give me rest for Jesus Christ's sake, to whom, with Thee and thy Holy Spirit, be all honor and glory, now and forever! *Amen.*

Queen Anne's Prayer for Protection

Queen Anne (1665–1714) of England, Scotland, and Ireland, later Queen of Great Britain, came to the throne in 1702. Called "Good Queen Anne," she was a Stuart educated in the Protestant faith and was known as a deeply religious monarch. The most important public event of her reign was the Act of Union with Scotland in 1707.

Almighty and Eternal God, the Disposer of all the affairs in the world, there is not one circumstance so great as not to be subject to Thy power, nor so small but it comes within Thy care; Thy goodness and wisdom show themselves through all Thy works, and Thy loving kindness and mercy appear in the several dispensations of Thy Providence. May we readily submit ourselves to Thy pleasure and sincerely resign our wills to Thine, with all patience, meekness, and humility; through Jesus Christ our Lord. *Amen.*

Horatio, Lord Nelson at Trafalgar

Horatio, Lord Nelson, the great British naval hero, lived from 1758 to 1805. On the morning of October 21, 1805, before the Battle of Trafalgar, he gave the signal to bear down on the enemy. He then retired to his cabin and wrote this prayer.

May the Great God, whom I worship, grant to my country and for the benefit of Europe in general, a great and glorious victory, and may no misconduct in any one tarnish it; and may humanity after victory be the predominant feature in the British fleet! For myself individually, I commit my life to Him that made me; and may His blessing alight on my endeavors for serving my country faithfully! To Him I resign myself, and the just cause which is entrusted to me to defend. *Amen! Amen! Amen!*

Evening Prayer at Brandywine

Joab Prout, Chaplain of the Continental Army, delivered this prayer on September 10, 1777, the evening before the Battle of Brandywine, before the assembled troops led by General Washington, who knelt with the others. Lafayette was there, as were Pulaski, Kosciusko, "Mad" Anthony Wayne, and other heroes of the Revolution.

Great Father, we bow before Thee. We invoke thy blessing, we deprecate thy wrath, we return Thee thanks for the past, we ask thy aid for the future. For we are in times of trouble, O Lord! and sore beset by foes, merciless and unpitying; the sword gleams over our land, the dust of the soil is dampened with the blood of our neighbors and friends.

O, God of mercy, we pray thy blessing on the American arms. Make the man of our hearts strong in thy wisdom; bless, we beseech, with renewed life and strength, our hope and thy instrument, even George Washington.

Shower thy counsels on the honorable, the Continental Congress. Visit the tents of our host; comfort the soldier in his wounds and afflictions; nerve him for the hour of fight; prepare him for the hour of death.

And, in the hour of defeat, O God of Hosts! do Thou be our stay; and, in the hour of triumph, be Thou our guide.

Teach us to be merciful, though the memories of galling wrongs be at our hearts, knocking for admittance, that they may fill us with desires for revenge; yet let us be merciful, though they never spared us, in their hour of butchery and bloodshed.

And in the hour of death, do Thou guide us into the abode prepared for the blest; so shall we return thanks unto Thee, through Christ, our Redeemer; God prosper the cause. *Amen.*

Abraham Lincoln's Prayer for a Great Bereavement

This prayer is from Abraham Lincoln's letter to Mrs. Bixby, a mother whose five sons were killed in action during the Civil War.

I pray that our Heavenly Father may assuage the anguish of your bereavement and leave you only the cherished memory of the loved and lost, and the solemn pride that must be yours to have laid so costly a sacrifice upon the altar of freedom.

A Plantation Negro after Lincoln's Death

This beautiful prayer from the *Prayers of the Ages* was delivered by a plantation Negro the Sunday after the assassination of President Abraham Lincoln.

O Lord, we come to Thee holding up our souls as empty pitchers, to be filled from the fountains of Thy love. Didn't you tell us, Lord, if we were hungry you would feed us? Didn't you tell us, Lord, if we were thirsty you would give us drink from the waters of salvation? Didn't you tell us, Lord, if we were poor and weak, Come unto me, all ye feeble, and weary, and heavy-laden, and I will give you rest? Didn't you tell us, Lord, if we would be patient and wait, you would bring us out of all our troubles? And when the hour was come, as you raised up Moses to break the power of Pharaoh and let the people go, so you have sent us a deliverer, to lead us out of slavery: and while the good shepherd was with us, he led us over the wilderness, and toted the little ones in his arms, and gave us to browse in the green pastures.

But now, Lord, when his work was done, you saw it was done, and took him up higher, and gave him a seat among the archangels, and clothed him in white robes; and he pleads for us. When any of us are worthy, we shall see him where he is, and embrace him. And the Lord will say, "Who be these?"

And Abraham will answer, "These are they whom I brought out with much tribulation and anguish, from the house of bondage, and for whom I was killed."

Franklin D. Roosevelt's D-Day Prayer

Franklin Delano Roosevelt (1882–1945), thirty-second President of the United States, led the country almost to the end of World War II and was the first President to be elected for a third term. This prayer was delivered on D-Day, June 6, 1944, as the invasion of Normandy began.

Almighty God: Our sons, pride of our Nation, this day have set upon a mighty endeavor, a struggle to preserve our Republic, our religion and our civilization, and to set free a suffering humanity.

Lead them straight and true; give strength to their hearts, steadfastness in their faith.

They will need Thy blessings. Their road will be long and hard. For the enemy is strong. He may hurl back our forces. Success may not come with rushing speed, but we shall return again and again; and we know that by Thy grace, and by the righteousness of our cause, our sons will triumph.

They will be sore tried, by night and by day, without rest— until the victory is won. The darkness will be rent by noise and flame. Men's souls will be shaken with the violences of the war.

For these men are lately drawn from the ways of peace. They fight not for the lust of conquest. They fight to end conquest. They fight to let justice arise, and tolerance and good will among all Thy people. They yearn but for the end of battle, for their return to the haven of home.

Some will never return. Embrace these, Father, and receive them, Thy heroic servants, into Thy kingdom.

And for us at home—fathers, mothers, children, wives, sisters and brothers of brave men overseas—whose thoughts and prayers are ever with them—help us, Almighty God, to rededicate ourselves in renewed faith in Thee in this hour of great sacrifice. . . .

Because the road is long and the desire is great, I ask that our people devote themselves in a continuance of prayer. As we rise to each new day, and again when each day is spent, let words of prayer be on our lips, invoking Thy help in our efforts.

Give us strength, too—strength in our daily tasks to redouble the contributions we make in the physical and the material support of our armed forces.

And let our hearts be stout, to wait out the long travail, to bear sorrows that may come, to impart our courage unto our sons wheresoever they may be.

And, O Lord, give us Faith. Give us Faith in Thee; Faith in our sons; Faith in each other; Faith in our united crusade. Let not the keenness of our spirit ever be dulled. Let not the impacts of temporary events, of temporal matters, of but fleeting moment—let not these deter us in our unconquerable purpose.

With Thy blessing, we shall prevail over the unholy forces of our enemy. Help us to conquer the apostles of greed and racial arrogance. Lead us to the saving of our country, and with our sister Nations into a world unity that will spell a sure peace—a peace invulnerable to the schemings of unworthy men. And a peace that will let all men live in freedom, reaping the just rewards of honest toil.

Thy will be done, Almighty God.

Amen.

Prayer for the United States Navy

This prayer was first invoked by a navy chaplain at the Philadelphia Navy Yard in 1843 and has become part of the Navy's traditional religious expressions.

O eternal God, may the vessels of our Navy be guarded by Thy gracious Providence and care. May they not bear the sword in vain, but as the minister of God; be a terror to those who do evil and a defense to those who do well. Graciously bless the officers and the men of our Navy. May love of country be engraven on their hearts and may their adventurous spirits and severe toils be duly appreciated by a grateful nation. May their lives be precious in Thy sight, and if ever our ships of war should be engaged in battle, grant that their struggles may be only under an enforced necessity for the defense of what is right. Bless all nations and kindreds on the face of the earth and hasten the time when the principles of holy religion shall so prevail that none shall wage war any more for the purpose of aggression, and none shall need it as a means of defense. All of which blessings we ask through the merits of Jesus Christ our Lord. *Amen.*

West Point Cadet Prayer

This prayer is regularly used at Sunday services of the United States Military Academy at West Point.

O God, our father, Thou Searcher of men's hearts, help us to draw near to Thee in sincerity and truth. May our religion be filled with gladness and may our worship of Thee be natural. Strengthen and increase our admiration for honest dealing and clean thinking, and suffer not our hatred of hypocrisy and

pretense ever to diminish. Encourage us in our endeavor to
live about the common level of life. Make us to choose the
harder right instead of the easier wrong, and never to be content with a half-truth when the whole can be won. Endow us
with courage that is born of loyalty to all that is noble and
worthy, that scorns compromise with vice and injustice and
knows no fear when truth and right are in jeopardy. Guard us
against flippancy and irreverence in the sacred things of life.
... Help us, in our work and in our play, to keep ourselves
physically strong, mentally awake and morally straight. All of
which we ask in the name of the Great Friend and Master of
men. *Amen.*

Midshipmen's Prayer

This prayer has long been used at chapel services on Sunday at the
United States Naval Academy at Annapolis.

O God, our Father, make us worthy of the trust which our
Navy has placed in us. May we serve our country with all
our heart, with all our soul, and with all our might, that we
may speed the victory and help bring law and order once
again to a distressed world.

Help us, we implore Thee, to keep undulled and unsullied our
faith in democracy and freedom. May our sword be un-
sheathed in the cause of truth and may we remain undaunted
while we struggle for world peace.

We go forth with love undying and undimmed vision, with
the resolve that we shall never be neutral toward wickedness and oppression. Give us faith in the future as individually and collectively we march out as officers of the United
States Navy in the cause of moral order and Humanity re-
born! *Amen.*

Prayer of the House of Commons

This prayer is spoken at every sitting of the British House of Commons. It was composed by Sir Christopher Yelverton, M.P. for Northampton and Speaker of the House, *circa* 1578.

Almighty God, by whom alone kings reign and princes decree justice, and from whom cometh all counsel, wisdom and understanding,

We, Thine unworthy servants, here gathered together in Thy name, do most humbly beseech Thee to send down the heavenly wisdom from above, to direct and guide us in all our consultations.

And grant that, we having Thy fear always before our eyes, and laying aside all private interests, prejudices and private affections, the result of all our counsels may be the glory of Thy blessed name, the maintenance of true religion and justice, and the safety, honour and happiness of the King, the public welfare, peace and tranquility of the realm, and the uniting and knitting together of the hearts of all persons and estates within the same in true Christian love and charity towards one another, through Jesus Christ our Lord and Saviour.

PRAYERS FOR THOSE
IN DOUBT

Fᴀɪᴛʜ ɪs ᴀ ʟᴏᴀɴ. *Giving it is the only thing that man can do for God, as opposed to all of the things which God can do for man. Some men do not have the faith to give. These are the truly poor of the earth. They want to believe, but they cannot.*

The men who split the atom had not seen it, but they had faith that it was there. No one has seen electrical current run along a wire, but we have faith that it does because we have seen an incandescent bulb light at the end of the wire. Faith in God is a gift of grace. It cannot be bought, bartered, or begged.

I have met many insincere Christians (at times I've been one), but I have never met an insincere atheist. And I have never met a doubter who wasn't worried about his state of mind. These prayers, then, are for the doubters.

You will go far to find more moving words than Peter Marshall's in the second prayer of this section: "Father, I have lost the feeling of Thy presence. Yet deep in my heart I know that it is not because Thou didst leave me, but because I have wandered from Thee."

Martin Luther was assailed by doubt and, in his fear, he mur-

mured to God "...at times I doubt and am unable to trust Thee altogether." Many of the saints survived a crumbling of faith.

In my twenties—the period of great knowledge and no wisdom—I lost most of my faith. Not all, because I still prayed when I feared that there was No One to whom I could pray. At that time, I began all prayers with the plea "Please grant to all of us ever more faith in Thee, and in Thy church, and in each other."

Faith returned, in time. It came back full and strong and this made me happy because there is no such thing as partial faith. One believes completely or one does not believe at all.

For Strengthening of Faith

Behold, Lord, an empty vessel that needs to be filled. My Lord, fill it. I am weak in the faith; strengthen thou me. I am cold in love; warm me and make me fervent that my love may go out to my neighbor. I do not have a strong and firm faith; at times I doubt and am unable to trust thee altogether. O Lord, help me. Strengthen my faith and trust in thee. In thee I have sealed the treasures of all I have. I am poor; thou art rich and didst come to be merciful to the poor. I am a sinner; thou art upright. With me there is an abundance of sin; in thee is the fulness of righteousness. Therefore, I will remain with thee of whom I can receive, but to whom I may not give. *Amen.*

—Martin Luther
See biographical note on page 98.

Restoration

Peter Marshall, born in Scotland in 1902, started life as a miner, then came to America where he was ordained to the ministry of the Presbyterian Church in 1931. He served as Chaplain of the United States Senate from 1947 until his death in 1949. His wife Catherine wrote a heartwarming book dealing with his life which became a best seller, *A Man Called Peter.*

Father, I have lost the feeling of Thy presence. Yet deep in my heart I know that it is not because Thou didst leave me, but because I have wandered from Thee.

"All we like sheep have gone astray. We have turned every one to his own way." I confess that I have found that way hard and wearisome. My feet are tired of wandering. My heart is sick of being lost. I would return to Thee now and be led of Thee in Thy way, that I may walk once more with a sense of direction and a clear light upon my path.

O my Father, receive me—Thy prodigal child; prodigal because I have wandered in a far country, prodigal in my forgetfulness of Thee, prodigal in all the blessings I have taken for granted. Now, bowing before Thee, I acknowledge them all.

And now I arise and come back to Thee, my Father, knowing that Thou art even now running to meet me, placing over my shoulders the robe of Thy love, placing upon my hand the ring of Thy forgiveness, pressing upon me the kiss of a divine love that knows no limit—a love which loved me while I was yet a sinner—a love that brought Jesus to Calvary.

I thank Thee for that love; I thank Thee for this restoration. I thank Thee that Thou art still my Father, and I am still Thy child. *Amen.*

—Peter Marshall, from *The Prayers of Peter Marshall*

For One Troubled in Conscience

John Wallace Suter was born in Winchester, Massachusetts, in 1890. He was ordained into the Protestant Episcopal clergy in 1915 and has been custodian of the *Standard Book of Common Prayer* in Washington, D.C., since 1942.

O blessed Lord, the Father of mercies and the God of all comfort, we beseech Thee, look down in pity and compassion on Thy servant whose soul is full of trouble. Give *him* a right understanding of *himself,* and also of Thy will for *him,* that *he* may neither cast away his confidence in Thee nor place it anywhere but in Thee. Deliver *him* from the fear of evil, lift up the light of Thy countenance upon *him,* and give *him* Thine everlasting peace; through the merits and mediation of Jesus Christ our Lord. *Amen.*

—John Wallace Suter

A Quaker's Prayer

John Woolman (1720–1772) was born in Rancocas, New Jersey. A tailor by trade, he became an itinerant Quaker preacher and traveled through the Colonies preaching against slavery. He is best known for his *Journal,* first published after his death in 1774 and now a classic.

O Lord, my God! the amazing horrors of darkness were gathered round me, and covered me all over, and I saw no way to go forth; I felt the depth and extent of the misery of my fellow creatures separated from the Divine harmony, and it was heavier than I could bear, and I was crushed down under it; I lifted up my hand, I stretched out my arm, but there was none to help me; I looked round about, and was amazed. In the depths of misery, O Lord, I remembered that Thou art omnipotent; that I had called Thee Father; and I felt that I loved Thee, and I was made quiet in my will, and I waited for deliverance from Thee. Thou hadst pity upon me, when no man could help me; I saw that meekness under suffering was showed to us in the most affecting example of Thy Son, and Thou taughtest me to follow Him, and I said, "Thy will, O Father, be done!"

—John Woolman

For Submission

Blaise Pascal, French scientist and philosopher, was born in 1623 and died in 1662. As a child he was a mathematical prodigy, and his more significant literary work began with his entrance into the Jansenist community at Port Royal in 1655. Among his most famous works are his *Lettres provinciales* and *Pensées*.

O Lord, take from me that sorrow which the love of self may produce from my sufferings, and from my unsuccessful hopes and designs in this world, while regardless of Thy glory; but create in me a sorrow resembling Thine. Let me not henceforth desire health or life, except to spend them for Thee, with Thee, and in Thee. I pray not that Thou wouldst give me either health or sickness, life or death; but that Thou wouldst dispose of my health and my sickness, my life and my death, for Thy glory, for my own eternal welfare, for the use of the church, for the benefit of the saints, of whose number, by Thy grace, I hope to be. Thou alone knowest what is good for me; Thou art Lord of all; do, therefore, what seemeth Thee best. Give to me, or take from me; conform my will to Thine! and grant that with humble and perfect submission, and in holy confidence, I may be disposed to receive the orders of Thy eternal providence; and may equally adore every dispensation which will come to me from Thy hand, through Jesus Christ our Lord. *Amen.*

—Blaise Pascal

When Fear Overcomes

Thomas à Kempis (1380–1471) was born in Kempen, Prussia, and entered an Augustinian monastery in 1407. He was ordained in 1413 and chosen subprior of the monastery in 1425. Tradition has assigned to him the authorship of *The Imitation of Christ,* a devotional classic which has appealed to Christians everywhere for centuries.

O Lord my God, be not thou far from me; my God, have regard to help me; for there have risen up against me sundry thoughts and great fears afflicting my soul. How shall I pass through unhurt? How shall I break them to pieces? This is my hope, my one only consolation, to flee unto thee in every tribulation, to trust in thee, to call upon thee from my inmost heart, and to wait patiently for thy consolation. *Amen.*

—St. Thomas à Kempis

For Rest in God

Christina Georgina Rossetti (1830–1894) was a member of a distinguished family of poets, artists, painters. She long attended her invalid mother, and after a serious illness in 1874 she herself was left an invalid.

O Lord, who art as the shadow of a great rock in a weary land, who beholdest thy weak creatures, weary of labor, weary of pleasure, weary of hope deferred, weary of self: In thine abundant compassion and unutterable tenderness, bring us, we pray thee, unto thy rest. *Amen.*

—Christina G. Rossetti

The Power of Love

Leslie D. Weatherhead has been minister of the City Temple, London, since 1936. He was born in London in 1893 and saw service in World War I. He is widely known as an inspiring preacher and writer. His interest in psychology as an aid to the work of the minister is an outstanding feature of his ministry, and he is the author of many books, including *Psychology, Religion, and Healing.*

O God, give us, we beseech Thee, a new sense of Thy power. We are only little children. We cannot see very far. We stumble in the darkness of our ignorance and folly and sin; stumble against some law of Thy universe; catastrophe falls upon us which was beyond our power to foresee; illness takes our loved ones, death smites in a way which frightens us; the sins of others hurt and maim the purest; the whole world seems, in our moments of pessimism, in the grip of evil forces and we doubt Thy power of love.

Forgive us. Our standards are false; our values are false. The things we call power are weakness. The things we call weak are strong.

Turn our eyes to the Cross until we begin to understand the power of Love. Keep our faith pure and sweet and unspoiled by doubt even when we are wounded. Deepen our prayer life. Help us to keep our love unspoiled by bitterness. And show us Thy power until we share it; a power that nothing can quell or overcome, a love that goes on loving and never lets go in the face of all that hostility can accomplish.

So may we share in the triumph of Thy kingdom of love, when all hearts bow in willing bondage to Thee and all men join in loving service. Through Jesus Christ our Lord. *Amen.*

—Leslie D. Weatherhead, from *In This Manner Pray Ye*

For Those Who Struggle with Doubt

John Hunter (1871–1917) was ordained minister of the Congregational Church in 1893. He preached in the United States and in other countries, and wrote a number of religious books.

Almighty God, by whom the meek are guided in judgment and whose secret is with them that fear thee; we pray for all who, in these days of unsettlement and growing knowledge and changing opinion, are troubled by questioning and doubt. Inspire them with that loyalty of soul to which the things essential to health and peace of life are ever clear. Keep them humble, earnest, aspiring, and pure minded, that they may never be without the light which makes plain the path of duty. Rebuke in them all impatience, presumption, and despondency; all dishonesty and uncharitableness; endue them with the spirit of wisdom, and hope, and courage. Be thou their teacher and guide; for if thou dost teach them they cannot learn amiss, and if thou dost guide them they cannot go astray. Help us all to a truer, simpler, and more peaceful trust in thee. . . . What we need to know teach thou us; what we cannot know make us content to leave unknown, and to wait patiently on thee till the shadows flee away. *Amen.*

—John Hunter, from *Devotional Service*

Spiritual Doubts and Difficulties

Ashton Oxenden (1808–1892) was born in Canterbury, England, and ordained in the Church of England in 1833. He was elected Bishop of Montreal and Metropolitan of Canada in 1869, remaining Primate of Canada until his death. He wrote numerous theological works of great simplicity and directness which won enormous popularity.

O Thou who art my Guide and Friend, my Counsellor and my Support, to Thee I come in this my time of need. Lord, Thou knowest how sorely I am tried by spiritual doubts and fears. Have compassion on me. Pity Thy poor, weak servant; and in Thy own good time make every difficulty to vanish.

In the meanwhile support me by Thy grace. Hold Thou me up, lest I sink. Let not the waves overwhelm me. Speak to my heart, and make me to feel Thy love towards me. Show me that Thou art indeed my Father. Lord, I believe: help Thou mine unbelief.

Remove every cloud that now darkens my soul; and shine upon me, O Thou Sun of Righteousness with healing in Thy wings. Take away all that hinders me from enjoying peace, and restore unto me the joy of Thy salvation. Give me grace to cast myself unreservedly on Thee, who art my Saviour and my Friend; and to Thee be all the praise, now and for evermore. *Amen.*

—Ashton Oxenden

Let Me Not Be Discouraged

Søren Aabye Kierkegaard (1813–1855) was a noted Danish existentialist philosopher and writer on theology. He held that religion was a matter for the individual and that the relation of the individual to God involves suffering. He has been discovered by the English-speaking world after nearly three-quarters of a century of complete neglect. Among his important works are *Either-or* and *Edifying Discourses*.

Father in Heaven! As a father sends his son out into the world, so also hast Thou sent man down here; he is, it seems, separated from Thee by a world; he does not see Thee with his eyes; he does not hear Thy voice with his ears of flesh. He stands now in the world, the way opens before him—so long weakened in the discouraging moment which will not give him time, so impassive in the moment of enervating impatience which will not give him time; give then to Thy child freedom from discouragement in the vast world, freedom from discouragement when false leads seem so numerous and the right road so difficult to find. Give him the freedom from discouragement when dread and care seem to be undergirded by the destructive furor of the elements and the terror of events and by the despair of human misery; give then to Thy child the courage to remember and believe that as a father sends his child into the world, Thou hast also sent man down here. God of compassion! As the prodigal son found everything changed on his return, even the disposition of his brother, but not that of his father whose fatherly love he received and who welcomed with a festival, whose fatherly love gave him courage in his discouragement at the festival. Even so, when a man turns back toward Thee, Thou givest him courage on his road to conversion, for his return is not joyous like that of the well-loved child returning home, but it is painful like that of the prodigal son, and he is not thus expected by a loving father who with joy awaits his loving son and is joyous at seeing him again. Ah, that he may have courage to believe that a compassionate Father, who in His solicitude dreads his perdition, is awaiting him.

—Søren Kierkegaard, from *Papirer*

I Have Lost My Confidence

Jeremy Taylor (1613–1667), English churchman and author, was chaplain to Archbishop Laud and Charles I. He is best remembered for his enduring inspirational works. These include *The Golden Grove, Holy Living*, and *Holy Dying*.

Thy judgments, O Lord God, are declared in thunder, and with fear and with dread Thou shakest all my bones, and my soul trembles when I consider the great day in which Thou shalt judge all the world, and that infinite justice which will not spare the mighty for his greatness, nor the poor for his poverty; and thy unlimited power, which can mightily destroy all them that will not have Thee to reign over them.

There is no holiness, O God, if Thou withdrawest thy hand; no wisdom profits if thy government ceaseth. No courage can abide, no watchfulness keep us safe, unless Thou dost continue to strengthen us, to purify us, to make us stand. When Thou leavest us we fall and perish; when thy grace and mercy visit us, we are lifted up and stand upright. We are unstable, and insecure, unless we be confirmed by Thee; but we seek to Thee for thy help; and yet depart from the ways of thy commandments.

O how meanly and contemptibly do I deserve to be thought of! how little and inconsiderable is the good which I do! and how vast, how innumerable, how intolerable are the evils which I have done! I submit, O God, to the depth of thy righteous and unsearchable judgment: for I have been searching for a little, some little good in me; but I find nothing. Much, indeed, of good I have received; but I have abused it. Thou hast given me thy grace; but I have turned it into wantonness: Thou hast enabled me to serve Thee; but I have served myself; but never but when I was thy enemy; so that in me, that is, in my flesh, dwelleth no good thing.

I am a deep abyss, O God, of folly and calamity; I search my heart, and can find no good thing; I search and I cannot find out all the evil. Thou didst create in me a hope of glory; but I have lost my confidence; and men have, sometimes, spoken good things of me; but I know not where they are: Who shall raise me up, when I fall down before thy face in the presence of the assembled world?

Pity my shame, O God; bind up my wounds; lift me from the dust; and make me what Thou wilt delight in. Take away the hindrance, "the sin that so easily besets me," and bring me unto Jesus, who died for a guilty world; unite me unto Him; and then although in myself I am nothing, yet in Him shall be what I ought to be, and what Thou wilt esteem entitled to thy love.

—Jeremy Taylor

For a Troubled Spirit

John Wesley (1703–1791), theologian, evangelist, and founder of Methodism, was ordained priest in 1728. He swept aside ecclesiastical and High-church views in 1739. Subsequently he traveled on foot and on horseback through England, Ireland, and Scotland organizing the Methodist Church. He was a prolific writer as well as a prodigious worker, and authored books on a variety of subjects.

O Most Blessed and gracious God, who only canst heal a wounded spirit and quiet a troubled mind, unto Thee do I cry for help.

O Thou great Physician of body and soul, uphold and comfort my weak and dejected spirit. As Thou alone canst relieve me, so unto Thee do I call for relief. O hear my most earnest supplication, and make me to possess an easy, quiet and cheerful spirit, as my trust is in Thee.

It is good that thou both hope and quietly wait for the salvation of the Lord.

Return unto thy rest, O my soul; and be no longer disquieted within me.

Return unto thy rest, O my soul, in God; for He is thy resting-place and thy salvation.

—John Wesley, from *John Wesley's Prayers*

God Be with Us

Robert Louis Stevenson (1850–1894) was born in Edinburgh, Scotland. Frail of health from infancy, he turned from the study of civil engineering to travel and literature and produced many famous essays, stories, and poetry. He spent the latter part of his life in voluntary exile in Samoa, living at Vailima, 500 feet above the sea. Here is a section from his *Prayers Written at Vailima*.

We beseech Thee, Lord, to behold us with favour, folk of many families and nations gathered together in the peace of this roof, weak men and women subsisting under the covert of Thy patience. Be patient still; suffer us yet a while longer —with our broken purposes of good, with our idle endeavours against evil, suffer us a while longer to endure and (if it may be) help us to do better. Bless to us our extraordinary mercies; if the day come when these must be taken, brace us to play the man under affliction. Be with our friends, be with ourselves. Go with each of us to rest; if any awake, temper to them the dark hours of watching; and when the day returns, return to us, our sun and comforter, and call us up with morning faces and morning hearts—eager to labor—eager to be happy, if happiness still be our portion—and if the day be marked for sorrow, strong to endure it.

—Robert Louis Stevenson

His Own Received Him Not

William E. Orchard, born in England in 1877, was ordained a Presbyterian minister but early became a Dissenter and has long been a controversial figure in British religious circles. He moved toward Catholicism, yet worked among the Free Churches of England for many years before he became a Catholic. His great book of prayers, *The Temple,* remains one of his most important contributions. The following three prayers are taken from *The Temple.*

O God, who cometh to us in an hour when we think not, and in such a way as we least expect; we are all gathered to wait and watch for Thy coming. Disappoint us not because we disappointed Thee when Thou camest to Thine own before. Refuse not to return to us because we knew not the day of Thy visitation, nor the things that belonged to our peace. We had expected a king coming in glory, girt with royal robes; not a wayfaring man who turned aside to tarry for a night. We looked for a mighty conqueror travelling victoriously, who would demand our submission in tones we dared not disobey; not for a suppliant standing at our gate pleading in lowliness and garbed in humility. We awaited one whose raiment would shine like the sun and whose crown was rich with precious stones and purest gold; not one clothed in mockery and crowned with thorns. We sought a Saviour whose magic touch would heal all our sickness, whose medicine would minister to a mind diseased; we never dreamed we might be called to drink a cup of tears and share a baptism of blood.

Yet come again to us. We look no more for seeming strength or outward power, but for a heart which cares, a face which answers ours. *Amen.*

—William E. Orchard

Behold, Thou Wert Within

O God, too near to be found, too simple to be conceived, too good to be believed; help us to trust, not in our knowledge of Thee, but in Thy knowledge of us; to be certain of Thee, not because we feel our thoughts of Thee are true, but because we know how far Thou dost transcend them. May we not be anxious to discern Thy will, but content only with desire to do it; may we not strain our minds to understand Thy nature, but yield ourselves and live our lives only to express Thee.

Shew us how foolish it is to doubt Thee, since Thou Thyself dost set the questions which disturb us; reveal our unbelief to be faith fretting at its outworn form. Be gracious when we are tempted to cease from moral strife: reveal what it is that struggles in us. Before we tire of mental search enable us to see that it was not ourselves but Thy call which stirred our souls.

Turn us back from our voyages of thought to that which sent us forth. Teach us to trust not to cleverness or learning, but to that inward faith which can never be denied. Lead us out of confusion to simplicity. Call us back from wandering without to find Thee at home within. *Amen.*

—William E. Orchard

For Strength in the Hour of Crisis

O God, who hast sent us to school in this strange life of ours, and hast set us tasks which test all our courage, trust and fidelity; may we not spend our days complaining at circumstance or fretting at discipline, but give ourselves to learn of life and to profit by every experience. Make us strong to endure.

We pray that when trials come upon us we may not shirk the issue or lose our faith in thy goodness, but committing our souls unto thee who knowest the way that we take, come forth as gold tried in the fire.

Grant by thy grace that we may not be found wanting in the hour of crisis. When the battle is set, may we know on which side we ought to be, and when the day goes hard, cowards steal from the field and heroes fall around the standard, may our place be found where the fight is fiercest. If we faint, may we not be faithless; if we fall, may it be while facing the foe. *Amen.*

—William E. Orchard
See biographical note on page 128.

Prayer of Intercession

Joseph Fort Newton was born in Decatur, Texas, in 1880 and ordained into the Baptist ministry in 1893. A noted preacher and prolific writer, he has served many churches and is the author of a long list of inspirational books, including *Altar Stairs,* from which this prayer is taken.

Thou, O God, art our Father, and our hearts cry out for thy living presence; be to us the light that reveals and the grace that renews. How lovely are the hours of thy revealing, when the sky is clear and the sunlight lies radiant upon the hills and the birds sing in our hearts! But for those hours how could we live through the long, slow days when the heavens are gray and the hills whence cometh our strength are shrouded in mist?

Lord, sanctify to us alike the light and shadow of life, alike its fruitions and failures, and may it bring us nothing of joy or woe that shall not be a ministry of grace to our spirits. Unless thou keep us, O Lord, our life will lose its secret of power and its soul of hope; hide us in the sanctuary of thy love. Visit in thy mercy all who are in dire plight of faith by reason of bitter sorrow, all for whom the sun is veiled by the pale cast of fear and foreboding.

Minister to us, our Father; help us to know thee, not as in the word of a prophet, but by what we are and have within us of thine eternal life. Teach us to love thee with the love of Jesus, in whom thou hast revealed thyself as in no other, our friend, our brother and our Saviour; in whose name we offer our prayer. *Amen.*

—Joseph Fort Newton

Lead, Kindly Light

John Henry Newman (1801–1890), English theologian, was leader of the Oxford Movement. He contracted malaria in Sicily on a vacation trip in 1833. Still convalescing, he took passage on a fruit boat to Marseilles which was becalmed for a whole week at sea. During this time Newman composed "Lead, Kindly Light." He was in a state of spiritual unease as well as bodily unrest. He felt there was much wrong with the Church of England and that the burden of reform would fall upon him. He finally accepted Catholicism in 1845 and became a cardinal.

Lead, kindly Light, amid th' encircling gloom,
  Lead thou me on!
The night is dark, and I am far from home,
  Lead thou me on!
Keep thou my feet! I do not ask to see
The distant scene, one step enough for me.

I was not ever thus, nor prayed that thou
  Shouldst lead me on;
I loved to choose and see my path; but now
  Lead thou me on!
I loved the garish day; and, spite of fears,
Pride ruled my will: remember not past years.

So long thy power hath blest me, sure it still
  Will lead me on
O'er moor and fen, o'er crag and torrent, till
  The night is gone;
And with the morn those angel faces smile,
Which I have loved long since, and lost awhile.
                                      —John Henry Newman

THE SAINTS AT PRAYER

I ENVY THE SAINTS, *and this envy leads me to play the detractor. I like to imagine them as dull people with one-track minds. This, of course, isn't true, but it makes me feel better. I visualize them with all of their energies devoted to the solitary purpose of saving their immortal souls—flexing their spiritual muscles to the disgust of anemic Christians like me.*

When I browse through Alban Butler's The Lives of the Saints, *I flip the pages slowly, always looking for one who first succumbed to the pleasures of the flesh before seeing the Light. Failing that, I will settle for a good human saint like Peter, who sometimes said the wrong thing at the right time. More than once, Our Lord had to ask Peter, "What is this to thee?"*

Some of the lady saints seem to have been born to sainthood, and when one is born to be pure in heart and to love God and obey His Commandments perhaps it requires less devotion to be a saint. Once, when my wife said, "I've been a good wife to you for twenty-seven years," I replied, "Were you ever tempted not to?" She thought for a moment and said, "No."

"Then," I said, "you will get no medals from me. You were good because you had no inclination to be otherwise."

Saints are like that. The ones who had to fight Satan the hardest are the ones who excite my admiration. In this section you will find prayers devised by the saints—some of whom were born with shiny halos, and others who had to polish the gold ring anew every morning before slipping it on the forehead, rakishly.

Polycarp's Prayer at the Stake

Polycarp, one of the early Christian martyrs, was put to death in 155. He was a disciple of St. John the Evangelist and had seen some of the Apostles. He was brought before the proconsul at Smyrna during the persecution of the Church by Marcus Aurelius. Commanded to curse Christ, he replied, "Six and eighty years have I served Him, and He has done me nothing but good. How could I curse my Lord and Saviour!"

He refused to be fastened to the stake as the people gathered fuel with which to burn him, and observed the preparations for his execution serenely. He spoke the following praise from the flames which allegedly did not destroy him, making it necessary to stab him to death.

Thou God and Father of Thy beloved and blessed Son, our Lord Jesus Christ, through whom we have received knowledge of Thee, O God of the Angels and powers and of all creation and of all just men who live in Thy presence, I thank Thee that Thou hast graciously vouchsafed this day and this hour to allot me a portion among the number of martyrs, among the people of Christ, unto the resurrection of everlasting life: among these may I be received in thy sight, this day, as a fruitful and acceptable sacrifice, wherefore, for all this, I praise Thee, I bless Thee, I glorify Thee through the eternal High Priest, Jesus Christ, Thy beloved Son; to whom, with Thee and the Holy Ghost, be all glory, world without end. Amen.

—St. Polycarp

Prayer for Children

Clement of Alexandria was born about the middle of the second century and died about 220. He was ordained a priest of the church of Alexandria about 190. This prayer, from Book III of Clement of Alexandria, is the most ancient hymn of the primitive church and dates from about 150 years after the Apostles.

Shepherd of tender youth,
Guiding in love and truth
    Through devious ways;
Christ our triumphant King!
We come Thy name to sing,
And here our children bring
    To shout Thy praise.

Thou art our holy Lord!
The all-subduing Word,
    Healer of strife!
Thou didst Thyself abase!
Thou mightest save our race
    And give us life.

Thou art wisdom's High Priest!
Thou hast prepared the feast
    Of holy love;
And in our mortal pain
None calls on Thee in vain;
Help Thou dost not disdain—
    Help from above.

Ever be Thou our guide,
Our Shepherd and our pride,
    Our staff and song.
Jesus, Thou Christ of God!
By the perennial word
Lead us where Thou hast trod;
    Make our faith strong.

So now, and till we die,
Sound we Thy praise on high,
    And joyful sing.
Infants, and the glad throng,
Who to Thy church belong,
Unite and swell the song
    To Christ our King.
                        —St. Clement

Invocations of the Blessed Virgin

Saint Basil the Great (330–379) was Bishop of Caesarea in Cappodocia,
Doctor of the Church, and one of the Four Fathers of the Greek Church.
His revision of the liturgy is still occasionally used in the Byzantine rite.
Although the liturgy also bears the name of St. John Chrysostom (345–
407), the greatest of the Greek Fathers, St. Basil is generally credited
with sole authorship. These "Invocations of the Blessed Virgin" are from
the Ordering of the Divine Liturgy.

I

O Blessed Mother of God:
Open the gate of compassion
To us whose hope is in thee,
That we may not be confounded,
But be preserved from adversity, through thee,
Who art the Salvation of Christian folk.

II

O thou who art
A well of tenderness,
Vouchsafe unto us thy compassion,
Mother of God!

Look down upon thy people
Who have sinned,
And show thy pardon as of old:

For in thee do we put our trust
And hail thee blessed
As once did Gabriel,
Chief captain of the bodiless Hosts.

III

It is very meet to bless thee
Who didst bring forth God,
Ever blessed and most spotless
And the Mother of our God.
More honorable than Cherubim,
And more than the Seraphim
Glorious incomparably, thou,
Who, inviolate, didst bring forth God The Word,
And art indeed Mother of God:
Thee
Do we magnify!

O Full of Grace!
Thou art the joy of all creation,
Of the assembly of the Angels
And the race of men—
Thou, hallowed Temple,
Spiritual Paradise,
And boast of maidenhood, whence God took Flesh,
When He, Who was before the worlds our God,
Became a Child.

Thy womb He made His Throne,
And He enlarged thy bosom
Broader than the heavens.

O Full of Grace!
Thou art the joy of all creation.
Glory be to thee!

IV

Arise! shine,
O new Jerusalem!
For the Glory of The Lord is risen upon thee!..
Now rejoice and be glad,
O city of Sion:
Appear in thy splendor,
Pure Mother of God,
For He Whom thou barest is risen!

O Thou, Great Passover,
And hallowed above all,
O Christ!
O Thou the Wisdom and The Word,
The Power of God!
Grant that we may partake of Thee
More truly,
In that day of Thy Kingdom
Which shall have no night!

V

Steadfast Protectress of Christians,
Constant Advocate with the Creator,
Disdain not the cry of the sinful,
But of thy goodness,
Be ready to succor us,
Who do call with all confidence to thee:

Make haste to hear our petition.
Make haste to supplicate for us,
O Mother of God,
Who ever didst protect them that pay honor to thee!

VI

More honorable than Cherubim,
And more than Seraphim incomparably glorious,
Thou, who, inviolate,
Forth didst bring God The Word,
And art indeed Mother of God:
Thee do we magnify!

Glory be to The Father
And to The Son,
And to The Holy Ghost,
Both now, and forever,
Henceforth eternally: *Amen.*
                    —St. John Chrysostom and St. Basil

A Priest before the Sacrifice of the Mass

St. John Chrysostom, one of the Fathers of the Greek Church, was born in Antioch in 345. He was chosen Bishop of Constantinople in 398. An eloquent speaker, he was known as "the Mouth of Gold" of the Eastern Church. A great lover of the Holy Sacrifice of the Mass, he was instrumental in abbreviating the long liturgy of the Eastern Churches. Banished because of enmity of those whose vices he criticized, he died as a result of privation in 407.

No one who is bound by earthly desires and lusts is worthy to come near to Thee, to approach Thee, to minister to Thee, O King of Glory: for to serve Thee is a thing great and terrible, even to the heavenly powers. Yet through Thy unspeakable and immeasurable love of men, Thou Who without change or loss didst become Man, and didst take the title of our High Priest, hast given us the ministry of this liturgic and unbloody Sacrifice, being Thyself Lord of all things. For Thou only, O Lord our God, dost reign in Heaven and on earth, Who sittest upon the Throne of the Cherubim, Lord of the Seraphim, King of Israel, Who only art holy, and restest among the holy. I therefore pray Thee, Thou the only gracious and merciful Lord, look down upon me a sinner, and Thine unprofitable servant, cleanse my soul and my heart from an evil conscience; and by the Power of Thy Holy Spirit, grant me, whom Thou hast endued with the Grace of the Priesthood, to stand before this Thy Holy Table, and to consecrate Thy Sacred and Spotless Body and Precious Blood. For to Thee I approach, with bowed neck, and beseech Thee to turn not Thy Face away from me, nor reject me from among Thy children, but rather deign that these Gifts be offered by me a sinner, Thy unworthy servant. For Thou Thyself dost offer and art offered, dost receive and art received, Christ our God. And to Thee we give praise together with Thine Eternal Father and Thine All-Holy, Good and Life-Giving Spirit, now and forever, eternally: *Amen.*

—St. John Chrysostom

For God's Mercy

St. Augustine was the greatest of the Fathers of the Early Church and has exerted profound and continuing influence upon both Catholic and Protestant theology. Born in Tagaste, Algeria, in 354, he was converted as a young man from Manichaeism and a life of carnal lust. He taught rhetoric in Rome and Milan and was made Bishop of Hippo in Africa in 396, where he died in 430. Here he wrote his immortal works, *The City of God, Confessions,* and many other theological treatises.

O God, our Father, Who dost exhort us to pray, and Who dost grant what we ask, if only, when we ask, we live a better life: Hear me—who am trembling in this darkness, Stretch forth Thy Hand unto me! Ah, hold forth Thy Light before me: ah, recall me from my wanderings, that, Thou being my guide, I may be restored to myself and Thee, through Jesus Christ, Thy Son, my Lord: *Amen.*

Woe is me! Lord: have pity on me: woe is me! Lord: I hide not my wounds: Thou art the Physician, I the sick; Thou merciful, I miserable.

Is not the life of man upon the earth a temptation? Who is he that wishes for vexations and difficulties? Thou commandest them to be endured, not to be loved. For no man loves what he endures, though he may love to endure. For notwithstanding he rejoices to endure, he would rather there were naught for him to endure. In adversity, I desire prosperity; in prosperity, I fear adversity. What middle place, then, is there between these, where human life is not a temptation? Woe unto the prosperity of this world, once and again, from fear of misfortune and of corruption of joy! Woe unto the adversities of this world, once and again, and for the third time, from the desire of prosperity, and because adversity itself is a hard thing, and makes of endurance shipwreck!

Is not the life of man upon earth a temptation, and that without intermission? And my whole hope is only in thy exceeding great mercy: give what Thou commandest and command what Thou wilt.   —St. Augustine, from *Miserere Mei, Deus*

An Intercession

Watch Thou, dear Lord, with those who wake or watch or weep to-night, and give Thine angels charge over those who sleep. Tend Thy sick ones, O Lord Christ. Rest Thy weary ones. Bless Thy dying ones. Pity Thine afflicted ones. Shield Thy joyous ones. And all, for Thy Love's sake.

—St. Augustine

See biographical note on page 141.

To the Mother of God

St. Cyril of Alexandria is best known as the opponent of Nestorius, Bishop of Constantinople, in the dispute over the unity of Person in Christ and therefore the denial to Mary of her title "Mother of God." Nestorius, who took the position that Christ was two persons, was tried in 431 by hundreds of bishops assembled in Ephesus. From the sermon preached by Cyril, then Patriarch of Alexandria and presiding officer of the council, these salutations to Mary as "Mother of God" are taken. Nestorius was declared heretical as a result. Cyril himself was attacked by the Nestorian faction and imprisoned, but his authority prevailed and a reconciliation was later effected. Cyril died in 444.

Hail, O Mary, Mother of God,
Virgin and Mother!
Morning Star, perfect vessel.

Hail, O Mary, Mother of God!
Holy Temple
in which God Himself was conceived.

Hail, O Mary, Mother of God!
chaste
and pure dove.

Hail, O Mary, Mother of God!
effulgent light, from thee
proceedeth the Sun of Justice.

Hail, O Mary, Mother of God!
Thou didst enclose in thy sacred womb
the One Who cannot be encompassed.

Hail, O Mary, Mother of God!
With the shepherds we sing
the praise of God;
with the angels, the song of thanksgiving,

> *"Glory to God in the highest*
> *and peace on earth*
> *to men of good will!"*

Hail, O Mary, Mother of God!
from thee flowed the True Light,
Jesus Christ,
our Lord.

Hail, O Mary, Mother of God!
through thee came to us The Conqueror
and triumphant Vanquisher of hell.

Hail, O Mary, Mother of God!
through thee blossoms the glory of The Resurrection.

Hail, O Mary, Mother of God!
Thou hast saved every faithful Christian.

Hail, O Mary, Mother of God!
Who can praise thee worthily,
O glorious Virgin Mary?

Holy Mary, Mother of God,
pray for us sinners
now and at the hour of our death. Amen.
                    —St. Cyril of Alexandria

A Morning Hymn

St. Patrick, apostle and patron saint of Ireland, was born near the Severn
River in Britain of a family of Celto-Roman descent. From the time of
his conversion he was a mighty warrior for God. He landed in 429 at
Wicklow Head, where he was at once attacked by the Irish chiefs. His
struggles in Ireland ended with victory. He converted the Irish people,
ended druid deviltry, and subdued savage and warlike chiefs and kings.
He built churches all over Ireland and died on March 17, 461, to become
the first of the Irish saints.

I arise today
Through a Mighty Strength,
Strong Virtue of Invocation of the Trinity:
    Through belief in The Threeness,
    Through the confession of The Oneness
    Of the Creator of Creation.

I arise today
Through a Mighty Strength:
    The Strength of The Incarnation of Christ,
    The Strength of Christ in His Baptism,
    The Strength of His Crucifixion and His Burial,

The Strength of His Resurrection and His Ascension,
The Strength of His Coming on Judgment Day.

I arise today
Through a Mighty Strength:
    The virtue of the love of Seraphim,
    In the Obedience of Angels,
    In the hope of Resurrection unto reward,
    By virtue of prayers of Patriarchs,
    By virtue of predictions of God's prophets,
    By virtue of preaching of His Apostles,
    In virtue of the faith of confessors,
    The purity of holy virgins,
    And deeds of righteous men.

I arise today
To witness a Mighty Strength:
    The Power that created Heaven,
    The Power that created the light of the sun,
    The Power that created the brightness of the
        moon,
    The Power that created the splendor of fire,
    The Power that created flashing lightning,
    The Power that caused the swiftness of winds,
    The Power that laid the depths of seas,
    The Power that founded earth's stability,
    The Power that formed all rocks.

I arise today
Through a Mighty Strength:
    God's Power to guide me,
    God's Might to uphold me,
    God's Wisdom to teach me,
    God's Eyes to watch over me,

God's Ear to hear me,
God's Word to give me speech,
God's Hand to guard me,
God's Way to lie before me,
God's Shield to shelter me,
God's Host to secure me:

Against the snares of devils,
Against the seductions of vices,
Against the lusts of nature,
Against everyone who shall wish me ill,
Whether far or near, many or few.

I invoke to my aid
All such virtues of Mighty Strength:
Against every merciless, hostile power,
Which may assail my body and my soul,
Against the incantations of false prophets,
Against the blackness of heathens,
Against idolatry's deceits,
Against the spells of women, druids, and smiths,
Against all knowledge that blinds the soul of man.

I arise today
Through a Mighty Strength:
Christ to protect me today
Against every poison,
Against burning,
Against drowning,
Against deathly wounds,
That I may receive abundant reward.

Christ with me, Christ before me,
Christ with me, Christ above,
Christ at my right, Christ at my left,

Christ in the fort, Christ in the chariot seat,
Christ in the poop,
Christ to every eye that sees me,
Christ in every ear that hears me,
That I may receive abundant reward.

I arise today through a Mighty Strength:
The Strength of invocation of the Trinity.
I believe the Trinity in the Unity,
The Creator of the universe:
Amen.

—St. Patrick

Prayer for Divine Aid

St. Bernard of Clairvaux, known as the "last of the Fathers" of the Church, was born in Dijon, France, in 1091. He became a monk at nineteen, and all six of his brothers and his sister followed him into the religious life. He founded the Cistercian monastery of Clairvaux and was its first abbé. Bernard preached the Second Crusade. He continued his writing throughout his life.

Help us, O Lord our God, since we cannot flee from the body, nor the body flee from us: We must needs carry it about, because it is bound up with us. It, we cannot destroy: we are forced to preserve it. But the world surrounds us, and assails us through the five gateways of sense. Alas! everywhere we are in conflict, everywhere darts fly against us, everywhere there are temptations, there are snares! Deliver us, we beseech Thee, from our enemies: defend us from all dangers to the soul and to the body, Lord, that at length we may come to Thine Eternal Rest, through Jesus Christ, our Lord: *amen.*

—St. Bernard

Prayer to Almighty God

Founder of the Benedictine Order, St. Benedict also built the famed Abbey at Monte Cassino. His sanctity was fabulous even during his lifetime, and he is credited with restoring to life the son of a peasant who implored Benedict to bring his son back to him. Benedict died in 543 (?), his hands outstretched in prayer.

Vouchsafe, O Gracious,
O Holy Father,
Upon me to bestow:

Intellect to understand Thee,
Perceptions to perceive purely Thee,
Reason to discern Thee,
Diligence to seek Thee,
Wisdom to find Thee,
A spirit to know Thee;

A heart to meditate upon Thee,
Ears to hear Thee,
Eyes to behold Thee,
A tongue to proclaim Thee,
A conversation pleasing unto Thee,
Patience to wait for Thee,
And perseverance to look for Thee.

Grant me
A perfect end—
Thy Holy Presence.

Grant me
A blessed resurrection,
And Thy Recompense,
Everlasting Life.
Amen.

—St. Benedict

Easter Prayer

St. Gregory was in his youth Prefect of Rome. Born to wealth and high station, he gave all to the poor and made his home into a monastery. He became Pope, converted the Arian Lombards, and began the conversion of England, a lifetime ambition. He preached and wrote a great deal. His name is associated (perhaps incorrectly) with the arrangement of so-called Gregorian mode or chant. He died in 604, one of the greatest of the Popes.

It is very meet and right, with all powers of heart and mind, and with the service of the lips, to praise the invisible God, the Father Almighty, and His Only-Begotten Son, our Lord Jesus Christ, Who paid the debt of Adam for us to the Eternal Father, and effaced the bond of the ancient guilt by the Blood poured forth in loving-kindness. For this is the Paschal festival in which Thou first didst bring our fathers, the children of Israel, out of Egypt and madest them to pass over the Red Sea dry-shod. This, then, is the night which cleared away the darkness of sin by a pillar of radiance. This is the night throughout the world which now restores to Grace and unites to holiness believers in Christ, separated from worldly vices and from the gloom of sin. This is the night in which Christ broke the bonds of death and ascended from the grave, the conqueror. For to be born had been no blessing to us, unless we could have been redeemed. Oh, the wondrous condescension of Thy loving-kindness towards us! Oh, the inestimable tenderness of Thy Love! To redeem the servant, Thou gavest up the Son. This holy night, then, puts to flight offenses, washes away sins, and restores innocence to the fallen and joyousness to the sad. Oh, truly blessed night, which spoiled the Egyptians and enriched the Hebrews—the night in which Heaven and earth are reconciled! We pray Thee, Lord, therefore, that Thou wouldst preserve Thy servants in the peaceful enjoyment of this Easter happiness; through Jesus Christ our Lord, Who Livest and Reignest with God the Father, in the Unity of the Holy Ghost, God now and forever: *amen.*

—St. Gregory

The Pater Noster

St. Francis was born in 1182, the son of a wealthy merchant in the town
of Assisi. Rebuked for taking merchandise from the stalls to give to a
beggar, he renounced the ties of the world and founded the Franciscan
order. His piety brought him an ever-growing following. His great love of
God according to tradition produced the miraculous appearance of open
and bleeding wounds in his hands and feet, the stigmata. He died in 1226
and has been honored since throughout the world.

Our Father Most Holy, our Creator, Redeemer, and Comforter:
Who art in heaven, in the Angels and in the Saints, illuminating
them unto knowledge, for Thou O Lord, art Light; inflaming
them unto Love, for Thou, O Lord, art Love; dwelling in them
and filling them with blessedness, for Thou, O Lord, art the
Highest Good, the Eternal Good, from Whom is all good, and
without Whom is no good.

Hallowed be Thy name. May Thy knowledge shine in us that
we may know the breadth of Thy Benefits, the length of Thy
Promises, the Height of Thy Majesty, and the depth of Thy
Judgments.

Thy Kingdom come, that Thou mayest reign in us by Grace,
and mayest make us come to Thy Kingdom, where there is the
clear vision of Thee, the perfect love of Thee, the blessed company of Thee, the eternal enjoyment of Thee.

Thy will be done on earth as it is in heaven, that we may love
Thee with the whole heart by thinking always of Thee, with
the whole soul, by desiring always Thee; with the whole mind,
by directing all our intentions to Thee, and seeking Thy Honor
in all things and with all our strength, by spending all the
powers and senses of body and soul in the service of Thy Love,
and not in anything else; and that we may love our neighbors
even as ourselves, drawing to the best of our power, all to Thy

Love; rejoicing in the good of others as in our own, and com-
passionating them in troubles, and giving offense to no one,
unjustly.

Give us this day, through memory, through understanding,
through reverence for the Love which He had for us, and for
those things which He said, and which He did, and which He
suffered for us.

Our daily bread, The Beloved Son, our Lord Jesus Christ.

And forgive us our trespasses, by Thy ineffable Mercy, in virtue of the Passion of Thy Beloved Son, our Lord Jesus Christ,
and through the merits and intercession of the most Blessed
Virgin Mary, and of all the Elect.

As we forgive them that trespass against us: and what we do
not fully forgive, when it please Thee, that for Thy Sake we
truly may love our enemies, and devoutly intercede for whom
Thou wouldst with Thee; that we may render no evil for evil,
but in Thee may strive to do good to all Thou wouldst.

And lead us not into temptation, hidden or visible, sudden or
continuous:

But deliver us from evil—past, present, and to come: *amen.*
                                              —St. Francis of Assisi

Praised Be God

O most high, almighty, good Lord God, to Thee belong praise, glory, honor, and all blessing!

Praised be my Lord God with all His creatures, and especially our brother the sun, who bringeth us the day and who bringeth us the light; fair is he and shineth with a very great splendor: O Lord, he signifieth to us Thee!

Praised be my Lord for our sister the moon, and for the stars, the which He hath set clear and lovely in heaven.

Praised be my Lord for our brother the wind, and for air and cloud, calms and all weather by the which Thou upholdest life in all creatures.

Praised be my Lord for our sister water, who is very serviceable unto us and humble and precious and clean.

Praised be my Lord for our brother fire, through whom Thou givest us light in the darkness; and he is bright and pleasant and very mighty and strong.

Praised be my Lord for our mother the earth, the which doth sustain us and keep us, and bringeth forth divers fruits and flowers of many colors, and grass.

Praised be my Lord for all those who pardon one another for His love's sake, and who endure weakness and tribulation; blessed are they who peaceably shall endure, for Thou, O most Highest, shalt give them a crown.

Praised be my Lord for our sister, the death of the body, from which no man escapeth. Woe to him who dieth in mortal sin! Blessed are they who are found walking by thy most holy will, for the second death shall have no power to do them harm.

Praise ye and bless the Lord, and give thanks unto Him and serve Him with great humility. *Amen.*

—St. Francis of Assisi
See biographical note on page 150.

Invocations to the Immaculate Virgin
to Achieve Purity

There is perhaps no saint more generally venerated than Anthony of Padua, who was not an Italian, as is generally supposed, but actually was son of an army officer from Portugal. His canonization took only a year, so widely was his sanctity known.*

I

O Mary, Virgin before the divine birth, guard my body and soul! Hail Mary, full of Grace! the Lord is with thee. Blessed art thou among women, and blessed is the fruit of thy womb, Jesus! Holy Mary, Mother of God, pray for us sinners now and in the hour of our death. *Amen.*

II

O Mary, Virgin during the Divine Birth, guard my body and soul! Hail Mary, full of Grace! the Lord is with thee. Blessed art thou among women, and blessed is the fruit of thy womb, Jesus! Holy Mary, Mother of God, pray for us sinners now and in the hour of our death. *Amen.*

III

O Mary, Virgin after the Divine Birth, guard my body and soul! Hail Mary, full of Grace! the Lord is with thee. Blessed art thou among women, and blessed is the fruit of thy womb, Jesus! Holy Mary, Mother of God, pray for us sinners now and in the hour of our death. *Amen.*

—St. Anthony of Padua

* *He was also my mother's favorite saint, and once, when I lost two dollars on my way to a grocery store, my mother asked me to say a prayer to St. Anthony of Padua and then to go back over the ground to the store. The two dollars fluttered between two flagstones on a street crowded with shoppers.*

—*Jim Bishop*

A Confession

Thomas à Kempis (c. 1380–1471), born near Düsseldorf of peasant stock, became an Augustinian monk, priest, then subprior. Quiet and studious, he wrote a number of books, most of them about the monastic life.

I offer up unto Thee my prayers and intercessions, for those especially who have in any manner hurt, grieved, or found fault with me, or who have done me any damage or displeasure.

For all those also whom, at any time, I may have vexed, troubled, burdened, and scandalized, by words or deeds, knowingly or in ignorance; that Thou wouldst grant us all equally pardon for our sins, and for our offenses against each other.

Take away from our hearts, O Lord, all suspiciousness, indignation, wrath, and contention, and whatsoever may hurt charity and lessen brotherly love.

Have mercy, O Lord, have mercy on those that crave Thy mercy, give grace unto them that stand in need thereof, and make us such as that we may be worthy to enjoy Thy grace, and go forward to life eternal. *Amen.*

—St. Thomas à Kempis

For Enlightenment of Mind

Enlighten me, Blessed Jesus, with the brightness of Thy inner light, and cast forth all darkness from the habitation of my heart. Restrain my many wandering thoughts, and carry away the temptations which strive to do me hurt. Fight Thou mightily for me, and drive forth the evil beasts, so call I alluring lusts, that peace may be within thy walls and plenteousness of praise within Thy palaces, even in my pure conscience.

Command Thou the winds and the storms, say unto the sea, "Be still," say unto the stormy wind, "Hold thy peace," so shall there be a great calm.

Oh send forth Thy light and Thy truth, that they may shine upon the earth; for I am but earth without form and void until Thou give me light. Pour forth Thy grace from above; water my heart with the dew of heaven; give the waters of devotion to water the face of the earth, and cause it to bring forth good and perfect fruit. Lift up my mind which is oppressed with the weight of sins, and raise my whole desire to heavenly things; that having tasted the sweetness of the happiness which is from above, it may take no pleasure in thinking of things of earth.

Draw me and deliver me from every unstable comfort of creatures, for no created thing is able to satisfy my desire and to give me comfort. Join me to Thyself by the inseparable bond of love, for Thou alone art sufficient to him that loveth Thee, and without Thee all things are vain toys.

—St. Thomas à Kempis, from *Imitation of Christ*
See biographical note above.

Against Darkness of Mind

St. Thomas, born near Aquino in 1225, entered the order of St. Dominic at the age of nineteen. In a period of intellectual clarification, St. Thomas is held responsible for much of the accomplishment of that time. His learning was so extraordinary that Dante considered him greater than Aristotle. The *Summa Theologica* is his greatest achievement. He declared that his wisdom came from prayer, of which this prayer is most typical.

Ineffable Creator, our Lord, our God, Who didst create the choirs of Angels out of Thy Wisdom's treasuries, and Who didst dispose them over the Heaven in a wonderful order, Thou Whose Name is the true Fountain of Light and of Wisdom the true Fountain; transcendent Source of all things:

Vouchsafe upon the darkness of our minds to shed the Beams of Thy Brightness: from us take the darkness both of sin and the darkness of our natural ignorance.

Thou Who makest the mouths of the speechless skilled in speech: Teach our mouths, pour upon our lips the Grace of Thy Benediction. Give us keenness of understanding, ability to remember, discernment in exposition, readiness in learning, and abundant Grace in utterance. Bestow upon us, at the out-set of our journey, gifts; as we journey, guide us, and bring to a perfect end our course: Through Jesus Christ, our Lord: *amen.*

—St. Thomas Aquinas

For Compliance with God's Will

Ignatius Loyola was a soldier at the court of the King of Spain. Lying wounded after a siege, he was brought a book one day which changed his life. It was the life of a saint. He was the founder of the Society of Jesus and wrote the famed *Spiritual Exercises.* He died in 1556 in his sixty-fifth year.

O Lord, so great to all Thy servants: Dispose of my life, of my liberty, of all that pertains to me. O my Creator: Speak to Thy creature! Behold my soul before Thee: my will is as a scale in a state of perfectly equal balance, which shall waver to one side or the other only when Thou placest in it the weight of Thy Will or Wish. I ignore all natural inclinations. My will is sus-pended and in a state of perfect indifference. I have but one will and desire: to obey, to please Thee. Enable me closely to approach to Thee, to lose none of Thy Words, to be better disposed for receiving of the Gifts of Thy Divine and Supreme Goodness: *amen.*

—St. Ignatius Loyola

In a Time of Desolations

St. Teresa wrote as no other saint has before or after on the spiritual life. *The Interior Castle* and *The Way of Perfection* are classics. Born in 1515, she founded the Reformed Order of Carmelites and died in 1582. El Greco in his painting of her tried to find in her the undiscoverable symbol of Faith.

Lord of all created things, my God, my Blessedness: How long must I yet wait before Thou dost show Thyself to me? How can one who has naught on earth find life apart from Thee? How tedious and full of sufferings is such a life in which one does really not live but experiences on every side utter abandonment, utter desolation! How long, O Lord, ah, how long will it yet last? What must I do, my Highest Good? Must I desire, really, never to yearn for Thee?

My God and my Creator: Thou dost wound, but Thou dost offer also the healing's means. Thou dost wound, yet there can be seen no wound. Thou slayest, and Thou grantest life anew. In Thy Omnipotence, according to Thy Good Will, Thou disposest, O Lord, of all.

Dost Thou, my God, then will that I, contemptible creature that I am, should endure such tribulation? So be it, then, my God, since Thou dost will it, for my will is other, none than Thine. But, oh, my Creator! the excess of my pain drives me to cry out and bewail my helplessness: Thy Good Pleasure it be to relieve me.

The fettered soul yearns for freedom, but wills it no sooner than to Thee is pleasing. My soul: let then the Will of God be accomplished in thee: alone, that concerns thee. Serve The Lord, trust in His Mercy: this will soothe thy pains.

O my God, my King! I naught can do, unless Thy Mighty Hand, unless Thy Heavenly Power, assist me.

With Thine Aid, I can do all.

—St. Teresa of Avila

An Act of Commiseration

Born in 1567 at Thorens in Savoy to the Comtesse de Sales, who offered her child to God before his birth, St. Francis became a priest against the wishes of his father. He converted thousands of Calvinists and helped found the Order of the Visitation of Our Lady. He died in 1622 at Lyons. His classic work is *Introduction to the Devout Life*.

How shall I be able to alleviate, in some degree, the sufferings of my afflicted Saviour? Oh, that I could, with richest and most costly garment, cover His Nakedness. Would, O my Jesus, that I had some precious balm to pour into Thy Wounds! Why may I not approach Thy cross and be privileged to support Thy Sacred Body in my arms, and hinder the weight from tearing open so roughly and so frightfully the Wounds in Thy Hands and Feet? But, more than all, why can I not dissuade sinners from so deeply grieving Thy Sacred Heart, which would account all the anguish and torments inflicted on Thy Body as nothing, if only sinners could be converted through their infliction from their evil ways? Why can I not be a holy and fervent preacher, sent to excite them to penance? How earnestly would I not cry out to the wicked, "Live no longer so wickedly!" and to the offenders, "Set not up the horns of your pride and treachery!"

O Lord: Be merciful to me, for henceforth I resolve to be more faithful to Thee. I will satisfy myself no longer with desires, but will put my resolutions into practice. I promise to relieve the poor, to do penance, and to sin no more. I will instruct the erring, and will say to my own heart, and to the hearts of the others: "Can you treat your Saviour more cruelly than birds of prey do the tender doves? Can you act so heartlessly to this Divine Dove, Who nestles on the cross, as to tear His Heart with the teeth of your impiety?" No, Lord: Henceforth, I will comfort and help Thy poor, by my deeds as truly as my words, and I will strive, with all earnestness, to destroy and to overcome sin, both in myself and in others.

—St. Francis de Sales

For the Divine Union

St. John of the Cross (1542–1591), confidant and aide of St. Teresa of Avila, was cofounder of the barefoot Carmelites. No saint seems to have achieved greater sanctification; none has been more learned in mystical theology.

Lord: Let us so act that by means of Love we even may come to see ourselves in Thy Beauty in Life Eternal: that is, that I may be so transformed in Thy Beauty that, being alike in beauty, we may both see ourselves in Thy Beauty, since I shall have Thine Own Beauty; so that, when one of us looks at the other, each may see in the other his beauty, the beauty of both being Thy Beauty alone, and I being absorbed in Thy Beauty; and thus I shall see Thee in Thy Beauty, and Thou wilt see me in Thy Beauty; and I shall see myself in Thee in Thy Beauty; and Thou wilt see Thyself in me in Thy Beauty; and thus I may be like to Thee in Thy Beauty, and Thou mayest be like to me in Thy Beauty, and my beauty may be Thy Beauty, and Thy Beauty my beauty; and thus I shall be Thou in Thy Beauty, and Thou wilt be I in Thy Beauty, because Thy Beauty itself will be my beauty, and thus we shall see the other in Thy Beauty.

—St. John of the Cross, from *The Spiritual Canticle*

Prayer during Suffering

St. Bernadette, whose life has been made known to millions of all faiths through the medium of the motion picture, is one of the most recently canonized saints. It was in 1858 in the provincial town of Lourdes in the French Pyrenees that this simple peasant girl first saw the Lady in White. As a result of this visitation the vast basilica was built which has since witnessed countless miracles of healing.

My God, I promise Thee, with the assistance of Thy Grace, to show my love for Thee by accepting without a murmur the trials and disappointments Thou mayest see well to send me, whether due to my superiors, or my companions, or even to the evil one himself.

O Jesus! make me realize more fully the jealousy of Divine Love! Detach my affections from the creature; raise them up and bind them to Thyself!

O Mary! Blessed Mother! grant that love may hallow my every action and suffering!

—St. Bernadette of Lourdes

GREAT PROTESTANT

PRAYERS

ALL PRAYER, except "The Lord's Prayer," has been devised by man. Jesus spoke "The Lord's Prayer" Himself. Other than that one, all the formal prayers which are recited in churches and temples in many tongues around the world come from the mind of man.

A good prayer is several things. First of all, it is a petition to God. Secondly, it is a hymn of glory to Him. Third, it is a confession of humility on the part of the petitioner and resignation to the Divine Will. Fourth, it recites the favors required of God by man.

In this group you will find many such prayers. They are eloquent and direct in their appeal, and they are recited in thousands of Protestant churches. Protestantism in all its fascinating diversity, from High Episcopal to Quaker, is represented here. In discarding some of the old forms, Protestants feel that they have infused their services with a new vitality and sincerity. Some of these prayers are very old. A few are new. Some are long; a few can be uttered in a single breath. The section opens with a calendar of prayers for special and religious holidays throughout the year.

Since the death of Jesus Christ, the sun has risen in the east more than 700,000 times, and with each new sunrise man has been inspired to sing his love for God in fresh words. But try though he may, there aren't enough new words, and man unwittingly repeats the old ones. But though the words be old, the spirit is each time new.

The New Year

Another year has passed, O Heavenly Father! We thank Thee that it was a time of grace, and we are not terrified by the thought that it was also a time for which we shall render an account; for we trust in Thy mercy. The New Year confronts us with its demands; and though we cannot enter upon it without humility and concern, because we cannot and will not forget the lusts of the eye that ensnared us, the sweets of revenge that seduced us, the wrath that made us irreconcilable, the coldness of heart in which we fled from Thee, yet we do not enter it altogether empty-handed. For we take with us the memory of fearful doubts which were set at rest, of anxieties which were solaced, of the downcast mind which was cheered and strengthened, of the glad hope which was not put to shame. Aye, and when in our melancholy moods we seek strength and encouragement in the thought of the great men, Thy chosen instruments, who in sharp trials and profound anxieties kept their souls free, their courage unbroken, the heavens open above them, then we also wish to add to theirs our testimony, convinced that even if our courage is but discouragement in comparison with theirs, and our strength weakness, nevertheless, Thou art ever the same, the same mighty God who tries the spirits of men in combat, the same Father without whose knowledge no sparrow falls to the ground. *Amen.*

—Søren Kierkegaard, from *Edifying Discourses*
(translated by David F. and Lillian M. Swenson)
See biographical note on page 123.

Ash Wednesday

James Martineau (1805–1900), Unitarian theologian and brother of Harriet Martineau, was an inspiring English preacher and teacher. He was also author of many influential philosophical works, as well as prayers. Here is his prayer for the first day of Lent, Christian period of penitence.

O God, our everlasting hope, who holdest us in life, and orderest our lot; we ask not for any prosperity that would tempt us to forget thee. As disciples of One who had not where to lay his head, may we freely welcome the toils and sufferings of our humanity, and seek only strength to glorify the cross thou layest on us. Every work of our hand may we do unto thee; in every trouble, trace some lights of thine; and let no blessing fall on dry and thoughtless hearts. Redeeming the time, may we fill every waking hour with faithful duty and well-ordered affections, as the sacrifice which thou hast provided. Strip us, O Lord, of every proud thought; fill us with patient tenderness for others, seeing that we also are in the same case before thee; and make us ready to help, and quick to forgive. And then, fix every grace, compose every fear, by a steady trust in thine eternal realities, behind the changes of time and delusions of men. Thou art our Rock: we rest on thee. *Amen.*

—James Martineau, from *Home Prayers*

Collect for Ash Wednesday

This is used in the United States every day in Lent until Palm Sunday, in England and Scotland until Good Friday, in Canada and Ireland every day in Lent.

Almighty and everlasting God, who hatest nothing that thou hast made, and dost forgive the sins of all those who are penitent; Create and make in us new and contrite hearts, that we, worthily lamenting our sins and acknowledging our wretchedness, may obtain of thee, the God of all mercy, perfect remission and forgiveness; through Jesus Christ our Lord. *Amen.*   —from *The Book of Common Prayer*

Lenten Prayer

Walter Russell Bowie was born in Richmond, Virginia, in 1882. He became an Episcopalian priest in 1909 and was on the faculty of Union Theological Seminary for many years.

O Lord our Master, who through the forty days didst forget the body because thy Spirit was caught up in God: Teach us with whole hearts to seek the heavenly communion, so that being delivered from subjection to the flesh we may be released into the spiritual liberty that belongs to the children of God. In thine own Name we ask it. *Amen.*
                           —Walter R. Bowie, from *Lift Up Your Hearts*

Palm Sunday

Palm Sunday is one of the chief days of Holy Week, the week before Easter. The other days are Monday, Thursday, Good Friday, and Holy Saturday.

Our Father, as on this day we celebrate our Redeemer's entry into Jerusalem, so grant, O Lord, that now and ever he may triumph in our hearts. Let the King of grace and glory enter in, that we may lay ourselves and all we are in full and joyful homage before him; through the same Jesus Christ our Lord. *Amen.*   —from *Book of Worship for Free Churches*

Collect for Palm Sunday

This prayer is translated from the Gelasian and Gregorian Sacramentaries.

Almighty and everlasting God, who, of thy tender love towards mankind hast sent thy Son our Saviour Jesus Christ to take upon him our flesh, and to suffer death upon the cross, that all mankind should follow the example of his great humility: Mercifully grant that we may both follow the example of his patience, and also be made partakers of his resurrection; through the same Jesus Christ our Lord. Amen.

— from *The Book of Common Prayer*

Good Friday

Good Friday, anniversary of Jesus' death on the cross and the Friday before Easter, is a day of mourning and penitence. In Roman Catholic and Orthodox churches there is no Mass, and communion is not given. An old English custom of Good Friday was making hot cross buns. Good Friday is a legal holiday in many countries and in some sections of the United States.

Almighty God, who in the life and teaching of thy Son hast showed us the true way of blessedness: Thou hast also showed us in his sufferings and death that the path of duty may lead to the Cross and the reward of faithfulness may be a crown of thorns. Give us grace to learn these harder lessons. May we take up our cross and follow Christ in the strength of patience and the constancy of faith; and may we have such fellowship with him in his sorrow that we may know the secret of his strength and peace, and see, even in our darkest hour of trial and anguish, the shining of the eternal light. *Amen.*

— from *Book of Worship for Free Churches*

Good Friday

As we look upon Thy Cross, O Christ, filled with wonder and with awe at the love that brought Thee to it, humbly we confess that we have no offering meet for such a love, no gift fit for such a sacrifice.

Thou wert willing to go to the Cross so that men might forever be haunted by its sign, might return to the foot of that Cross to be melted and broken down in the knowledge of Thy love for us and all men everywhere.

When we see a love like that—the love of God yearning for the hearts of His children—we know that only love can respond.

We acknowledge, O Lord, that there is so little in us that is lovable. So often we are not lovely in our thoughts, in our words, or in our deeds. And yet Thou dost love us still, with a love that neither ebbs nor flows, a love that does not grow weary, but is constant—year after year, age after age.

O God, may our hearts be opened to that love today. With bright skies above us, the fields and woods and gardens bursting with new life and beauty, how can we fail to respond? With the clear notes of bird songs challenging us to praise, with every lowly shrub and blooming tree catching new life and beauty, our hearts indeed would proclaim Thee Lord, and we would invite Thee to reign over us and make us truly Thine own. May Thy healing love invade our inmost hearts, healing sorrow, pain, frustration, defeat and despair.

May this day create within us a love for Thee of stronger stuff than vague sentimentality—a love which seeks to know Thy will and do it. So grant that this day of hallowed remembrance may be the beginning of a new way of life for each of us, a new kind of living that shall be the best answer to the confusion and to the challenge of evil in our day. This we ask in Jesus' name. *Amen.*

—Peter Marshall, from *The Prayers of Peter Marshall*
See biographical note on page 117.

Easter

Easter, chief Christian festival and anniversary of the resurrection of Jesus Christ, comes between March 22 and April 25, inclusive. There is a preparatory period of penitence, beginning with Septuagesima Sunday, seventeen days before Lent, and ending in Holy Week.

O God, who, through the mighty resurrection of thy Son Jesus Christ from the dead, hast delivered us from the power of darkness into the kingdom of thy love: Grant, we beseech thee, that as by his death he has recalled us into life, so, by his presence ever abiding in us, he may raise us to joys eternal; through him who for our sakes died and rose again, and is ever with us in power and great glory; even the same Jesus Christ our Lord. *Amen.*

—from *Book of Common Order* (Church of Scotland)

Pentecost

Pentecost is the time of both Jewish and Christian feasts of great importance. On the Pentecost after the resurrection of Jesus (fifty days after the Passover in which he was crucified), the disciples received from the Holy Ghost the power of speaking in diverse tongues (*Acts* 2); the gift was accompanied by tongues of fire and the sound of a rush of wind. The Christian feast of Pentecost commemorates this event. It is the seventh Sunday after Easter and closes Eastertime.

God of all peace and consolation, who didst gloriously fulfil the great promise of the gospel by sending down the Holy Ghost on the day of Pentecost, to establish the Church as the house of his continual presence and power among men; mercifully grant unto us, we beseech thee, this same gift of the Spirit, to renew, illuminate, refresh, and sanctify our souls; to be over us and around us like the light and dew of heaven and to be in us evermore as a well of water springing up into everlasting life; through Jesus Christ our Lord. *Amen.*

—from *Book of Common Order* (Church of Scotland)

Whitsunday

This prayer was translated from the Gelasian Sacramentary and was included in both the 1549 and revised 1662 editions of *The Book of Common Prayer*. Whitsunday, an English name for Pentecost, symbolizes the white garments of the neophytes who were in ancient times baptized at the season of Pentecost after a penitential vigil.

O God, who as at this time didst teach the hearts of thy faithful people, by sending to them the light of thy Holy Spirit; Grant us by the same Spirit to have a right judgment in all things, and evermore to rejoice in his holy comfort; through the merits of Christ Jesus our Saviour, who liveth and reigneth with thee, in the unity of the same Spirit, one God, world without end. *Amen.*

—from *The Book of Common Prayer*

Thanksgiving Day

Thanksgiving Day is a national holiday in the United States, commemorating the harvest reaped by the Plymouth Colony in 1621, after a long, hard winter of near starvation. First celebrated by the Pilgrims that year, Thanksgiving Day as a national holiday was proclaimed by Washington on November 26, 1789, by Lincoln in 1863, and by all subsequent presidents. It falls on the fourth Thursday of November.

Almighty God, our heavenly Father, from whom cometh every good and perfect gift: Let thy blessing rest upon us in this festival of thanksgiving. We praise thee as the bountiful benefactor from whose gracious hand all our blessings have come. We remember thy loving-kindness and tender mercy toward us through all the years, and with grateful hearts we lift up to thee our songs of joy. For all the gifts thou hast bestowed upon us, and upon the whole family of man, we give thee humble and hearty thanks. May we show our gratitude by faithful lives devoted to thy service; through Jesus Christ our Lord. *Amen.*

—from *The Book of Church Services*

Let Us Give Thanks

Let us give thanks! For the old, sweet fashions of nature, for the ritual of its seasons, for the wonder of seedtime, summer, and autumn harvest; for the stores of material good for our use and blessings; for the spur of necessity which impels industry; for the sky over all, deepening as we gaze, and for that other heaven within, which widens into strange distances.

Let us give thanks! for the old world road along which we journey, trodden by so many feet before us; for the flowers of divine grace and human kindness along the way; for the thorns that require careful handling, and the disciplines and tasks that train us for strength and honor; for the Kindly Light that leads us; for the love that heals our hurts and the mercy that lifts us when we fall.

Let us give thanks! For our country and its laws; for home and family and the dear love of comrades; for the sorrows that subdue us to sobs and weld us in love unto our kind; . . . for all teachers of art and insight who interpret to us the way and the will of the eternal!

Let us give thanks! For the organization of life in education, art, and character; for the fellowship of man in spiritual faith, moral endeavor, and the quest of truth; for the dream that love will one day everywhere prevail to the confounding of all unkindness, all uncleanness; for God, the Father of all, who is the meaning of life, the home of the soul, and the hope that "love can never lose its own." *Amen.*

—Joseph Fort Newton, from *Altar Stairs*
See biographical note on page 130.

Advent

Advent is the season of the Christian ecclesiastical year lasting from the Sunday nearest November 30 to Christmas. It is a season of penitence to prepare for the holy day commemorating the coming of Christ, and its liturgical color is purple or violet. The first Sunday in Advent is the first day of the church calendar. The following two prayers are from William Orchard's *The Temple* and from *The Book of Common Prayer*.

O God, for whose advent Thy weary world has waited long, save us lest in these latter days the hope of Thee grow dim, and we, forgetting to watch with lamps trimmed and loins girded, find ourselves unprepared to meet Thee, when at midnight comes the cry.

For we know our hopes cannot lie. In the past we can discern that Thou hast surely come; in the prophets and in the Word made flesh; in the downfall of empires, and the rising of peoples; in the strange thoughts that stir the world, in the dawning sense of brotherhood. But not yet dost Thou wholly dwell amongst us.

We mourn the misunderstandings and suspicions that arm the nations, the growing alienation and strife between class and class, our failure to find a common faith or a religion to unite us all. Come and heal our divisions, and enable us to find that one highway along which we may march together to the Promised Land.

Grant that we may be found with those prophets and forerunners who, knowing the mind of God and the times of His restoration, prepared the way of the Lord.

Forbid that when Thou comest Thou shouldest not find faith upon the earth. *Amen.*

—William E. Orchard, from *The Temple*

Collect for the First Sunday in Advent

Almighty God, give us grace that we may cast away the works of darkness, and put upon us the armour of light, now in the time of this mortal life, in which thy Son Jesus Christ came to visit us in great humility; that in the last day, when he shall come again in his glorious majesty to judge both the quick and the dead, we may rise to the life immortal, through him who liveth and reigneth with thee and the Holy Ghost, now and ever. *Amen.*

—from *The Book of Common Prayer*

Bible Sunday

John Calvin (1509–1564), French theologian and reformer, worked for many years to bring together the scattered and unsystematic opinions of the Reformation into a body of doctrine known as Calvinism. His *Institutes of the Christian Religion* is one of the most influential books in history.

O Lord, heavenly Father, in whom is the fullness of light and wisdom: Enlighten our minds by thy Holy Spirit and give us grace to receive thy Word with reverence and humility, without which no man can understand thy truth. For Jesus Christ's sake. *Amen.*

—John Calvin

Christmas Eve

Father of us all, at this hour when the solitary are set in families, men gather again under the old roof, and wanderers and exiles think longingly of home, we think of Thee the home of us all, of the hearth fire of Thy love where all are welcome, of that last great Christmastide when He who was the Babe of Bethlehem shall have gathered all souls together one unbroken family, not one missing.

May the solemn associations of this hour be blessed to all of us this Christmas Eve. May kind thoughts find lodging in the hardest heart; may longing for purity be born in minds that are unclean; may the lonely and the labouring hear the angels sing tonight.

We are all still children, our Father; our knowledge and our years drop from us all tonight. We gather to Thee, as long ago to our mother's knee. Let us hear again the wonderful story of Thy love, let us listen to the songs of heaven, and in the light of Thy forgiveness have all our doubts and sins and fears dispelled. *Amen.*

—William E. Orchard, from *The Temple*
See biographical note on page 128.

Christmas

Morgan Phelps Noyes was born in Warren, Pennsylvania, in 1891. Long a minister in the Presbyterian Church in Montclair, New Jersey, he also was for many years on the faculty of Union Theological Seminary. His *Prayers for Services: A Manual for Leaders of Worship* is considered one of the outstanding works of its kind for the use of the Protestant clergy.

O God, who centuries ago blessed our earth with a vision of thy love in the form of a little child; who sent to rebuke earth's selfishness a humble Man to go about doing good and to speak the words of life; who revealed thyself, the Conqueror of evil, in one the weapons of whose warfare were deeds of kindliness and mercy—graciously grant us the Christmas power as we remember him. Fill our hearts with the gladness of his coming. Teach us the enduring joy of his service. Lead us into the Christmas peace which passeth understanding, the peace of Christ. *Amen.*

—Morgan Phelps Noyes, from *Prayers for Services*

The First Sunday after Christmas

In *The Book of Common Prayer* special collects are to be found for many Sundays after Christmas. This beautiful prayer is used for the first Sunday after Christmas.

Almighty God, who hast given us thine only-begotten Son to take our nature upon him, and as at this time to be born of a pure virgin; Grant that we being regenerate, and made thy children by adoption and grace, may daily be renewed by thy Holy Spirit; through the same our Lord Jesus Christ, who liveth and reigneth with thee and the same Spirit ever, one God, world without end. *Amen.*

—from *The Book of Common Prayer*

Canticle

All Canticles take their origin from the *Song of Solomon,* another name for which is "Canticle." This Canticle, *Benedicite, omnia opera Domini,* from *The Book of Common Prayer* has much in common with St. Francis of Assisi's "Canticle for the Sun."

O All ye Works of the Lord, bless ye the Lord; praise him, and magnify him for ever.

O ye Angels of the Lord, bless ye the Lord; praise him, and magnify him for ever.

O ye Heavens, bless ye the Lord; praise him, and magnify him for ever.

O ye Waters, that be above the firmament, bless ye the Lord; praise him, and magnify him for ever.

O all ye Powers of the Lord, bless ye the Lord; praise him, and magnify him for ever.

O ye Sun and Moon, bless ye the Lord; praise him, and magnify him for ever.

O ye Stars of Heaven, bless ye the Lord; praise him, and magnify him for ever.

O ye Showers and Dew, bless ye the Lord; praise him, and magnify him for ever.

O ye Winds of God, bless ye the Lord; praise him, and magnify him for ever.

O ye Fire and Heat, bless ye the Lord; praise him, and magnify him for ever.

O ye Winter and Summer, bless ye the Lord; praise him, and magnify him for ever.

O ye Dews and Frosts, bless ye the Lord; praise him, and magnify him for ever.

O ye Frost and Cold, bless ye the Lord; praise him, and magnify him for ever.

O ye Ice and Snow, bless ye the Lord; praise him, and magnify him for ever.

O ye Nights and Days, bless ye the Lord; praise him, and magnify him for ever.

O ye Light and Darkness, bless ye the Lord; praise him and magnify him for ever.

O ye Lightnings and Clouds, bless ye the Lord; praise him and magnify him for ever.

O let the Earth bless the Lord; yea, let it praise him and magnify him for ever.

O ye Mountains and Hills, bless ye the Lord; praise him, and magnify him for ever.

O all ye Green Things upon the earth, bless ye the Lord; praise him, and magnify him for ever.

O ye Wells, bless ye the Lord; praise him, and magnify him for ever.

O ye Seas and Floods, bless ye the Lord; praise him, and magnify him for ever.

O ye Whales, and all that move in the waters, bless ye the Lord; praise him, and magnify him for ever.

O all ye Fowls of the Air, bless ye the Lord; praise him, and magnify him for ever.

O all ye Beasts and Cattle, bless ye the Lord; praise him, and magnify him for ever.

O ye Children of Men, bless ye the Lord; praise him, and magnify him for ever.

O let Israel bless the Lord; praise him, and magnify him for ever.

O ye Priests of the Lord, bless ye the Lord; praise him, and magnify him for ever.

O ye Servants of the Lord, bless ye the Lord; praise him, and magnify him for ever.

O ye Spirits and Souls of the Righteous, bless ye the Lord; praise him, and magnify him for ever.

O ye holy and humble Men of Heart, bless ye the Lord; praise him, and magnify him for ever.

—from *The Book of Common Prayer*

Our Father

When His disciples asked Jesus how to pray, He delivered the prayer which has become a model of prayer for all time and part of the religious service of all Christianity.

Our Father, Who art in heaven, hallowed be Thy name. Thy kingdom come, Thy will be done, on earth as it is in heaven. Give us this day our daily bread and forgive us our debts as we forgive our debtors. And lead us not into temptation, but deliver us from evil, for Thine is the kingdom, and the power, and the glory forever. *Amen.*

Benediction

The peace of God which passeth all understanding, keep our hearts and minds in the knowledge and love of God, and of his Son Jesus Christ our Lord, and the blessing of God Almighty, the Father, the Son, and the Holy Ghost, be amongst you and remain with you always. *Amen.*

—from *The Book of Common Prayer*

Declaration of Faith

This declaration of faith is a variation of the Nicene Creed or Apostles' Creed. In different versions this is used by Catholics and Protestants.

I believe in God, our Father, infinite in wisdom, goodness and love, and in his Son, our Saviour, the Lord Jesus Christ, who for us men and our salvation lived and died and liveth evermore, exalted at the right hand of the Father, whose kingdom shall have no end.

And I believe in the Holy Spirit of God, the Lord and Giver of Life, proceeding from the Father and the Son, and with the Father and the Son exalted and glorified; taking of the things of Christ, revealing them to us; comforting, renewing, inspiring our spirits.

I believe in the persistence of personality and the immortality of the soul and I am resolved through the grace given unto me to order my life in the works of faith and in the ways of the holy commandments, looking for the victory of righteousness over evil, life over death, and for the life of the world to come.

Morning Prayer

This is the most widely known of all the morning prayers in use in the Protestant Church.

O Lord, our heavenly Father, Almighty and everlasting God, who hast safely brought us to the beginning of this day; Defend us in the same with thy mighty power, and grant that this day we fall into no sin, neither run into any kind of danger, but that all our doings, being ordered by thy governance, may be righteous in thy sight; through Jesus Christ our Lord. *Amen.*

—from *The Book of Common Prayer*

In a Humble Sense

This prayer is originally from Bishop Gibson's *Morning and Evening Prayer for a Family.* He was Bishop of London from 1723 to 1748.

Most merciful God, who art of purer eyes than to behold iniquity, and hast promised forgiveness to all those who confess and forsake their sins: We come before thee in a humble sense of our own unworthiness, acknowledging our manifold transgressions of thy righteous laws. But, O gracious Father, who desirest not the death of a sinner, look upon us, we beseech thee, in mercy, and forgive us all our transgressions; make us deeply sensible of the great evil of them, and work in us a hearty contrition; that we may obtain forgiveness at thy hands, who art ever ready to receive humble and penitent sinners; for the sake of thy Son Jesus Christ, our only Saviour and redeemer. *Amen.*

—from *The Book of Common Prayer* (U.S.)

We Confess

This prayer is a shorter version of the general confession of the Episcopal Liturgy.

O Almighty Father, Lord of heaven and earth: We confess that we have sinned against thee in thought, word and deed. Have mercy upon us, O God, after thy great goodness; according to the multitude of thy mercies, do away our offences and cleanse us from our sins; for Jesus Christ's sake. *Amen.*

—from *The Book of Common Prayer* (U.S.)

A *Prayer of Thanksgiving*

This is the "Common and Proper Preface for Christmas" of the Lutheran faith. It is a prayer of thanksgiving—in imitation of our Lord who gave thanks when he took the bread and cup to institute the Holy Communion. "The Sanctus" is the great hymn of the communion service, the climax of the thanksgiving.

It is truly meet, right and salutary, that we should at all times, and in all places, give thanks unto Thee, O Lord, Holy Father, Almighty Everlasting God:

For in the mystery of the Word made flesh, Thou hast given us a new revelation of Thy glory; that seeing Thee in the Person of Thy Son, we may be drawn to the love of those things which are not seen. Therefore with Angels and Archangels, and with all the company of heaven, we laud and magnify Thy glorious Name; evermore praising Thee, and saying:

(THE SANCTUS)

Holy, holy, holy, Lord God of Sabaoth; Heaven and earth are full of Thy glory; Hosanna in the highest.

Blessed is He that cometh in the Name of the Lord. Hosanna in the highest.

—from *Common Service Book of the Lutheran Church*

Eucharistic Prayer

In the Protestant celebration of the Eucharist this sacrament is believed mystically to unite the believers with Christ and with each other, as opposed to the traditional belief held by Catholics in the sacrament as a sacrifice and a transubstantiation of the elements into the Body and Blood of Christ.

Lift up your hearts:
We lift them up unto the Lord.
It is very meet, right and our bounden duty, that we should at all times, and in all places, give thanks unto Thee, Holy Father, Almighty, Everlasting God; through Jesus Christ Thy Son, who being very and eternal God, came down from heaven in perfect love, and became Man for us men and for our salvation.

Not as we ought, but as we are able, we bless Thee for His holy incarnation; for His life on earth; for His precious sufferings and death upon the cross; for His resurrection from the dead; for His glorious ascension to Thy right hand; and for the promise of His coming again.

Thee, mighty God, heavenly King, we magnify and praise. With angels and archangels, and all the hosts of heaven, we worship and adore Thy glorious name, joining in the everlasting hymn of the cherubim and seraphim, singing unto Thee:

Holy, holy, holy, Lord God of hosts; heaven and earth are full of Thy glory. Hosanna in the highest. Blessed is he that cometh in the name of the Lord. Hosanna in the highest.
　　　　　　—from *Book of Common Order* (Church of Scotland)

Communion

Communion is partaking of the Christian sacrament, which repeats the action of Jesus at his last supper with his disciples, when he broke bread saying, "This is my body," and gave them wine saying, "This is my blood." In the Protestant sacrament there is a mystical union of believers with Christ and with each other.

O God, who art, and wast, and art to come; before whose face the generations rise and pass away: Age after age the living seek thee and find that of thy faithfulness there is no end. Our fathers in their pilgrimage walked by thy guidance, and rested on thy compassion; still to their children be thou the cloud by day and the fire by night. Where but in thee have we a covert from the storm or a shadow from the heat of life? In our manifold temptations thou alone knowest and art ever nigh; in sorrow, thy pity revives the fainting soul; in our prosperity and ease, it is Thy Spirit only that can keep us from our pride and keep us humble. O thou only source of peace and righteousness, take now the veil from every heart, and join us in one communion with thy prophets and saints, who have trusted in thee and were not ashamed. Not of our worthiness, but of thy tender mercy, hear our prayer; for the sake of Jesus Christ thy Son our Lord. *Amen.*

> —from *The Book of Common Worship* (Presbyterian)
> (Originally from James Martineau: *Home Prayers*)

Post-Communion Prayers

The following prayer may be said after all have communicated and the Sacrament has been given.

O God our Father, we give thee hearty thanks for the most blessed communion of which thou hast this day made us partakers. We again dedicate ourselves to thy service in body, soul, and spirit. Make thy grace always sufficient for us. Perfect thy strength in our weakness. Succour us amid the manifold temptations and sorrows of our lives. Give us power to endure unto the end as good soldiers of Jesus Christ, and let the light of thy countenance be upon us now and evermore.

> —from *Book of Common Order* (Church of Scotland)

Penitence

This collect was translated from the Gregorian Sacramentary and appeared in the 1549 and 1662 editions of *The Book of Common Prayer* in revised form.

O God, whose nature and property is ever to have mercy and to forgive; Receive our humble petitions; and though we be tied and bound with the chain of our sins, yet let the pitifulness of thy great mercy loose us; for the honour of Jesus Christ, our Mediator and Advocate. *Amen.*

—from *The Book of Common Prayer*

The Burial of the Dead

O Merciful God, the Father of our Lord Jesus Christ, who is the Resurrection and the Life; in whom whosoever believeth, shall live, though he die; and whosoever liveth, and believeth in him, shall not die eternally; who also hath taught us, by his holy Apostle Saint Paul, not to be sorry, as men without hope, for them who sleep in him; We humbly beseech thee, O Father, to raise us from the death of sin unto the life of righteousness; that, when we shall depart this life, we may rest in him, as our hope is this our brother doth; and that, at the general Resurrection in the last day, we may be found acceptable in thy sight; and receive that blessing, which thy well-beloved Son shall then pronounce to all that love and fear thee, saying, Come, ye blessed children of my Father, receive the kingdom prepared for you from the beginning of the world. Grant this, we beseech thee, O merciful Father, through Jesus Christ, our Mediator and Redeemer. *Amen.*

—from *The Book of Common Prayer*

For Those Who Have Passed On

Before thee, O Heavenly Father, we remember those who have passed from our midst into the fuller light of thy eternal Presence. We thank thee for their loyalty to duty and their power of self-surrender, and for the discipline by which thou hast made them fit in a short time for the higher service in thy kingdom. May we have the assurance of their continued fellowship in thee, and realize that there is no separation between those that love, even though converse and communion be no longer possible according to the flesh. Hear, O God our Father, the prayers that follow our beloved ones upon their unseen way, and grant that both we and they, in every condition thy wisdom ordains, may grow and continue in the knowledge of thee which alone is eternal life. *Amen.*

—John Hunter, from *Devotional Services*
See biographical note on page 122.

For the Sick and Sorrowing

The following three prayers are used in the Protestant faith on occasions of sickness and ill-health.

Most gracious God, who art the strength of the weak and the refuge of the sorrowful; we bear on our hearts before thee the sick, the sad and the sorrowing, and all who are anywise suffering in body, or mind, or worldly estate (especially our brethren who are absent by reason of sickness or infirmity). Draw near to the sick with sustaining strength and healing, speak to the downcast and desolate in comfort and peace, and to those who are appointed to die grant the safekeeping of thy love and in due time a peaceful entrance into rest; through Jesus Christ our Lord. *Amen.*

—from the *Ordinal and Service Book* (Church of Scotland)

For Those Who Suffer

O Thou, who understandest the frailty of the human heart, hear our prayer for those who have been unfortunate in life and bruised in spirit; those who have toiled without success; those who have endured with no outside encouragement; those who have given up all earthly prospects to comfort the aged and care for the maimed; those who are lonely in heart; for them we know not what to ask, but thou knowest, O Lover of Souls. *Amen.*

—from *Acts of Devotion*

For Healing

Almighty God, who didst send thy son Jesus Christ to be the great physician of our souls and bodies: Grant us thy peace. Thou who givest rest to those who wait upon thee, grant us thy courage. In quietness and confidence may we find strength. Give wisdom and skill to the doctors and nurses. We give ourselves into thy sustaining presence, knowing that in thee is our peace; through Jesus Christ our Lord. *Amen.*

—from *The Book of Common Worship*

In the Sacrament of Motherhood

This prayer dedicated to the Mother and Child is one of the most beautiful and moving of its kind.

O most blessed Lord, uphold my soul in every time of need, or adversity; give me at this time increased holiness, strengthen my weakness; give me courage to face any pain, offering it up to Thee. Make me realize the privilege of bearing a child even as Thy blessed Mother bore one.

Give me, O Lord, a little of Thy infinite love and wise understanding, and whisper to my soul the secrets of perfect mother-hood, which Thou alone canst teach.

Give to my child a great capacity for goodness and a happy disposition, so that it may enter life here well equipped to with-stand the world and the devil, and thus come to life immortal.

Into Thy hands, O Lord, do I commend my body and soul. *Amen.*

—from *Prayers of Health and Healing*

For the Churches of Christendom

This prayer by the Federal Council of Churches first appeared in 1940. The Federal Council of Churches has been replaced by the National Council of Churches of Christ in the United States, which now is the leading Protestant church organization in this country.

Let us give thanks for the gifts and graces of each great division of Christendom:

For the ROMAN CATHOLIC CHURCH; its glorious traditions, its disciplines in holiness, its worship, rich with the religious passion of the centuries; its noble company of martyrs, doctors and saints;

> *We thank Thee, O Lord, and bless Thy Holy Name.*

For the EASTERN ORTHODOX CHURCH; its secret treasure of mystic experience; its marvelous liturgy; its regard for the collective life and its common will as a source of authority;

> *We thank Thee, O Lord, and bless Thy Holy Name.*

For the great PROTESTANT COMMUNIONS;

For the CONGREGATIONALIST jealousy for the rightful independence of the soul and of the group;

For the stress in the BAPTIST CHURCHES upon personal regeneration and upon the conscious relation of the mature soul to its Lord;

For the power of the METHODISTS to awaken the conscience of Christians to our social evils; and for their emphasis upon the witness of personal experience, and upon the power of the disciplined life;

For the PRESBYTERIAN reverence for the sovereignty of God and their confidence in his faithfulness to his covenant; for their sense of the moral law, expressing itself in constitutional government;

For the witness to the perpetual real presence of the inner light in every human soul borne by the RELIGIOUS SOCIETY OF FRIENDS and for their faithful continuance of a free prophetic ministry;

For the LUTHERAN CHURCH; its devotion to the grace of God and the word of God, enshrined in the ministry of the word and sacraments;

For the ANGLICAN CHURCH; its reverent and temperate ways, through its Catholic heritage and its Protestant conscience; its yearning concern over the divisions of Christendom, and its longing to be used as a house of reconciliation.

We thank Thee, O Lord, and bless Thy Holy Name.
—from Federal Council of Churches Bulletin

For Brotherhood of Man

O God, who hast made man in thine own likeness and who dost love all whom thou hast made: Teach us the unity of thy family and the breadth of thy love. By the example of thy Son, Jesus our Saviour, enable us, while loving and serving our own, to enter into the fellowship of the whole human family, and forbid that, from pride of race or hardness of heart, we should despise any for whom Christ died or injure any in whom he lives. *Amen.*

—from *The Book of Common Worship*

For Unity

The following three prayers for the brotherhood of man have particular timeliness and urgency in our search for world unity and abiding peace

O God, the Father of our Lord Jesus Christ, our only Saviour, the Prince of Peace, give us grace seriously to lay to heart the great dangers we are in by our unhappy divisions. Take away all hatred and prejudice, and whatsoever else may hinder us from godly union and concord; that as there is but one body, and one Spirit, and one hope of our calling, one Lord, one faith, one baptism, one God and Father of us all, so we may henceforth be all of one heart, and of one soul, united in one holy bond of truth and peace, of faith and charity, and may, with one mind and one mouth, glorify thee; through Jesus Christ our Lord.

Amen.

—From *Liturgy of St. James* (second century)

For International Friendship

Almighty God, in whose hand are all the nations of the earth, grant to them all thy guidance and help that they may seek prosperity in promoting the welfare of their people and of all mankind. Grant to all peoples and races that they may feel their kinship with each other since all men are alike the children of the same eternal Father. Restrain them from jealousy, hatred or selfish ambition. Awaken in them the spirit of justice, fraternity and concord. Unite them by the bonds of international friendship, that they may work together for the betterment of the whole world. Make wars to cease, and hasten the day when there shall be everywhere peace on earth, and good will among men; this we ask in the name of the Prince of Peace. *Amen.*

—from *The Book of Church Services*
(National Council of Congregational Churches)

A Prayer for the President

O Lord, our heavenly Father, the high and mighty Ruler of the Universe, who dost from thy throne behold all the dwellers upon earth; Most heartily we beseech thee, with thy favour to behold and bless thy servant The President of the United States, and all others in authority; and so replenish them with the grace of the Holy Spirit, that they may always incline to thy will, and walk in thy way. Endue them plenteously with heavenly gifts; grant them in health and prosperity long to live; and finally, after this life, to attain everlasting joy and felicity; through Jesus Christ our Lord. *Amen.*

—from *The Book of Common Prayer*

Prayer for America

The Book of Common Prayer has gone through many editions. This prayer was composed and included in this prayer book when it was first published in America.

Almighty God, who hast given us this good land for our heritage; We humbly beseech thee that we may always prove ourselves a people mindful of thy favour and glad to do thy will. Bless our land with honourable industry, sound learning, and pure manners. Save us from violence, discord, and confusion; from pride and arrogancy, and from every evil way. Defend our liberties, and fashion into one united people the multitudes brought hither out of many kindreds and tongues. Endue with the spirit of wisdom those to whom in thy Name we entrust the authority of government, that there may be justice and peace at home, and that, through obedience to thy law, we may show forth thy praise among the nations of the earth. In the time of prosperity, fill our hearts with thankfulness, and in the day of trouble, suffer not our trust in thee to fail; all which we ask through Jesus Christ our Lord. *Amen.*

—from *The Book of Common Prayer*

The General Prayer

This prayer from the *Common Service Book of the Lutheran Church* has been used in almost its present form since 1553.

Almighty and most merciful God, the Father of our Lord Jesus Christ: We give Thee thanks for all Thy goodness and tender mercies, especially for the gift of Thy dear Son, and for the revelation of Thy will and grace; and we beseech Thee so to implant Thy word in us, that, in good and honest hearts, we may keep it, and bring forth fruit by patient continuance in well-doing.

Most heartily we beseech Thee so to rule and govern Thy Church universal, that it may be preserved in the pure doctrine of Thy saving word, whereby faith toward Thee may be strengthened, and charity increased in us toward all mankind.

Send forth Thy light and Thy truth unto the uttermost parts of the earth. Raise up faithful pastors and missionaries to preach the Gospel in our own land and to all nations; and guide, protect, and prosper them in all their labors.

Bless, we pray Thee, the institutions of the Church; its colleges, its seminaries, and all its schools; that they may send forth men and women to serve Thee, in the Ministry of the Word, the Ministry of Mercy, and all the walks of life.

Let the light of Thy word ever shine within our homes. Keep the children of the Church in the covenant which Thou hast made with them in Holy Baptism; and grant all parents grace to bring them up in faith toward Thee and in obedience to Thy will.

Grant also health and prosperity to all that are in authority, especially to the President (and Congress) of the United States, the Governor (and Legislature) of this Commonwealth, and to all our Judges and Magistrates; and endue them with grace to rule after Thy good pleasure, to the maintenance of righteousness, and to the hindrance and punishment of wickedness, that we may lead a quiet and peaceable life, in all godliness and honesty.

All who are in trouble, want, sickness, anguish of labor, peril of death, or any other adversity, especially those who are in suffering for Thy Name and for Thy truth's sake, comfort, O God, with Thy Holy Spirit, that they may receive and acknowledge their afflictions as the manifestation of Thy fatherly will.

And although we have deserved Thy righteous wrath and manifold punishments, yet, we entreat Thee, O most merciful Father, remember not the sins of our youth, nor our many transgressions; but out of Thine unspeakable goodness, grace and mercy, defend us from all harm and danger of body and soul. Preserve us from false and pernicious doctrine, from war and bloodshed, from plague and pestilence, from all calamity by fire and water, from hail and tempest, from failure of harvest and from famine, from anguish of heart and despair of Thy mercy, and from an evil death. And in every time of trouble, show Thyself a very present Help, the Saviour of all men, and especially of them that believe.

Cause also the needful fruits of the earth to prosper, that we may enjoy them in due season. Give success to all lawful occupations on land and sea, to all pure arts and useful knowledge; and crown them with Thy blessing.

Here special Supplications, Intercessions,
and Prayers may be made.

These, and whatsoever other things Thou wouldest have us ask of Thee, O God, vouchsafe unto us for the sake of the bitter sufferings and death of Jesus Christ, Thine only Son, our Lord and Saviour, Who liveth and reigneth with Thee and the Holy Ghost, ever one God, world without end.

Then shall the minister, and the congregation, say

THE LORD'S PRAYER

—from *Common Service Book of the Lutheran Church*

The Southwell Litany

George Ridding (1828–1904) was born in Winchester, England, and became the first Bishop of Southwell in 1884. He had a long career as a schoolmaster as well as churchman. His Southwell litany is a favorite among many Protestant clergymen.

O Lord, open thou our minds to see ourselves as thou seest us, or even as others see us and we see others, and from all unwillingness to know our infirmities,

Save us and help us
We humbly beseech thee, O Lord.

From weariness in continuing struggles, from despondency in failure and disappointment, from over-burdened sense of unworthiness, from morbid fancies of imaginary backslidings, raise us to a lively hope and trust in thy presence and mercy, in the power of faith and prayer, and from all exaggerated fears and vexations,

Save us and help us
We humbly beseech thee, O Lord.

From pride and self-will, from desire ever to have our own way in all things, from overweening love of our own ideas and blindness to the value of others; from resentment against opposition and contempt for the claim of others; enlarge the generosity of our hearts and enlighten the fairness of our judgments; and from all selfish arbitrariness of temper,

Save us and help us
We humbly beseech thee, O Lord.

Give us knowledge of ourselves, our powers and weaknesses, our spirit, our sympathy, our imagination, our knowledge, our truth; teach us by the standard of Thy Word, by the judgments of others, by examinations of ourselves; give us earnest desire to strengthen ourselves continually by study, by diligence, by prayer and meditation; and from all fancies, delusions, and prejudices of habit, or temper, or society,

Save us and help us
We humbly beseech thee, O Lord.

Finally, O Lord, we humbly beseech thee, blot out our past transgressions, heal the evils of our past negligences and ignorances, make us amend our past mistakes and misunderstandings, uplift our hearts to new love, new energy and devotion, that we may be unburthened from the grief and shame of past faithlessnesses to go forth in thy strength to persevere through success and failure, through good report and evil report, even to the end; and in all the time of our tribulation, in all the time of our prosperity,

> *Save us and help us*
> *We humbly beseech thee, O Lord. Amen.*
> —Bishop George Ridding

The Wesleyan Litany

The Litany, or General Supplication, was composed by John Wesley and later adopted into *The Book of Common Prayer*. It is used after morning service on Sundays, Wednesdays, and Fridays.

O God the Father of Heaven; have mercy upon us miserable sinners.

O God the Father of Heaven; have mercy upon us miserable sinners.

O God the Son, Redeemer of the world; have mercy upon us miserable sinners.

O God the Son, Redeemer of the world; have mercy upon us miserable sinners.

O God the Holy Ghost, proceeding from the Father and the Son; have mercy upon us miserable sinners.

O God the Holy Ghost, proceeding from the Father and the Son; have mercy upon us miserable sinners.

O holy, blessed, and glorious Trinity, three Persons, and one God; have mercy upon us miserable sinners.

O holy, blessed, and glorious Trinity, three Persons, and one God; have mercy upon us miserable sinners.

Remember not, Lord, our offences, nor the offences of our forefathers; neither take thou vengeance of our sins: Spare us,
good Lord, spare thy people, whom thou hast redeemed
with thy most precious blood, and be not angry with us
forever.

Spare us, good Lord.

From all evil and mischief; from sin, from the crafts and assaults of the devil, from thy wrath, and from everlasting
damnation,
Good Lord, deliver us.

From all blindness of heart; from pride, vainglory, and hypocrisy; from envy, hatred, and malice, and all uncharitableness,
Good Lord, deliver us.

From all inordinate and sinful affections; from all the deceits of
the world, the flesh, and the devil,
Good Lord, deliver us.

From lightning and tempest; from plague, pestilence, and famine; from battle and murder, and from sudden death,
Good Lord, deliver us.

From all sedition, privy conspiracy, and rebellion; from all
false doctrine, heresy, and schism; from hardness of heart
and contempt of thy Word and Commandment,
Good Lord, deliver us.

By the mystery of thy holy Incarnation; by thy holy Nativity
and Circumcision; by thy Baptism, Fasting, and Temptation,
Good Lord, deliver us.

By thine Agony and Bloody Sweat; by thy Cross and Passion;
by thy precious Death and Burial; by thy glorious Resurrection and Ascension; and by the coming of the Holy
Ghost,
Good Lord, deliver us.

In all time of our tribulation; in all time of our prosperity; in
the hour of death, and in the day of judgment,
Good Lord, deliver us.

We sinners do beseech thee to hear us, O Lord God; and that
it may please thee to rule and govern thy holy Church universal in the right way;
We beseech thee to hear us, good Lord.

That it may please thee to bless and preserve all Christian
Rulers and Magistrates, giving them grace to execute jus-
tice, and to maintain truth;
We beseech thee to hear us, good Lord.

That it may please thee to illuminate all Bishops, Elders, and
Deacons, with true knowledge and understanding of thy
Word; and that both by their preaching and living they
may set it forth, and show it accordingly;
We beseech thee to hear us, good Lord.

That it may please thee to send forth laborers into thy harvest;
We beseech thee to hear us, good Lord.

That it may please thee to bless and keep all thy people;
We beseech thee to hear us, good Lord.

That it may please thee to give to all nations, unity, peace and
concord;
We beseech thee to hear us, good Lord.

That it may please thee to give us an heart to love and to fear
thee, and diligently to live after thy commandments;
We beseech thee to hear us, good Lord.

That it may please thee to give to all thy people increase of
grace, to hear meekly thy Word, and to receive it with
pure affection, and to bring forth the fruits of the Spirit;
We beseech thee to hear us, good Lord.

That it may please thee to bring into the way of truth all such
as have erred, and are deceived;
We beseech thee to hear us, good Lord.

That it may please thee to strengthen such as do stand; and to
comfort and help the weak-hearted; and to raise up them
that fall; and finally to beat down Satan under our feet;
We beseech thee to hear us, good Lord.

That it may please thee to succor, help, and comfort all who are
in danger, necessity and tribulation;
We beseech thee to hear us, good Lord.

That it may please thee to preserve all that travel by land or by
water, all women in the perils of childbirth, all sick persons
and young children; and to show thy pity upon all prisoners and captives;
We beseech thee to hear us, good Lord.

That it may please thee to defend, and provide for, the fatherless children, and widows, and all that are desolate and
oppressed;
We beseech thee to hear us, good Lord.

That it may please thee to have mercy upon all men;
We beseech thee to hear us, good Lord.

That it may please thee to forgive our enemies, persecutors,
and slanderers, and to turn their hearts;
We beseech thee to hear us, good Lord.

That it may please thee to give and preserve to our use the
kindly fruits of the earth, so that in due time we may enjoy
them;
We beseech thee to hear us, good Lord.

That it may please thee to give us true repentance; to forgive
us all our sins, negligences and ignorances; and to endue
us with the grace of thy Holy Spirit, to amend our lives
according to thy holy Word;
We beseech thee to hear us, good Lord.

Son of God, we beseech thee to hear us.

Son of God, we beseech thee to hear us.

O Lamb of God, that takest away the sins of the world;
Grant us thy peace.

O Lamb of God, that takest away the sins of the world;
Have mercy upon us.

—John Wesley

GREAT CATHOLIC PRAYERS 195

GREAT CATHOLIC
PRAYERS

T HESE PRAYERS EVOKE MEMORIES. *My people were Roman Catholic. I am Roman Catholic. Some of my formative years were spent at St. Patrick's School in Jersey City. Thus, when I read the prayers I know best, I find that my mind is flooded with scenes of other days.*

For example, at the bottom of a Litany to the Sacred Heart of Jesus, you will find the words, "Jesus, meek and humble of heart, make our hearts like unto thine." It is probably far from the most inspired of prayers but, when my eyes crossed those words, my stomach knotted and then relaxed. My eyes squeezed shut with a forty-year-old longing.

It is one of the earliest aspirations I learned. I would guess that I was eight or nine years of age when I said it, over and over, in the dimness of the church, the smell of incense in my nostrils, my eyes closed to the priest who held the monstrance high, with the Holy Eucharist inside, making the sign of the cross. The reason for the closed eyes was that I was unworthy to watch.

I can see the cool gray granite of the church pillars, and I can see Mr. Kerrigan, in shirt sleeves and vest, leaning back

*hard to pull the deep-toned church bell. The soft snap of rub-
ber heels on tile belongs to the tall Sister Grace Agatha. So does
the click of the rosary hanging from her waist.*

*Other prayers brought other memories, as other prayers in
other sections of this book may rekindle the darkened corners
of your mind. Of the prayers in this section, the most beautiful,
to my way of thinking, is the "Act of Contrition."*

The Lord's Prayer

"The Lord's Prayer" or "Our Father" is called in Latin "Pater" or "Pater
Noster." Roman Catholics have never added the doxology which was
adopted by most Protestants from a version of *Matthew* reading "For
Thine is the kingdom, and the power, and the glory, for ever and ever."

Our Father Who art in heaven, hallowed be Thy name; Thy
kingdom come; Thy will be done on earth as it is in heaven.
Give us this day our daily bread; and forgive us our trespasses
as we forgive those who trespass against us; and lead us not
into temptation, but deliver us from evil. *Amen.*

The Angelic Salutation

"The Angelic Salutation" or "Ave Maria" is based on the greeting of
the angel Gabriel to the Virgin Mary (*Luke* 1:28) and is also commonly
known as the "Hail Mary."

Hail, Mary, full of grace! the Lord is with thee: blessed art thou
amongst women, and blessed is the fruit of thy womb, Jesus.
Holy Mary, Mother of God, pray for us sinners, now and at the
hour of our death. *Amen.*

The Apostles' Creed

"The Apostles' Creed" appeared in its present form in the fifth century, and has two main differences from the Nicene Creed: (1) "He descended into hell," omitted in the Nicene; (2) "resurrection of the body," in the Nicene "of the dead." It is used by Roman Catholics privately and at baptism; it is also widely used by Protestants of many denominations.

I believe in God the Father Almighty, Creator of heaven and earth:

And in Jesus Christ his only Son our Lord: Who was conceived by the Holy Ghost, Born of the Virgin Mary: Suffered under Pontius Pilate, Was crucified, died, and was buried: He descended into hell; The third day he rose again from the dead: He ascended into heaven, sitteth on the right hand of God the Father Almighty: From thence he shall come to judge the living and the dead.

I believe in the Holy Ghost: The holy Catholic Church; The Communion of Saints: The Forgiveness of sins; The Resurrection of the body: And Life everlasting. *Amen.*

Regina Coeli

"Regina Coeli," or "Queen of Heaven," are the opening words of the Eastertide anthem of the Blessed Virgin. Of unknown authorship, the song first came into use in the twelfth century. Legend has it that St. Gregory the Great heard the first three lines one Easter morning in Rome while walking barefoot in a religious procession and then composed the next line on the spot.

> Queen of heaven, rejoice! Alleluia!
> For He, Whom thou didst merit to bear, Alleluia!
> Hath risen, as He said. Alleluia!
> Rejoice and be glad, O Virgin Mary! Alleluia!
> For Our Lord has truly risen. Alleluia!

Let us pray

O God, Who didst vouchsafe to give joy to the world by the resurrection of Thy Son our Lord Jesus Christ, grant, we beseech Thee, that by the intercession of His virgin mother, Mary, we may receive the joys of eternal life, through the same Christ, Our Lord. *Amen.*

Gloria

This prayer of praise has been used in its present form since the sixth century.

Glory be to the Father, and to the Son, and to
the Holy Ghost. As it was in the beginning, is now,
and ever shall be, world without end. *Amen.*

Anima Christi

This prayer dates from the first half of the fourteenth century, but its authorship is not known for certain.

Soul of Christ, be my sanctification.
Body of Christ, be my salvation.
Blood of Christ, fill all my veins.
Water from Christ's side, wash out my stains.
Passion of Christ, my comfort be.
O good Jesus, listen to me.
In thy wounds I fain would hide,
Ne'er to be parted from thy side.
Guard me should the foe assail me.
Call me when my life shall fail me.
Bid me come to Thee above,
With thy Saints to sing thy love
World without end. *Amen.*

Morning Prayers

The *Missal* is the English translation from the Latin of all directions and text necessary for the celebration of the Roman Catholic Mass throughout the year, also various blessings, prayers, and votive Masses.

In the name of the Father, and of the Son, and of the Holy Ghost. *Amen.*

Our Father, etc.
Hail Mary, etc.
The Apostles' Creed
Doxology (Glory be, etc.)

O my God, I believe in thee, because thou art truth itself.

O my God, I hope in thee because of thy promises to me.

O my God, I love thee above all things, because thou art so good; teach me to love thee daily more and more.

O my God, I offer thee all my thoughts, words, actions, and sufferings; and I beseech thee give me thy grace that I may not offend thee this day, but may faithfully serve thee and do thy holy will in all things.

I desire to gain all the indulgences that I can.

Holy Mary, be a mother to me.
All ye angels and saints of God, pray for me.

May Our lord bless us and keep us from all evil, and bring us to life everlasting.

May the souls of the faithful departed, through the mercy of God, rest in peace. *Amen.*

O Lord God Almighty, Who hast caused us to reach the beginning of this day, save us today by thy power, that we may turn not aside to any sin, but that our words, thoughts and deeds may ever be ruled by thy justice.

O Lord God, King of heaven and earth, vouchsafe this day to direct and sanctify, to rule and govern our hearts and bodies, our thoughts, words and deeds, according to Thy law and in the works of Thy commandments; that here and forever, with Thy help, we may be protected and saved, O Thou Saviour of the World, Who liveth and reigneth for ever and ever. *Amen.*

May Holy Mary and all saints intercede for us to the Lord, that we may merit to be aided and saved by Him Who liveth and reigneth for ever and ever. *Amen.*

—from *Small Missal*

Evening Prayers

In the name of the Father, and of the Son, and of the Holy Ghost. *Amen.*

The Lord's Prayer (Our Father, etc.)
Hail Mary, etc.
The Apostles' Creed.
Doxology (Glory be, etc.)

O my God, I return Thee thanks for all the benefits which I have ever received from Thee, and particularly this day. Give me light to see what sins I have committed this day, and grant me grace to be truly sorry for them.

(*Pause and reflect on the faults committed during the day*)

O my God, I am very sorry that I have offended Thee; I love Thee with all my heart because Thou art so good, and I will not sin again.

Into Thy hands, O Lord, I commend my spirit; Lord Jesus, receive my soul.

Holy Mary, be a mother to me.

May the blessed Virgin Mary, St. Joseph, and all the saints pray for us to our Lord, that we may be preserved this night from sin and all evil. *Amen.*

O my good angel, whom God has appointed to be my guardian, watch over me during this night.

All ye angels and saints of God, pray for me.

May our Lord bless us and preserve us from all evil,
and bring us to life everlasting.

May the souls of the faithful departed, through the
mercy of God, rest in peace. *Amen.*

—from *Small Missal*

A Grace before Meals

Bless us, O Lord, and these Thy gifts, which we are about
to receive from Thy bounty. Through Christ our Lord. *Amen.*

A Grace after Meals

We give Thee thanks, O almighty God, for all Thy mercies.
Who liveth and reigneth for ever and ever. *Amen.*

May the souls of the faithful departed, through the mercy of
God, rest in peace.

The Confiteor

"The Confiteor" is a general confession of sins and is used at the beginning of Mass and on various other occasions as a preparation for receiving grace.

I confess to Almighty God, to blessed Mary, ever Virgin, to
blessed Michael, the Archangel, to blessed John the Baptist, to
the holy Apostles Peter and Paul, and to all the Saints that I
have sinned exceedingly in thought, word and deed, through
my fault, through my fault, through my most grievous fault.
Therefore I beseech blessed Mary, ever Virgin, blessed Michael
the Archangel, blessed John the Baptist, the holy Apostles
Peter and Paul, and all the Saints, to pray to the Lord our God
for me.

May the Almighty God have mercy on me, and forgive me
my sins, and bring me to everlasting life. *Amen.*

Act of Contrition

A sinner must repent before he can be reconciled with God. Therefore he must either make an act of perfect contrition or supplement the imperfect contrition by receiving the Sacrament of Penance. This prayer is part of the Sacrament.

O my God, I am heartily sorry that I have offended Thee and I detest all my sins because I dread the loss of heaven and the pains of hell, but most of all because I have offended Thee, Who art all Good and deserving of all my love. I firmly resolve, with the help of Thy grace, to confess my sins, to do penance, and to amend my life. *Amen.*

Our National Patron Saints

Roman Catholics believe that faithful Christians on earth and the saints are all members of the Church. Those living on earth may ask those in heaven for their prayers and share in their merits. The Virgin Mary is the chief saint. Each member of a church has at least one patron saint from baptism and another is added at confirmation. Cities, towns, and nations all have their patron saints, and a complete list would run to thousands of names. Some of the chief countries and their saints are listed below.

Grant us, we beseech Thee, O Lord, the pardon of our sins; and through the intercession of our patron Saints, give to us such devotion that we may become partakers of their companionship. Our own defects hold us back, but may their merits assist us; our own actions accuse us before Thee, but may their pleading obtain our pardon. To them, O Lord, Thou hast given the palm of heavenly triumph; do not deny to us the forgiveness of our offenses, so that we may become their fellow citizens in Thy Kingdom.

—Roman Catholic Prayers

Some Patron Saints (as listed in the *Catholic Encyclopedia*)

Austria—Our Lady
Belgium—St. Joseph
Borneo—St. Francis Xavier
Canada—St. Anne and St. George
Chile—St. James
China—St. Joseph
The Congo—Our Lady
Denmark—St. Ansgar
East Indies—St. Thomas the Apostle
England—St. George
Finland—St. Henry of Upsal
France—St. Denis and St. Joan of Arc
Germany—St. Michael and St. Boniface
Greece—St. Nicholas of Myra
Holland—St. Willibrod
Hungary—St. Stephen the King

Ireland—St. Patrick
Italy—St. Francis of Assisi and St. Catherine of Siena
Mexico—Our Lady of Guadalupe
Norway—St. Olaf
Piedmont—St. Maurice
Poland—St. Stanislaus of Cracow
Portugal—St. George and St. Vincent of Saragossa
Russia—St. Andrew
Scotland—St. Andrew the Apostle
South America—St. Rose of Lima
Spain—St. James the Great
Sweden—St. Bridget
Switzerland—St. Nicholas of Fluë
United States—The Immaculate Conception
Wales—St. David

A Litany

The litany was developed for use in processions, the Eastern liturgy making frequent use of litanies recited by deacons. In the Roman Catholic Church the one liturgical litany, the "Litany of the Saints," dates from the fifth century. After it were modeled the "Litany of the Most Holy Name of Jesus," developed in the fifteenth century, the "Litany of the Blessed Virgin," developed in the sixteenth century, the "Litany of the Sacred Heart," and the litany directly below—compiled from the *Liturgy of St. John Chrysostom.*

Blessed be the kingdom of the Father, the Son, and the Holy Ghost, now and for ever, world without end. *Amen.*

In peace, let us pray to the Lord.

Kyrie eleison.

For the peace from on high, and for the salvation of our souls, let us pray to the Lord.

Kyrie eleison.

For the peace of the whole world, for the good estate of all the holy churches of God, and for the unity of all, let us pray to the Lord.

Kyrie eleison.

For this holy house and for those who enter therein with faith, reverence, and fear of God, let us pray to the Lord.

Kyrie eleison.

For our most holy pope, for our God-beloved bishop, for the venerable order of priests, for religious and deacons in Christ, for all the clergy and people, let us pray to the Lord.

Kyrie eleison.

Let us pray for mercy, life, peace, health, salvation, protection, forgiveness and remission of sins of the servants of God, the dwellers in this place.

Kyrie eleison.

Let us pray for the blessed and ever-memorable benefactors of this church, for all our brethren and fathers departed who rest in peace near this place, and for all the orthodox throughout the world.

Kyrie eleison.

Let us pray for those who offer fruits and who do good in this holy and most venerable church, for the workmen, singers, and all the people here present who await from God great and rich mercy.

Kyrie eleison.

For this realm, for every city and country, and for all the faithful who dwell therein, let us pray to the Lord.

Kyrie eleison.

For a good state of climate, abundance of the fruits of the earth, and peaceful seasons, let us pray to the Lord.

Kyrie eleison.

For sailors, travellers, the sick, sufferers, prisoners, for the salvation of all, let us pray to the Lord.

Kyrie eleison.

That we may be delivered from all affliction, wrath, peril, and necessity, let us pray to the Lord.

Kyrie eleison.

Help, save, pity and guard us, O God, by thy grace.

Kyrie eleison.

Remembering our all-holy, immaculate, most worshipful and glorious Lady, the Mother of God and ever-virgin Mary, and all the saints, let us commend ourselves, each other, and all our life to Christ our God.

Lord almighty, God of our fathers, we pray thee to hear and have mercy upon us.

Help, save, pity and guard us, O God, by thy grace.

Kyrie eleison.

That this whole day be perfect, holy, peaceful, and sinless, let us ask the Lord.

Grant, O Lord.

For an angel of peace, a faithful guide and guardian of our souls and bodies, let us ask the Lord.

Grant, O Lord.

For pardon and forgiveness of our sins and offenses, let us ask the Lord.

Grant, O Lord.

For what is good and profitable to our souls, and for peace in the world, let us ask the Lord.

Grant, O Lord.

That our God send us his divine grace and the gifts of the Holy Ghost, let us ask the Lord.

Grant, O Lord.

That the rest of our lives be spent in peace and repentance, let us ask the Lord.

Grant, O Lord.

For a Christian end to our lives, without pain or blame, and peaceful, and for a good defense at his dread tribunal, let us ask the Lord.

Grant, O Lord.

Having prayed for union of faith and the communion of the
Holy Ghost, let us commend ourselves, each other, and our
whole life to Christ our God. Let us love one another, that we
may with one mind confess Father, Son and Holy Ghost, the
consubstantial and undivided Trinity.

And may the mercies of our great God and Saviour Jesus Christ
be with us all. *Amen.*

—from *Liturgy of St. John Chrysostom*

The Litany of the Sacred Heart of Jesus

Lord, have mercy on us.
  Christ, have mercy on us.
Lord, have mercy on us.
Christ, hear us.
  Christ, graciously hear us.
God the Father of heaven,
God the Son, Redeemer of the world,   *Have mercy on us.*
God the Holy Ghost,   [*repeat*]
Holy Trinity, one God,
Heart of Jesus, Son of the Eternal Father,
Heart of Jesus, formed by the Holy Ghost in the
        womb of the Virgin Mary.
Heart of Jesus, substantially united to the Word of
        God.
Heart of Jesus, of infinite majesty,
Heart of Jesus, Holy Temple of God,
Heart of Jesus, Tabernacle of the Most High,
Heart of Jesus, House of God, and Gate of Heaven,
Heart of Jesus, glowing furnace of charity,
Heart of Jesus, abode of justice and love,
Heart of Jesus, full of goodness and love,
Heart of Jesus, abyss of all virtues,

Heart of Jesus, most worthy of all praise,   *Have mercy on us.*

Heart of Jesus, King and centre of all hearts,   [*repeat*]

Heart of Jesus, wherein are all the treasures of wisdom and knowledge,

Heart of Jesus, wherein abides the fulness of the Godhead,

Heart of Jesus, in which the Father was well pleased,

Heart of Jesus, of whose fulness we have all received,

Heart of Jesus, desire of the eternal hills,

Heart of Jesus, patient and abounding in mercy,

Heart of Jesus, rich unto all that call upon Thee,

Heart of Jesus, source of life and holiness,

Heart of Jesus, atonement of our iniquities,

Heart of Jesus, glutted with reproaches,

Heart of Jesus, bruised for our sins,

Heart of Jesus, made obedient unto death,

Heart of Jesus, pierced by the lance,

Heart of Jesus, source of all consolation,

Heart of Jesus, our Life and Resurrection,

Heart of Jesus, our peace and reconciliation,

Heart of Jesus, Victim of sin,

Heart of Jesus, salvation of all who trust in Thee,

Heart of Jesus, hope of all who die in Thee,

Heart of Jesus, delight of all the saints, *Have mercy on us.*

Lamb of God who takest away the sins of the world, *Spare us, O Lord.*

Lamb of God, who takest away the sins of the world, *Graciously hear us, O Lord.*

Lamb of God, Who takest away the sins of the world, *Have mercy on us.*

Jesus, meek and humble of heart,

Make our hearts like unto Thine.

The Litany of the Most Holy Name of Jesus

Lord, have mercy on us.
>*Christ, have mercy on us.*
Lord, have mercy on us,
Jesus, hear us.
>*Jesus, graciously hear us.*

God the Father of heaven,   *Have mercy on us.*
God the Son, Redeemer of the world,   *[repeat]*
God the Holy Ghost,
Holy Trinity, one God,
Jesus, Son of the living God,
Jesus, splendor of the Father,
Jesus, brightness of eternal light,
Jesus, King of glory,
Jesus, sun of justice,
Jesus, Son of the Virgin Mary,
Jesus, most amiable,
Jesus, most admirable,
Jesus, mighty God,
Jesus, Father of the world to come,
Jesus, angel of great counsel,
Jesus, most powerful,
Jesus, most patient,
Jesus, most obedient,
Jesus, meek and humble of heart,
Jesus, lover of chastity,
Jesus, lover of us,
Jesus, God of peace,
Jesus, author of life,
Jesus, example of virtues,
Jesus, zealous lover of souls,
Jesus, our God,
Jesus, our refuge,
Jesus, Father of the poor,

Jesus, treasure of the faithful,   *Have mercy on us.*
Jesus, Good Shepherd,   *[repeat]*
Jesus, true light,
Jesus, eternal wisdom,
Jesus, infinite goodness,
Jesus, our way and our life,
Jesus, joy of Angels,
Jesus, King of Patriarchs,
Jesus, Master of the Apostles,
Jesus, Teacher of the Evangelists,
Jesus, strength of Martyrs,
Jesus, light of Confessors,
Jesus, purity of Virgins,
Jesus, crown of all Saints,   *Have mercy on us.*
Be merciful;
    Spare us, O Jesus,
Be merciful;
    Graciously hear us, O Jesus.
From all evil,   *Jesus, deliver us.*
From all sin,   *[repeat]*
From Thy wrath,
From the snares of the devil,
From the spirit of fornication,
From everlasting death,
From the neglect of Thy inspirations,
Through the mystery of Thy holy Incarnation,
Through Thy Nativity,
Through Thine infancy,
Through Thy most divine life,
Through Thy labors,
Through Thine Agony and Passion,
Through Thy cross and dereliction,
Through Thy sufferings,
Through Thy Death and Burial,
Through Thy Resurrection,

Through Thine Ascension,   *Jesus, deliver us.*
                                                [repeat]
Through Thine institution of the most holy Eucharist,
Through Thy joys,
Through Thy glory,
Lamb of God, Who takest away the sins of the world,
    Spare us, O Jesus.
Lamb of God, who takest away the sins of the world,
    Graciously hear us, O Jesus.
Lamb of God, who takest away the sins of the world,
    Have mercy on us, O Jesus.
Jesus, hear us.
    Jesus, graciously hear us.

The Litany of the Blessed Virgin

We fly to thy patronage, O holy Mother of God. Despise
not our petitions in our necessities; but deliver us from
all dangers, O ever-glorious and blessed Virgin.

Lord, have mercy on us.
Christ, have mercy on us.
Lord, have mercy on us.
Christ, hear us.
Christ, graciously hear us.
God, the Father of heaven, *Have mercy on us.*
God, the Son, Redeemer of the world, *Have mercy on us.*
God, the Holy Ghost, *Have mercy on us.*
Holy Trinity, one God, *Have mercy on us.*
Holy Mary, *Pray for us.*
Holy Mother of God, *Pray for us.*

Holy Virgin of virgins,   *Pray for us.*
Mother of Christ,   *[repeat]*

Mother of divine grace,   *Pray for us.*
Mother most pure,   *[repeat]*
Mother most chaste,
Mother inviolate,
Mother undefiled,
Mother most amiable,
Mother most admirable,
Mother of good counsel,
Mother of our Creator,
Mother of our Savior,
Virgin most prudent,
Virgin most venerable,
Virgin most renowned,
Virgin most powerful,
Virgin most merciful,
Virgin most faithful,
Mirror of justice,
Seat of wisdom,
Cause of our joy,
Spiritual vessel,
Vessel of honor,
Singular vessel of devotion,
Mystical rose,
Tower of David,
Tower of ivory,
House of gold,
Ark of the covenant,
Gate of heaven,
Morning star,
Health of the sick.
Refuge of sinners,
Comforter of the afflicted,
Help of Christians,
Queen of angels,
Queen of patriarchs,
Queen of prophets,

Queen of apostles,	*Pray for us.*
Queen of martyrs,	[*repeat*]
Queen of confessors,	
Queen of virgins,	
Queen of all saints,	
Queen conceived without original sin,	
Queen assumed into heaven,	
Queen of the most holy Rosary,	
Queen of peace,	

Lamb of God, who takest away the sins of the world,
   Spare us, O Lord!

Lamb of God, who takest away the sins of the world,
   Graciously hear us, O Lord!

Lamb of God, who takest away the sins of the world,
   Have mercy on us, O Lord!

We fly to thy patronage, O holy Mother of God. Despise not our petitions in our necessities; but deliver us from all dangers, O ever-glorious and blessed Virgin.

   Pray for us, O holy Mother of God.
   That we may be made worthy of the promises of Christ.

Let us pray

Pour forth, we beseech Thee, O Lord, Thy grace into our hearts; that as we have known the Incarnation of Christ Thy Son by the message of an angel, so by His Passion and Cross, we may be brought to the glory of His resurrection; through the same Christ our Lord. *Amen.*

   May the divine assistance remain always with us.
   Amen.

   And may the souls of the faithful departed, through the
      mercy of God, rest in peace.
   Amen.

Te Deum

The "Te Deum," traditionally supposed to have been composed by St. Ambrose, was at the beginning of the twentieth century proved to have been written by Niketas, who also composed many other hymns. The "Te Deum" is the traditional prayer of triumph, sung at coronations, celebrations of victory, and other occasions of joy.

We praise Thee, O God: we acknowledge Thee to be the Lord.
Thee, the Father everlasting, all the earth doth worship.
To Thee all angels; to Thee the heavens and all the powers:
To Thee the cherubim and seraphim continually cry:
Holy, holy, holy, Lord God of Sabaoth.
Heaven and earth are full of the majesty of Thy glory.
Thee, the glorious choir of the apostles,
Thee, the admirable company of prophets,
Thee, the white-robed army of martyrs, praise.
Thee, the holy Church throughout the world doth acknowl-
       edge:
The Father of infinite majesty;
The adorable, true and only Son;
Also, the Holy Ghost, the Comforter.

Thou, O Christ, art the King of glory,
Thou art the everlasting Son of the Father.
When Thou didst take upon Thee to deliver man,
Thou didst not disdain the Virgin's womb.
Having overcome the sting of death, Thou didst open the king-
       dom of heaven to all believers.
Thou sittest at the right hand of God, in the glory of the Father.
We believe that Thou shalt come to be our Judge.
We therefore pray Thee to help Thy servants, whom Thou hast
       redeemed with Thy Precious Blood.
Make them to be numbered with Thy saints in glory ever-
       lasting.
Save Thy people, O Lord, and bless Thy inheritance.
Govern them and raise them up forever.

Every day we bless Thee.
And we praise Thy name forever; yea, forever and ever.
Vouchsafe, O Lord, this day, to keep us from sin.
Have mercy on us, O Lord, have mercy on us.
Let Thy mercy, O Lord, be upon us, as we have hoped in Thee.
In Thee, O Lord, I have hoped, let me never be confounded.

—Niketas

The Memorare

This is a popular prayer to Our Lady, attributed to St. Bernard of Clairvaux. Its use was greatly popularized in the early seventeenth century.

Remember, O most gracious Virgin Mary, that never was it known that any one who fled to thy protection, implored thy help, or sought thy intercession, was left unaided. Inspired with this confidence, I fly unto thee, O Virgin of virgins, my mother; to thee I come, before thee I stand, sinful and sorrowful; O Mother of the Word Incarnate, despise not my petitions; but in thy clemency hear and answer me. *Amen.*

Tantum Ergo

This is the "Tantum Ergo" of St. Thomas Aquinas and is part of the Corpus Christi hymn, being sung at Benediction of the Blessed Sacrament.

Let us venerate on bended knee this august Sacrament;
And let the old order give place to the new rite;
Let faith supply for the defect of the senses.
To God the Father and to the Son, be praise and jubilation,
Adoration, honor, power and benediction;
And let equal praise be given to Him who proceeds from both. *Amen.*

Prayer

O God, who in this wonderful Sacrament hast left us a memorial of Thy Passion: grant us, we beseech Thee, so to reverence the sacred mysteries of Thy Body and Blood, that we may continually find in our souls the fruit of Thy Redemption. Who livest and reignest, world without end. *Amen.*

—St. Thomas Aquinas

GREAT JEWISH
PRAYERS

THE VISIBLE LINK *between the Jews and God was the great Temple of Solomon. In it reposed the Ark of the Covenant, and in the Ark were the stone tablets of the Commandments. The Temple foundations were made of stones bigger than twentieth-century automobiles. Above the east wall of Jerusalem, a cluster of gold grapes, four stories high, caught the morning sun as it tipped the top of the Mount of Olives. In the Temple 7,000 Levitical priests assisted at the holy sacrifices. When the Temple was destroyed by the Romans the Synagogue became the central locale of worship.*

It was David who acquired the property for the Temple. It was Solomon who built it. The Temple had such an enormous hold on the world of Jewry that now, 1,900 years after it was destroyed, it is still the symbol which fills the Jewish heart with longing to return to the Holy City.

There is greatness and grandeur, wisdom and sorrow in Jewry, and there is pride too. It shows up in the prayers of the faithful, which are among the oldest and most venerated in the history of man. If you are a Gentile, you will find, in reading this section, that there is a familiar ring to the phrasing of the prayers: the abasement before God, the plea for help, the complete adoration of the Divine Presence.

Rosh Hashana (New Year)

Rosh Hashana, the Jewish New Year, is also known as the Day of Remembrance. Second in importance only to the Day of Atonement (Yom Kippur), it is observed usually in September, on the first of the seventh month (Tishri) of the Jewish calendar.

Our God and God of our Fathers, sound the great Shofar for our freedom, lift up the ensign to gather our exiles; bring our scattered ones among the nations near unto thee, and gather our dispersed from the ends of the earth. Lead us with exultation unto Zion thy city, and unto Jerusalem the place of thy sanctuary with everlasting joy; and there we will prepare before thee the offerings that are obligatory for us, as is commanded us in thy Law through the hand of Moses thy servant from the mouth of thy glory, as it is said, and in the day of your gladness and in your set feasts, and in the beginnings of your months, ye shall blow with the trumpets over your burnt offerings, and over the sacrifices of your peace offerings; and they shall be to you for a memorial before your God: I am the Lord your God. For thou hearest the sound of the Shofar and givest heed to the trumpet-blast, and there is none like unto thee. Blessed art thou, O Lord, who in mercy hearest the sound of the trumpet-blast of thy people Israel.

Accept, O Lord our God, thy people Israel and their prayer; restore the service to the oracle of thy house; receive in love and favor both the fire-offerings of Israel and their prayer; and may the service of thy people Israel be ever acceptable unto thee.

—from the Traditional *Musaf* Service for the New Year

The Grandeur of the Holy Day

This prayer, dating back to the eleventh century, describes the procedure of the heavenly court on the Day of Judgment. It is one of the most emotional of Jewish prayers offered in the Synagogue.

Let us tell how utterly holy this day is and how awe-inspiring. It is the day when thy dominion shall be exalted, thy throne shall be established on mercy, and thou shalt occupy it in truth. True it is that thou art judge and arbiter, discerner and witness, inscribing and recording all forgotten things. Thou openest the book of records and it reads itself; every man's signature is contained in it.

The great shofar is sounded; a gentle whisper is heard; the angels, quaking with fear, declare: "The day of judgment is here to bring the hosts of heaven to justice!" Indeed, even they are not guiltless in thy sight. All mankind passes before thee like a flock of sheep. As a shepherd seeks out his flock, making his sheep pass under his rod, so dost thou make all the living souls pass before thee; thou dost count and number thy creatures, fixing their lifetime and inscribing their destiny.

On Rosh Hashanah their destiny is inscribed, and on Yom Kippur it is sealed, how many shall pass away and how many shall be brought into existence; who shall live and who shall die; who shall come to a timely end, and who to an untimely end; who shall perish by fire and who by water; who by sword and who by beast; who by hunger and who by thirst; who by earthquake and who by plague; who by strangling and who by stoning; who shall be at ease and who shall wander about; who shall be at peace and who shall be molested; who shall have comfort and who shall be tormented; who shall become poor and who shall become rich; who shall be lowered and who shall be raised.

But repentance, prayer and charity cancel the stern decree.
—from *High Holyday Prayer Book*

Sounding of the Shofar

The following verses are from the Shofar service of the Jewish New Year.
Featured by the blowing of a ram's horn, this service symbolizes the contrite and the confessing. It is a call to the slumbering conscience of man
to search his heart and meditate over his journey in life.

Give heed to the sound of the Shofar,
The sharp, piercing blasts of the Shofar,
Rending the air with its message,
Its portent of heav'nly salvation,
Summoning man to his Father
To render Him homage, devotion.
Renounce ye your sins and transgressions,
False aims and vainglorious striving;
Infuse in your hearts a new spirit
To build a new earth and new heaven.
Heed ye the sound of the Shofar,
The blast that is blown, O my people.

Give heed to the blasts of the Shofar,
The shrill quiv'ring notes of the Shofar,
Sounding its message of warning,
Its cry of alarm and awakening—
Urging us work with our brothers
To combat the ills that beset man.
Accept ye the challenge to triumph
O'er forces of wrath and destruction.
Remove from your midst crime and warfare,
All poverty, greed, and contention.
Heed ye the sound of the Shofar,
The blast that is blown, O my people.

Give heed to the sound of the Shofar,
The loud clarion call of the Shofar,
Bringing bright hope to a people
Long scattered and stricken with sorrow;

Comforting Israel with promise
Of healing divine and redemption.
Renew ye your faith in God's covenant
That made you a nation through Torah.
Return to your God and establish
A Kingdom of Peace for all people.
Heed ye the sound of the Shofar.
The blast that is blown, O my people.

—from *High Holiday Prayer Book*

Yom Kippur (Day of Atonement)

Yom Kippur, the Day of Atonement, is the most sacred Hebrew Holy
Day, and falls at the end of September or beginning of October, ten
days after Rosh Hashana (New Year). It is a day of fasting and prayer
for forgiveness of sins committed during the year. The following prayer
is a recitation of confession repeated throughout all of the services on
Yom Kippur.

Our God and God of our fathers, pardon our iniquities on
this Day of Atonement; blot out our transgressions and our
sins, and make them pass away from before thine eyes; as it is
said, I, even I, am he that blotteth out thy transgressions for
mine own sake; and I will not remember thy sins. And it is
said, I have blotted out, as a cloud, thy transgressions, and as
a mist, thy sins: return unto me, for I have redeemed thee. And
it is said, For on this day shall atonement be made for you, to
cleanse you; from all your sins shall ye be clean before the
Lord. Sanctify us by thy commandments, and grant our portion in thy Law; satisfy us with thy goodness, and gladden us
with thy salvation; and purify our hearts to serve thee in truth;
for thou art the forgiver of Israel and the pardoner of the
tribes of Jeshurun in every generation, and beside thee we have
no king who pardoneth and forgiveth. Blessed art thou, O

Lord, thou King who pardonest and forgivest our iniquities
and the iniquities of thy people, the house of Israel, who makest
our trespasses to pass away year by year, King over all the
earth, who sanctifiest Israel and the Day of Atonement.

Our God and God of our fathers, let our prayer come before
thee; hide not thyself from our supplication, for we are not
arrogant and stiff-necked, that we should say before thee, O
Lord our God and God of our fathers, we are righteous and
have not sinned; but verily, we have sinned.

We have trespassed, we have been faithless, we have robbed,
we have spoken basely, we have committed iniquity, we have
wrought unrighteousness, we have been presumptuous, we
have done violence, we have forged lies, we have counseled
evil, we have spoken falsely, we have scoffed, we have revolted,
we have blasphemed, we have been rebellious, we have acted
perversely, we have transgressed, we have persecuted, we have
been stiff-necked, we have done wickedly, we have corrupted
ourselves, we have committed abomination, we have gone
astray, and we have led astray.

We have turned aside from thy commandments and good
judgments, and it hath profited us nought. But thou art righteous in all that is come upon us; for thou hast acted truthfully,
but we have wrought unrighteousness.

What shall we say before thee, O thou who dwellest on
high, and what shall we recount unto thee, thou who abidest
in the heavens? dost thou not know all things, both the hidden
and the revealed?

Thou knowest the secrets of eternity and the most hidden
mysteries of all living. Thou searchest the innermost recesses,
and triest the reins and the heart. Nought is concealed from
thee, or hidden from thine eyes.

May it then be thy will, O Lord our God and God of our
fathers, to forgive us for all our sins, to pardon us for all our
iniquities, and to grant us remission for all our transgressions.

Kol Nidre Prayer

This prayer is given at the Evening Service on Yom Kippur. In ancient times, as in our day, vows unto the Lord were often rashly made. In the precarious eras in which our forefathers lived, circumstances beyond their control frequently denied them the opportunity of fulfilling their vows. Recognizing that the broken word profaned the soul, they developed the earnest desire to have such vows nullified on the Day of Atonement, when men yearned to be at peace with God and their fellow men. The following legal formula, known as the Kol Nidre, was the result. It applies only to those vows which an individual makes to his God and in which no other persons are involved.

Our God and God of our fathers, as evening casts its shadows over the earth, ushering in the most solemn day of the year, we join with our fellow Jews throughout the world in prayer and meditation. We put aside all petty thoughts and vain desires. What is our life, and of what avail our strength? What is our wealth, and to what purpose our power? We lift up our eyes unto Thee, O Lord, and yearn for Thy light and inspiration. On this Kol Nidre Night, sanctified by sacred memories, united with the generations of the past, recalling the piety and devotion of our ancestors, we stand in Thy presence stripped of all pretence and revealed in all our weakness. O Thou who seest all, Thou knowest how frail and fragile we are.

We aim toward lofty heights, but temptation overcomes us. Greed and vanity blind our eyes, envy and arrogance eat into the marrow of our bones, false ambitions bring us bitter remorse, and selfishness dwarfs our souls. We are creatures of haphazard living. We stumble and fall; we grope and wander. O Lord, strengthen us in our weak moments and guide our faltering footsteps. Speak to our hearts with the still small voice of Thy Spirit so that we may search our ways and return unto Thee. Cause us to be forgiving even as we ask to be forgiven. Cause us to discover the faults of our ways and the errors into which we have fallen, so that we may not repeat the trespasses for which we repent this day.

Amidst the uncertainties and tragedies of life, we need Thee, O God. Only when we are aware of Thee do we have fortitude, vision and hope. Out of the depths of our hearts do we call upon Thee. O hearken unto our voice and attend our prayer. Turn us unto Thee, O Lord, so that we may be at peace with ourselves and with our fellow men. On this sacred night, may we heed the admonition of Thy prophet, to cast away our sins and transgressions and make us a new heart and a new spirit. *Amen.*

—from *High Holiday Prayer Book*

Kol Nidre Meditation

Kol Nidre—chant of ages,
Chant of grief and chant of triumph,
Echoing, this night of mem'ries,
In the ears and heart of Israel,
Once again you draw together
All dispersed and all God's faithful
To return and humbly seek Him,—
Suppliants for His grace and pardon.
Faced by grim, appalling forces
In these days of woeful living,
Do we plead before God's mercy
For His strength, His help, His guidance.
With your plaintive chant, Kol Nidre,
Rise our prayers to heaven ascending,
For a surcease of man's sorrows,
For the dawn of peace and freedom,
When all hearts are purged of hatred,
Passions, lusts that rend asunder.
Then all men will stand together
To acknowledge God, their Father.

—from *High Holiday Prayer Book*

Sukkoth (Feast of Tabernacles)

Sukkoth, the Feast of Tabernacles, is one of the most joyous of the Jewish holidays. It begins on the fifteenth day of the Tishri, five days after Yom Kippur, and lasts for nine days until the Simhath Torah, or rejoicing over the Law.

O Living God, we thank Thee that Thou hast not left us to grope after Thee in the dark; that Thy law has been a lamp unto our feet, and a light unto our path. In this harvest season, when Thy people had gathered in their crops, Thy law did enjoin upon them to leave their homes and make their abode in frail booths. Thus didst Thou remind them of the transient nature of earthly possessions, of the insecurity of a life stayed on prosperity without faith in Thee.

Vouchsafe unto us, too, O Father, an understanding of this truth, so that no arrogance may tarnish the joy of success, no self-exaltation debase the love of achievement. Teach us to be humble. Keep far from us the pride of possession and the despair of want. In poverty save us, O God, from bitterness; in abundance rescue us from self-indulgence. Incline our hearts unto Thee and keep us from covetousness. Kindle within us a passion for a better world. Enlarge our sympathies, make us eager to ease the sorrow and distress of men and thus learn to know the joy of service. Lift up our eyes that, like our fathers, we too may see, through the leafy booth, the light of sun and star so that our souls may soar to Thee.

—from *Union Prayer Book*

Rock of Ages

This famous hymn, known as "Mooz Tsur," has become a regular part of the Hanukkah services. The Festival of Lights, Hanukkah, or the Feast of the Maccabees, was begun by Judas Maccabaeus and his brothers in 165 B.C. to celebrate the dedication of the new sacrificial altar in the Temple of Jerusalem after the successful revolt against Antiochus in which the pagan altar he had decreed for the Jews was overthrown.

Rock of Ages, let our song
   Praise Thy saving power;
Thou amidst the raging foes,
   Wast our shelt'ring tower.
Furious they assailed us,
But Thine arm availed us.
      And Thy word
      Broke their sword
When our own strength failed us.

Kindling new the holy lamps,
   Priests approved in suffering,
Purified the nation's shrine,
   Brought to God their offering.
And His courts surrounding,
Hear, in joy abounding,
      Happy throngs
      Singing songs
Far and wide resounding.

Children of the martyr-race,
   Whether free or fettered,
Wake the echoes of the songs
   Where ye may be scattered,
Yours the message cheering,
That the time is nearing
      Which shall see
      All men free,
Tyrants disappearing.
                 —from *Union Prayer Book*

Purim (Feast of Esther)

Purim is the Jewish festival celebrated on the fourteenth and fifteenth of Adar, sixth month of the calendar. It commemorates the deliverance of the Persian Jews from massacre by Haman, according to the *Book of Esther*. It is a day of joy, marked by merrymaking and feasting. Other features are exchange of gifts, giving of alms to the poor, and the presentation of Purim plays by children.

Thou, O Lord, pleadest the cause of the just, and defeatest the devices of the cruel. The counsel of the heathen, Thou bringest to nought; the devices of the crafty, Thou makest of no effect.

We bless Thee, O Lord our God, that Thou hast sustained us in life and preserved the house of Israel unto this day. Thou didst work miracles for our fathers in the days of old, and hast enabled us to survive the enemies of Thy truth. When Haman rose up against us, Thou didst cause the devotion of Mordecai and the loving-kindness of Esther to triumph over unjust wrath and hate. The righteous were delivered out of the hand of the wicked, and those who sought to destroy were themselves destroyed. Thou hast ever been Israel's salvation, our hope in every generation. None that trusts in Thee shall be put to shame.

We pray Thee, O Father, that in the presence of cruelty and wrong our hearts remain steadfast and true. When evil men plot against us and seek to uproot us, let not despair drain our strength nor fear chill our faith. Teach us to meet enmity with courage and hope, and to battle against adversity with resolute will and unyielding self-possession. Keep alive within us the vision of our higher purposes and nobler destiny, and renew our zeal for the divine tasks of life. Open our hearts to the cry of the persecuted and the despoiled. Hasten the day when hate and strife shall cease to divide the family of men, and justice and love reign supreme in the world.

—from *Union Prayer Book*

Passover Prayer

Passover, one of the most important of the Jewish festivals, begins on the evening of the first month of the Hebrew religious calendar, corresponding to March–April, and lasts for seven days. Orthodox Jews celebrate it in commemoration of their deliverance from the yoke of Egypt in Mosaic times. Seders, or Jewish home festivals, are held the first and second nights of the Passover, with various special dishes symbolizing the hardships of the Israelites during their bondage; the story of the Exodus is recited and praise given to God for their deliverance.

Lord of all generations, the past is Thy handiwork and the glories of the future Thy promise. On this festival of Passover, we are gathered in Thy house to recall Thy wonders of old. When we were slaves in Egypt and suffered the lash of taskmasters, Thou didst send thy servants, Moses and Aaron, to stand in the presence of Pharaoh and proclaim in Thy name: Let my people go that they may serve Me. The cruel heart of the tyrant and the might of his armies did not avail against Thy liberating word and Israel marched forth from Egypt with songs and rejoicing to find freedom in Thy service.

This was Thy will in ancient days and it is Thy law forever. Wherever the yoke of serfdom is broken, wherever tyrants are overthrown, wherever Thy children live as free men, there is Thy word fulfilled and Thy will triumphant. To every soul comes Thy command: Be servants unto Me alone and not slaves to man.

Teach us, O God, to accept and cherish Thy law of liberty. Guide us with Thy wisdom that we may grow in knowledge and in sympathy and keep our judgment free from passion or prejudice. May we strive for the redemption of our souls and thus become messengers of freedom to all Thy children.

In Thy power, O Lord, is the fate of nations. Thou who didst break Pharaoh's yoke and bid the slaves go free, be Thou our help in every time of peril. Let all men see that the might of armies and the power of tyrants must vanish like smoke before the force of Thy spirit. May the coming year bring a new Passover of freedom to all Thy children in every land. *Amen.*

—from *Union Prayer Book*

Shabuoth (Festival of Weeks)

The Feast of Weeks, of Harvest, and of the Firstfruits is the Palestinian celebration of the closing of the grain harvest and falls fifty days from the second day of Passover. From ancient times it was known also as the anniversary of the giving of the Law. Today synagogues and homes are decorated with flowers, study of the law takes place all night, and the confirmation of girls is celebrated.

O everliving God, Thou art our unfailing Guide; Thy word is the law of our life. On this festival of Shabuoth we commemorate the sacred day when Israel entered into covenant with Thee. Freed from Pharaoh's bondage our fathers journeyed through the wilderness till at last they stood in reverence at the foot of Sinai and heard the unforgettable words: I am the Lord thy God.

Wherever our fathers wandered they carried the memory of Thy revelation. Written upon the tablets of their heart was Thy behest that they dedicate their lives to Thee and merit the dignity of priesthood in Thy service. In Thy Name they strove to break the yoke of the oppressed, and to bring freedom to the captive. They gave bread to the hungry and shelter to the homeless. They sought an ever deeper knowledge of Thee and Thy will, that they might open the eyes of the blind and lead all men to the light of Thy presence.

On this day of Israel's dedication, we pray for renewed awareness of Thy revelation. When the world is filled with sor-

row and confusion and the path is hidden from our gaze, help
us to see Thine eternal purpose. Strengthen our confidence in
the triumph of justice among men and nations. Confirm our
faith in Thy covenant that we may continue to carry Thy message of brotherhood and peace among all the children of men.

—from *Union Prayer Book*

The Yigdal

The Yigdal appears at the beginning or end of the Morning Service in
the Orthodox observance on the Sabbath. Its authorship is uncertain,
although the Yigdal is supposed to have been written in Italy in the
fourteenth century and based on the thirteen articles of the Creed of
Maimonides.

1. The living God O magnify and bless,
   Transcending Time and here eternally.

2. One being, yet unique in unity;
   A mystery of Oneness and measureless.

3. Lo! form or body He has none, and man
   No semblance of His holiness can frame.

4. Before Creation's dawn He was the same;
   The first to be, though never He began.

5. He is the world's and every creature's Lord;
   His rule and majesty are manifest,

6. And through His chosen, glorious sons exprest
   In prophecies that through their lips are poured.

7. Yet never like to Moses rose a seer,
   Permitted glimpse behind the veil divine.

8. This faithful prince of God's prophetic line
   Received the Law of Truth for Israel's ear.

9. The Law God gave He never will amend,
   Nor ever by another Law replace.

10. Our secret things are spread before His face;
    In all beginnings He beholds the end.

11. The saint's reward He measures to his meed;
    The sinner repays the harvest of his ways.

12. Messiah He will send at end of days,
    And all the faithful to salvation lead.

13. God will the dead again to life restore
    In His abundance of Almighty love.
                              —from the traditional *Siddur*

Prayer on Awakening

The Talmud is the vast compilation of the oral law of the Jews in con-
tradistinction to the Scriptures or written laws. In the Middle Ages *The
Talmud* was sometimes censored and even burned by Christians, but
it has persisted and been recognized by Jews through the centuries as
the living law.

O my God, the soul which thou gavest me is pure; thou didst
create it, thou didst form it, thou didst breathe it into me; and
thou wilt take it from me, but wilt restore it unto me hereafter.
So long as the soul is within me, I will give thanks unto thee,
O Lord my God and God of my fathers, Sovereign of all works,
Lord of all souls! Blessed art thou, O Lord, who restores souls
unto dead bodies.
                              —from *The Talmud Berakhothbob*

Morning Song

Solomon ibn-Gabirol, the great master of Spanish-Jewish poetry, lived in Spain in the medieval period. This poem by him, part of the Morning Service, found its way into the ritual after having been written in a great period of Jewish literary activity.

> At the dawn, I seek Thee,
>   Refuge and rock sublime,—
> Set my prayer before Thee in the morning,
>   And my prayer at eventime.
>
> I before Thy greatness
>   Stand and am afraid:—
> All my secret thoughts Thine eye beholdeth
>   Deep within my bosom laid.
>
> And withal what is it
>   Heart and tongue can do?
> What is this my strength, and what is even
>   This the spirit in me too?
>
> But verily man's singing
>   May seem good to Thee;
> So will I thank Thee, praising, while there
>   dwelleth
>   Yet the breath of God in me.
>   —from *Sabbath and Festival Prayer Book*

Kiddush for Sabbath Evening

The following prayer is said in the Home by the Master of the House, previous to partaking of the Sabbath Meal.

"And it was evening and it was morning, the sixth day. And the heaven and the earth were finished and all their host. And on the seventh day God had finished his work which he had made; and he rested on the seventh day from all his work which he had made. And God blessed the seventh day, and he hallowed it, because he rested thereon from all his work which God had created and made."

Blessed art Thou, O Lord our God, King of the universe, who createst the fruit of the vine.

Blessed art thou, O Lord our God, King of the universe, who hast hallowed us by thy commandments and hast taken pleasure in us, and in love and favour hast given us thy holy Sabbath as an inheritance, a memorial of the creation—that day being also the first of the holy convocations, in remembrance of the departure from Egypt. For thou hast chosen us and hallowed us above all nations, and in love and favour hast given us thy holy Sabbath as an inheritance. Blessed art thou, O Lord, who hallowest the Sabbath.

Blessed art thou, O Lord our God, King of the universe, who bringest forth bread from the earth.

—from *The Daily Prayer Book of the United Hebrew Congregations*
of the British Empire

Sabbath Prayer

Among Jews as early as the period of the Kings it was customary to visit the Temple or a prophet on the Sabbath. The Sabbath day was filled with readings from the Scriptures and with their interpretation. The place of prayers was modest. The Reform Movement shortened and modified the service.

Our God and God of our fathers, grant that our worship on this Sabbath be acceptable to Thee. Sanctify us through Thy commandments that we may share in the blessings of Thy word. Teach us to be satisfied with the gifts of Thy goodness and gratefully to rejoice in all Thy mercies. Purify our hearts that we may serve Thee in truth. O help us to preserve the Sabbath as Israel's heritage from generation to generation, that it may ever bring rest and joy, peace and comfort to the dwellings of our brethren, and through it Thy name be hallowed in all the earth. Praised be Thou, O Lord, Who sanctifiest the Sabbath.

—from *Union Prayer Book*

Kiddush Services in the Home

Home services on Sabbath Eve were observed among Jews as far back as the time of the Second Temple and continued even after public services were introduced. The table is given a festive appearance. A wine cup and a loaf of bread for the blessing are set before the head of the household. The ceremony of ushering in the Sabbath is begun by the kindling of the lights, during which a blessing by the wife is silently asked upon the home and the dear ones.

May our home be consecrated, O God, by Thy light. May it shine upon us all in blessing as the light of love and truth, the light of peace and goodwill. *Amen.*

When all are seated, the head of the household says:

Come, let us welcome the Sabbath in joy and peace! Like a bride, radiant and joyous, comes the Sabbath. She brings blessings to our hearts; workday thoughts and cares are put aside. The brightness of the Sabbath light shines forth to tell that the divine spirit of love abides within our home. In that light all our blessings are enriched, all our griefs and trials are softened.

At this hour, God's messenger of peace comes and turns the hearts of the parents to the children, and the hearts of the children to the parents, strengthening the bonds of devotion to that pure and lofty ideal of the home found in Sacred Writ.

The head of the household lifts the wine cup and says:

Let us praise God with this symbol of joy, and thank Him for the blessings of the past week, for life, health, and strength, for home, love, and friendship, for the discipline of our trials and temptations, for the happiness that has come to us out of our labors. Thou hast ennobled us, O God, by the blessings of work, and in love and kindness Thou hast sanctified us by the blessing of rest through the commandment: "Six days shalt thou labor and do all thy work, but the seventh day is the Sabbath hallowed unto the Lord, Thy God."

Praised be Thou, O Lord our God, King of the universe, who hast created the fruit of the vine.

The wine cup is passed round the table and each in turn drinks from it. The head of the household then breaks the bread and, dipping a piece of it in salt, pronounces the blessing:

Praised be Thou, O Lord our God, King of the universe, who causest the earth to yield food for all.

Each one at the table likewise partakes of bread and salt. Then the parent, with hands upon the head of each child in turn, silently pronounces a blessing as follows:

May the God of our fathers bless you. May He who has guided us unto this day lead you to be an honor to our family. May He who has protected us from all evil make you a blessing to Israel and to all mankind. *Amen.*

—from *Union Prayer Book*

Olenu (The Adoration)

This prayer is repeated at the end of each of the three daily services by Reform Jews. It is considered one of the most sublime in the Jewish Liturgy, expressing as it does a lofty spiritual and social mood.

Let us adore the ever-living God, and render praise unto Him who spread out the heavens and established the earth, whose glory is revealed in the heavens above and whose greatness is manifested throughout the world. He is our God; there is none else.

We bow the head in reverence, and worship the King of kings, the Holy One, praised be He.

May the time not be distant, O God, when Thy name shall be worshipped in all the earth, when unbelief shall disappear and error be no more. Fervently we pray that the day may come when all men shall invoke Thy name, when corruption and evil shall give way to purity and goodness, when superstition shall no longer enslave the mind, nor idolatry blind the eye, when all who dwell on earth shall know that to Thee alone every knee must bend and every tongue give homage. O may all, created in Thine image, recognize that they are brethren, so that, one in spirit and one in fellowship, they may be forever united before Thee. Then shall Thy kingdom be established on earth and the word of Thine ancient seer be fulfilled: the Lord will reign forever and ever. On that day the Lord shall be One and His name shall be One.

—from *Union Prayer Book*

A Mother's Prayer

This is a particularly beautiful prayer taken from one of the early Jewish prayer books printed in English in the United States.

My God, to Thee my heart is uplifted, as I commend unto Thy protecting care those dearest on earth to me. Guard well my husband and my children, all the members of my family, and all the inmates of my home. Preserve them from sorrow and misfortune; hold suffering and ailment far from us, that we may fear neither the dangers of the day nor the terrors of the night.

May Thy providence hold watch and ward over us in the performance of our daily duties. Give me Thine aid in controlling vain promptings within me so that I may rule my life with virtue and uprightness before Thee. Preserve me from idleness and foolish yearning for worldly pleasure; teach me that in my home I shall find my purest joys, my most pleasurable emotions in acts of womanly devotion, self-forgetfulness and simplicity. Bless me and those I love with health and cheerfulness: shield us all from temptation and sin. Let us find favor and regard in Thine eyes and in the eyes of all good men. Sustain and strengthen my husband in his daily labors; give him courage and endurance. Preserve for ever the tranquility of our happy home and the peace that dwells in our hearts. For this I beseech Thee, for this have I set my heart before Thee, Lord, my rock and my redeemer. *Amen.*

—from *Jewish Home Prayer Book* (1887)

Introductory Prayer to the Kaddish

The Mourner's Kaddish, which follows this introductory Reform prayer, is one of the most sacred prayers of the Jewish faith and is daily recited by Jews throughout the world as an act of reverence to their departed father or mother during the period of mourning which lasts for a year. It is also said one day a year thereafter, on the Yahrzeit, or anniversary of a death.

All you who mourn the loss of loved ones, and, at this hour, remember the sweet companionship and the cherished hopes that have passed away with them, give ear to the word of comfort spoken in the name of God. Only the body has died and has been laid in the dust. The spirit lives in the shelter of God's love and mercy. Our loved ones continue, also, in the remembrance of those to whom they were precious. Their deeds of loving-kindness, the true and beautiful words they spoke are treasured up as incentives to conduct by which the living honor the dead. And when we ask in our grief: Whence shall come our help and our comfort? then in the strength of faith let us answer with the Psalmist: My help cometh from God. He will not forsake us nor leave us in our grief. Upon Him we cast our burden and He will grant us strength according to the days He has apportioned to us. All life comes from Him; all souls are in His keeping. Come then, and in the midst of sympathizing fellow worshipers, rise and hallow the name of God.

—from *Union Prayer Book*

Mourner's Kaddish

MOURNERS: Magnified and sanctified be his great Name in the world which he hath created according to his will. May he establish his kingdom during your days, and during the life of all the house of Israel, even speedily and at the near time, and say ye, *Amen*.

CONGREGATION AND MOURNERS: Let his great Name be blessed for ever and to all eternity.

MOURNERS: Blessed, praised and glorified, exalted, extolled and honoured, magnified and lauded be the Name of the Holy One, blessed be he; though he be high above all the blessings and hymns, praises and consolations, which are uttered in the world; and say ye, *Amen.*

CONGREGATION: Let the Name of the Lord be blessed from this time forth for evermore.

MOURNERS: May there be abundant peace from heaven and life for us and for all Israel; and say ye, *Amen.*

CONGREGATION: My help is from the Lord, who made heaven and earth.

MOURNERS: He who maketh peace in his high places, may he make peace for us and for all Israel; and say ye, *Amen.*

GREAT BIBLE PRAYERS

Here, gleaned from *the Old Testament and the New, are some of the most inspired prayers left as legacies to spiritually starving mankind. Some readers will be moved by one prayer, some by another. My personal selection for the greatest of these prayers from the Bible was used daily by my grandmother, Mary Murphy Bishop, and it consists of four words: "Thy Will be Done."*

In Christmas week of 1898, three of her children died of diphtheria. When the undertaker and his assistant carried the three white caskets into the house, Grandma came into the room, looked down on each little face impassively, dropped to her knees and lifted her arms to heaven and said, "Thy Will be Done."

She did not weep. As an afterthought, she said, "If You will grant me three more, I will name them after these, Margaret, Mary, and James." She was granted two more daughters, and she kept her promise. Then her husband died, and she was left with four children. She said the four words again.

It is possible that the prayer would not have meant as much to me had I not heard the story of courage which goes with it. However, I prefer to think that this is not true. Its complete resignation would have appealed to me in any case.

Abraham Talks with God

Abraham or Abram is progenitor of the Hebrews, according to the *Book of Genesis*. The prayer following was spoken by Abraham when Sodom and Gomorrah were threatened with destruction and God was on his way to look over Sodom and decide about the fate of the wicked city. Two angels have gone ahead to talk first with Lot. God remains for a time at the abode of Abraham, while Abraham speaks directly with the Lord.

And Abraham drew near, and said, Wilt thou also destroy the righteous with the wicked? Peradventure there be fifty righteous within the city: wilt thou also destroy and not spare the place for the fifty righteous that are therein? That be far from thee to do after this manner, to slay the righteous with the wicked: and that the righteous should be as the wicked, that be far from thee: Shall not the Judge of all the earth do right?

And the Lord said, If I find in Sodom fifty righteous within the city, then I will spare all the place for their sakes.

And Abraham answered and said, Behold now, I have taken upon me to speak unto the Lord, which am but dust and ashes: Peradventure there shall lack five of the fifty righteous: wilt thou destroy all the city for lack of five? And he said, If I find there forty and five, I will not destroy it.

And he spake unto him yet again, and said, Peradventure there shall be forty found there. And he said, I will not do it for forty's sake.

And he said unto him, Oh let not the Lord be angry, and I will speak: Peradventure there shall thirty be found there. And he said, I will not do it, if I find thirty there.

And he said, Behold now, I have taken upon me to speak unto the Lord: Peradventure there shall be twenty found there. And he said, I will not destroy it for twenty's sake.

And he said, Oh let not the Lord be angry, and I will speak yet but this once: Peradventure ten shall be found there. And he said, I will not destroy it for ten's sake.

—*Genesis* 18:23–32

Jacob's Prayer for Deliverance from Esau

Jacob was the younger of the twin sons of Isaac, son of Abraham. Esau, the Hairy One, was the other brother. After Jacob had gained the inheritance from Esau by trickery and had finally settled in Mahanaim some years later with two wives, many sons, and great wealth, he sent messengers to Esau to make his peace with him. Uncertain of Esau's reception of these overtures, Jacob prays to God.

And Jacob said, O God of my father Abraham, and God of my father Isaac, the Lord which saidst unto me, Return unto thy country, and to thy kindred, and I will deal well with thee: I am not worthy of the least of all the mercies, and of all the truth, which thou hast showed unto thy servant; for with my staff I passed over this Jordan; and now I am become two bands. Deliver me, I pray thee, from the hand of my brother, from the hand of Esau: for I fear him, lest he will come and smite me, and the mother with the children. And thou saidst, I will surely do thee good, and make thy seed as the sand of the sea, which cannot be numbered for multitude.

—*Genesis* 32:9–12

The Lord's Answer

And Jacob lifted up his eyes, and looked, and, behold, Esau came, and with him four hundred men. And he divided the children.... And he passed over before them, and bowed himself to the ground seven times, until he came near to his brother. And Esau ran to meet him, and embraced him, and fell on his neck, and kissed him: and they wept.

—*Genesis* 33:1, 3–4

A Prayer of Moses

Moses, lawgiver of Israel, led his people out of their Egyptian bondage to the land of Canaan, was divinely protected in childhood and led to become the greatest prophet of the Hebrews. His story is told in the books of *Exodus, Leviticus, Numbers* and *Deuteronomy*, but the prayer here quoted is from *Psalms* and bears the caption "A Prayer of Moses, the Man of God."

Lord, thou hast been our dwelling-place in all generations.

Before the mountains were brought forth, or ever thou hadst formed the earth and the world, even from everlasting to everlasting, thou art God.

Thou turnest man to destruction; and sayest, Return, ye children of men.

For a thousand years in thy sight are but as yesterday when it is past, and as a watch in the night.

Thou carriest them away as with a flood; they are as a sleep: in the morning they are like grass which groweth up.

In the morning it flourisheth, and groweth up; in the evening it is cut down, and withereth.

For we are consumed by thine anger, and by thy wrath are we troubled.

Thou hast set our iniquities before thee, our secret sins in the light of thy countenance.

For all our days are passed away in thy wrath; we spend our years as a tale that is told.

The days of our years are threescore years and ten; and if by reason of strength they be fourscore years, yet is their strength labor and sorrow: for it is soon cut off, and we fly away.

Who knoweth the power of thine anger? even according to thy fear, so is thy wrath.

So teach us to number our days, that we may apply our hearts unto wisdom.

Return, O Lord, how long? and let it repent thee concerning thy servants.

O satisfy us early with thy mercy; that we may rejoice and be glad all our days.

Make us glad according to the days wherein thou hast afflicted us, and the years wherein we have seen evil.

Let thy work appear unto thy servants, and thy glory unto
their children.

And let the beauty of the Lord our God be upon us: and
establish thou the work of our hands upon us; yea, the work
of our hands establish thou it.

—Psalm 90

Hannah's Prayer

Hannah was the mother of the great Hebrew prophet Samuel. Her song
is recalled in the "Magnificat." Hannah was one of the two wives of
Elkanah who lived near Shiloh, and being without child she wept before
the priest Eli at the temple in Shiloh and prayed.

And she was in bitterness of soul, and prayed unto the Lord,
and wept sore.

And she vowed a vow, and said, O Lord of hosts, if thou
wilt indeed look on the affliction of thine handmaid, and remember me, and not forget thine handmaid, but wilt give unto
thine handmaid a man child, then I will give him unto the Lord
all the days of his life, and there shall no razor come upon his
head.

—I Samuel 1:10–11

Hannah's Thanksgiving

(*And the Lord remembered her . . . she bare a son and called his name Samuel, saying, Because I have asked him of the Lord.*)

And Hannah prayed, and said, My heart rejoiceth in the Lord, mine horn is exalted in the Lord, my mouth is enlarged over mine enemies because I rejoice in thy salvation.

There is none holy as the Lord: for there is none beside thee: neither is there any rock like our God.

Talk no more so exceeding proudly; let not arrogancy come out of your mouth: for the Lord is a God of knowledge, and by him actions are weighed.

The bows of the mighty men are broken, and they that stumbled are girded with strength.

They that were full have hired out themselves for bread; and they that were hungry ceased: so that the barren hath born seven; and she that hath many children is waxed feeble.

The Lord killeth, and maketh alive: he bringeth down to the grave, and bringeth up.

The Lord maketh poor, and maketh rich: he bringeth low, and lifteth up.

He raiseth up the poor out of the dust, and lifteth up the beggar from the dunghill, to set them among princes, and to make them inherit the throne of glory: for the pillars of the earth are the Lord's, and he hath set the world upon them.

He will keep the feet of his saints, and the wicked shall be silent in darkness; for by strength shall no man prevail.

The adversaries of the Lord shall be broken to pieces; out of heaven shall he thunder upon them: the Lord shall judge the ends of the earth; and he shall give strength unto his King, and exalt the horn of his Anointed.

—*I Samuel* 2:1–10

David's Prayer

David was king of the ancient Hebrews about 1013 to 973 B.C. His reign marked the change of the Jews from a loose confederation of tribes to a settled nation. After the removal of the capital from Hebron to Jerusalem, the building of the Temple was projected as part of the process of making this city the eternal center of the Jews. This prayer was made in the presence of his son Solomon, to whom the plan for the Temple had been given, and the assembled Jewish people.

Blessed be Thou, Lord God of Israel our father, for ever and ever.

Thine, O Lord, is the greatness, and the power, and the glory, and the victory, and the majesty: for all that is in the heaven and in the earth is thine. Thine is the kingdom, O Lord, and Thou art exalted as head above all. Both riches and honour come of Thee, and Thou reignest over all; and in Thy hand is power and might, and in Thy hand it is to make great, and to give strength unto all. Now, therefore, our God, we thank Thee and praise Thy glorious name.

But who am I, and what is my people, that we should be able to offer so willingly after this sort? for all things come of Thee, and of Thine own have we given Thee. For we are strangers before Thee, and sojourners, as were all our fathers; our days on the earth are as a shadow, and there is none abiding. O Lord, our God, all this store that we have prepared to build thee an house for thy holy name, cometh of thine hand, and is all thine own.

I know also, my God, that thou triest the heart, and hast pleasure in uprightness. As for me, in the uprightness of mine heart I have willingly offered all these things: and now have I seen with joy thy people, which are present here, to offer willingly unto thee.

O Lord God of Abraham, of Isaac, and of Israel, our fathers, keep this for ever in the imagination of the thoughts of the heart of thy people, and prepare their heart unto thee: and give unto Solomon my son a perfect heart, to keep thy commandments, thy testimonies, and thy statutes, and to do all these things, and to build the palace, for the which I have made provision.

—*I Chronicles* 29:10–19

Solomon at the Consecration of the Temple

Solomon, son and successor of David as king of the Hebrews, acceded to the throne about 973 B.C. when still quite young. His wisdom was proverbial, and his reign saw the remarkable flourishing of his kingdom and the successful building of the Temple.

... O Lord God of Israel, there is no God like thee in the heaven, nor in the earth. ...

When the heaven is shut up, and there is no rain, because they have sinned against thee; yet if they pray toward this place, and confess thy name, and turn from their sin, when thou dost afflict them;

Then hear thou from heaven, and forgive the sin of thy servants, and of thy people Israel, when thou hast taught them the good way, wherein they should walk: and send rain upon thy land, which thou hast given unto thy people for an inheritance.

If there be dearth in the land, if there be pestilence, if there be blasting, or mildew, locusts, or caterpillars; if their enemies besiege them in the cities of their land, whatsoever sore or whatsoever sickness there be;

Then what prayer or what supplication soever shall be made of any man, or of all thy people Israel, when every one shall know his own sore and his own grief, and shall spread forth his hands in this house;

Then hear thou from heaven thy dwellingplace, and forgive, and render unto every man according unto all his ways, whose heart thou knowest; (for thou only knowest the hearts of the children of men:)

That they may fear thee, to walk in thy ways, so long as they live in the land which thou gavest unto our fathers.

—II Chronicles 6:14, 26–31

Prayer of Elijah for the Widow's Son

Elijah or Elias, who lived about 875 B.C., is one of the outstanding figures of the Old Testament. Elijah's mission was to destroy the worship of foreign gods and to restore justice in Israel. The raising of the widow's son from death with which the following prayer is concerned is one of numerous dramatic and miraculous incidents in the story of this great Hebrew prophet.

And he [Elijah] cried unto the Lord, and said, O Lord my God, hast thou also brought evil upon the widow with whom I sojourn, by slaying her son?

And he stretched himself upon the child three times, and cried unto the Lord, and said, O Lord my God, I pray thee, let this child's soul come into him again.

—I Kings 17:20–21

The Lord's Answer

And the Lord heard the voice of Elijah; and the soul of the child came into him again, and he revived.

—I Kings 17:22

Prayer of Hezekiah

The petition of Hezekiah ranks with *Psalm* 90, "A Prayer of Moses," and with "Habakkuk's Prayer" as among the most sublime prayers in the Old Testament. Hezekiah was the King of Judah about 715–687 B.C. During his reign, the Assyrians under Sennacherib twice invaded Judah. The first time the Assyrians were victorious and exacted a huge ransom. The second time a plague in the Assyrian army saved Judah. This is the occasion of the prayer here quoted.

The king prayed in the temple on receiving the boastful letter of Sennacherib, King of Assyria:

"O, Lord God of Israel, which dwelleth between the cherubims, thou art the God, even thou alone, of all the kingdoms of the earth; thou hast made heaven and earth.

"Lord, bow down thine ear, and hear: open, Lord, thine eyes, and see; and hear the words of Sennacherib, which hath sent him to reproach the living God. Of a truth, Lord, the Kings of Assyria have destroyed the nations and their lands, and have cast their gods into the fire: for they were no gods, but the work of men's hands, wood and stone; therefore they have destroyed them.

"Now, therefore, O Lord our God, I beseech thee, save thou us out of his hand, that all the kingdoms of the earth may know that thou art the Lord God, even thou only."

—*II Kings* 19:15–19

And it came to pass that night, that the angel of the Lord went out, and smote in the camp of the Assyrians, an hundred fourscore and five thousand: and when they arose early in the morning, behold, they were all dead corpses.

—*II Kings* 19:35

The Lament of Job

The *Book of Job* is of unknown authorship and date. It is cast in dialogue
and dramatic form, and the bulk of the book consists of speeches by
Job and three friends who try to comfort him after the loss of family and
fortune. Then Elihu speaks to Job, and finally the voice of God himself,
out of the whirlwind.

Job

My soul is weary of my life: I will leave my complaint upon
myself; I will speak in the bitterness of my soul.

I will say unto God, Do not condemn me; shew me wherefore thou contendest with me.

Is it good unto thee that thou shouldest oppress, that thou
shouldest despise the work of thine hands, and shine upon the
counsel of the wicked?

Hast thou eyes of flesh? or seest thou as man seeth?

Are thy days as the days of man? are thy years as man's days,

That thou inquirest after mine iniquity, and searchest after
my sin?

Thou knowest that I am not wicked; and there is none that can
deliver out of thine hand.

Thine hands have made me, and fashioned me together
round about; yet thou dost destroy me.

Remember, I beseech thee, that thou hast made me as the
clay; and wilt thou bring me into dust again?

Hast thou not poured me out as milk, and curdled me like
cheese?

Thou hast clothed me with skin and flesh, and hast fenced
me with bones and sinews.

Thou hast granted me life and favour, and thy visitation
hath preserved my spirit.

And these things hast thou hid in thine heart: I know that
this is with thee.

If I sin, then thou markest me, and thou wilt not acquit me
from mine iniquity.

If I be wicked, woe unto me; and if I be righteous, yet will I not lift up my head. I am full of confusion; therefore see thou mine affliction;

For it increaseth. Thou huntest me as a fierce lion; and again thou shewest thyself marvellous upon me.

Thou renewest thy witnesses against me, and increasest thine indignation upon me; changes and war are against me.

Wherefore then hast thou brought me forth out of the womb? Oh that I had given up the ghost, and no eye had seen me!

I should have been as though I had not been; I should have been carried from the womb to the grave.

Are not my days few? cease then, and let me alone, that I may take comfort a little.

Before I go whence I shall not return, even to the land of darkness and the shadow of death;

A land of darkness, as darkness itself; and of the shadow of death, without any order, and where the light is as darkness.

—*Job* 10:1–22

The Lord

Then the Lord answered Job out of the whirlwind, and said

Who is this that darkeneth counsel by words without knowledge?

Gird up now thy loins like a man; for I will demand of thee and answer thou me.

Where wast thou when I laid the foundations of the earth? declare, if thou hast understanding.

Who hath laid the measures thereof, if thou knowest? or who hath stretched the line upon it?

Whereupon are the foundations thereof fastened? or who laid the corner stone thereof,

When the morning stars sang together, and all the sons of God shouted for joy?

Or who shut up the sea with doors, when it brake forth as if it had issued out of the womb?

When I made the cloud the garment thereof, and thick darkness a swaddling band for it.

And brake up for it my decreed place, and set bars and doors,

And said, Hitherto shalt thou come, but no further; and here shall thy proud waves be stayed?

Hast thou commanded the morning since thy days; and caused the dayspring to know his place;

That it might take hold of the ends of the earth, that the wicked might be shaken out of it?

It is turned as clay to the seal, and they stand as a garment.

And from the wicked their light is withholden, and the high arm shall be broken.

Hast thou entered into the springs of the sea? or hast thou walked in the search of the depth?

Have the gates of death been opened unto thee? or hast thou seen the doors of the shadow of death?

Hast thou perceived the breadth of the earth? declare, if thou knowest it all.

Where is the way where light dwelleth? and as for darkness, where is the place thereof,

That thou shouldest take it to the bound thereof, and that thou shouldest know the paths to the house thereof?

Knowest thou it, because thou wast then born? or because the number of thy days is great?

—Job 38:1–21

Hath the rain a father? or who hath begotten the drops of dew?

Out of whose womb came the ice? and the hoary frost of heaven, who hath gendered it?

The waters are hid as with a stone, and the face of the deep is frozen.

Canst thou bind the sweet influences of Pleiades, or loose the bands of Orion?

Canst thou bring forth Mazzaroth in his season? or canst thou guide Arcturus with his sons?

—Job 38:28–32

Gavest thou the goodly wings unto the peacocks? or wings and feathers unto the ostrich?

Which leaveth her eggs in the earth, and warmeth them in dust,

And forgetteth that the foot may crush them, or that the wild beast may break them.

She is hardened against her young ones, as though they were not hers; her labour is in vain without fear;

Because God hath deprived her of wisdom, neither hath he imparted to her understanding.

What time she lifteth up herself on high, she scorneth the horse and his rider.

Hast thou given the horse strength? hast thou clothed his neck with thunder?

Canst thou make him afraid as a grasshopper? the glory of his nostrils is terrible.

He paweth in the valley, and rejoiceth in his strength: he goeth on to meet the armed men.

He mocketh at fear, and is not affrighted; neither turneth he back from the sword.

The quiver rattleth against him, the glittering spear and the shield.

He swalloweth the ground with fierceness and rage; neither believeth he that it is the sound of the trumpet.

He saith among the trumpets, Ha, ha; and he smelleth the battle afar off, the thunder of the captains, and the shouting.

Doth the hawk fly by thy wisdom, and stretch her wings toward the south?

Doth the eagle mount up at thy command, and make her nest on high?

She dwelleth and abideth on the rock, upon the crag of the rock, and the strong place.

From thence she seeketh the prey, and her eyes behold afar off.

Her young ones also suck up blood: and where the slain are, there is she.   —*Job* 39:13–30

Shall he that contendeth with the Almighty instruct him? he that reproveth God, let him answer it.

—*Job* 40:2

Job

Then Job answered the Lord, and said,
I know that thou canst do every thing, and that no thought can be withholden from thee.

Who is he that hideth counsel without knowledge? therefore have I uttered that I understood not; things too wonderful for me, which I knew not.

Hear, I beseech thee, and I will speak: I will demand of thee, and declare thou unto me.

I have heard of thee by the hearing of the ear: but now mine eye seeth thee.

Wherefore I abhor myself, and repent in dust and ashes.

—*Job* 42:1–6

Daniel's Prayer for Jerusalem

Daniel, a Jew of the sixth century B.C., spent his life at the court of Babylon, where he was known as Belteshazzar. Daniel was proverbial for his wisdom; he was famous for his interpretation of the dreams of Nebuchadnezzar and the handwriting on the wall of Belshazzar's palace during the feast, and his escape from the lion's den. Daniel always remained faithful to the Law and to Israel even though at the Babylonian court, and this prayer reflects his devotion.

O Lord, the great and dreadful God, keeping the covenant and mercy to them that love him, and to them that keep his commandments:

We have sinned, and have committed iniquity, and have done wickedly, and have rebelled, even by departing from thy precepts, and from thy judgments:

Neither have we hearkened unto thy servants the prophets, which spake in thy name to our kings, our princes, and our fathers, and to all the people of the land. . . .

O Lord, to us belongeth confusion of face, to our kings, to our princes, and to our fathers, because we have sinned against thee.

To the Lord our God belong mercies and forgivenesses, though we have rebelled against him;

Neither have we obeyed the voice of the Lord our God, to walk in his laws, which he set before us by his servants the prophets. . . .

O Lord, according to all thy righteousness, I beseech thee, let thine anger and thy fury be turned away from thy city Jerusalem, thy holy mountain: because for our sins, and for the iniquities of our fathers, Jerusalem and thy people are become a reproach to all that are about us.

Now therefore, O our God, hear the prayer of thy servant, and his supplications, and cause thy face to shine upon thy sanctuary that is desolate, for the Lord's sake.

O my God, incline thine ear, and hear; open thine eyes, and behold our desolations, and the city which is called by thy name: for we do not present our supplications before thee for our righteousnesses, but for thy great mercies.

O Lord, hear; O Lord, forgive; O Lord, hearken and do; defer not, for thine own sake, O my God: for thy city and thy people are called by thy name.

—*Daniel* 9:4–6, 8–10, 16–19

Jonah's Prayer from the Whale's Belly

Jonah was the famous Hebrew prophet sent to reform the city of Nineveh in the eighth century B.C. According to the Old Testament, to avoid his divine mission he sailed to Tarshish instead. The sailors threw him overboard with his consent because of the storm he brought down upon them. Swallowed by a whale, he was vomited up on shore after three days. He then preached to the people who repented. Jonah's coming forth from the whale's belly is famous in Christian belief as the prefiguration of the resurrection of Christ.

Then Jonah prayed unto the Lord his God out of the fish's belly,

And said, I cried by reason of mine affliction unto the Lord, and he heard me, out of the belly of hell cried I, and thou heardest my voice.

For thou hadst cast me into the deep, in the midst of the seas; and the floods compassed me about: all thy billows and thy waves passed over me.

Then I said, I am cast out of thy sight; yet I will look again toward thy holy temple.

The waters compassed me about, even to the soul: the depth closed me round about, the weeds were wrapped about my head.

I went down to the bottoms of the mountains: the earth with her bars was about me for ever: yet hast thou brought up my life from corruption, O Lord my God.

When my soul fainted within me I remembered the Lord: and my prayer came in unto thee, into thine holy temple.

They that observe lying vanities forsake their own mercy.

But I will sacrifice unto thee with the voice of thanksgiving; I will pay that that I have vowed. Salvation is of the Lord.

—Jonah 2:1–9

And the Lord spake unto the fish, and it vomited out Jonah upon the dry land.

—Jonah 2:10

The Prayer of Habakkuk

Habakkuk was a minor Hebrew prophet of unknown date, who has been the subject of many legends. "The Prayer of Habakkuk" has been regarded as one of the most lofty strains of Hebrew poetry. Awe-inspiring, it represents the majesty, power, and glory of Deity—one of the most moving prayers in all of Holy Writ.

O Lord, I have heard thy speech, and was afraid: O Lord, revive thy work in the midst of the years, in the midst of the years make known: in wrath remember mercy.

God came from Teman, and the Holy One from Mount Paran. His glory covered the heavens, and the earth was full of his praise.

And his brightness was as the light; he had horns coming out of his hand: and there was the hiding of his power.

Before him went the pestilence, and burning coals went forth at his feet.

He stood, and measured the earth: he beheld, and drove asunder the nations; and the everlasting mountains were scattered, the perpetual hills did bow: his ways are everlasting.

I saw the tents of Cushan in affliction: and the curtains of the land of Midian did tremble.

Was the Lord displeased against the rivers? was thine anger against the rivers? was thy wrath against the sea, that thou didst ride upon thy horses and thy chariots of salvation?

Thy bow was made quite naked, according to the oaths of the tribes, even thy word. Thou didst cleave the earth with rivers.

The mountains saw thee, and they trembled: the overflowing of the water passed by: the deep uttered his voice, and lifted up his hands on high.

The sun and moon stood still in their habitation: at the light of thine arrows they went, and at the shining of thy glittering spear.

Thou didst march through the land in indignation, thou didst thresh the heathen in anger.

Thou wentest forth for the salvation of thy people, even for salvation with thine anointed; thou woundedst the head out of the house of the wicked, by discovering the foundation unto the neck.

Thou didst strike through with his staves the head of his villages; they came out as a whirlwind to scatter me: their rejoicing was as to devour the poor secretly.

Thou didst walk through the sea with thine horses, through the heap of great waters.

When I heard, my belly trembled; my lips quivered at the voice: rottenness entered into my bones, and I trembled in myself, that I might rest in the day of trouble: when he cometh up unto the people, he will invade them with his troops.

Although the fig tree shall not blossom, neither shall fruit be in the vines; the labour of the olive shall fail, and the fields shall yield no meat; the flock shall be cut off from the fold, and there shall be no herd in the stalls:

Yet I will rejoice in the Lord, I will joy in the God of my salvation.

The Lord God is my strength and he will make my feet like hind's feet, and he will make me to walk upon mine high places. . . .

—*Habakkuk* 3:2–19

Magnificat

Mary's prayer of praise and thanksgiving at the Annunciation was uttered by the Blessed Virgin when she visited her cousin Elizabeth, as narrated by St. Luke. It is an ecstasy of praise for the favor bestowed upon Mary by God and also thanks for the mercies shown to Israel, as well as gratitude for the fulfilment of the promises made to Abraham and the patriarchs.

My soul doth magnify the Lord, and my spirit hath rejoiced in God my Saviour.

For he hath regarded the low estate of his handmaiden: for, behold, from henceforth all generations shall call me blessed.

For he that is mighty hath done to me great things; and holy is his name.

And his mercy is on them that fear him from generation to generation.

He hath shewed strength with his arm; he hath scattered the proud in the imagination of their hearts.

He hath put down the mighty from their seats, and exalted them of low degree.

He hath filled the hungry with good things; and the rich he hath sent empty away.

He hath holpen his servant Israel in remembrance of his mercy;

As he spake to our fathers, to Abraham and to his seed for ever.

—*Luke* 1:46–55

The Beatitudes

"The Sermon on the Mount" begins with "The Beatitudes," which are the eight solemn blessings cast in sublimely poetic form. The paramount idea of the Beatitudes is the spiritual character of the Messianic Kingdom. The eight conditions required are the very essence of Christian perfection. "The Beatitudes" are ranked with "The Decalogue" of the Old Testament and "The Lord's Prayer" for their depth and breadth of meaning and for their practical bearing on Christian life.

Blessed are the poor in spirit: for theirs is the kingdom of heaven.

Blessed are they that mourn: for they shall be comforted.

Blessed are the meek: for they shall inherit the earth.

Blessed are they which do hunger and thirst after righteousness: for they shall be filled.

Blessed are the merciful: for they shall obtain mercy.

Blessed are the pure in heart: for they shall see God.

Blessed are the peacemakers: for they shall be called the children of God.

Blessed are they which are persecuted for righteousness' sake: for theirs is the kingdom of heaven.

Blessed are ye, when men shall revile you, and persecute you, and shall say all manner of evil against you falsely, for my sake.

Rejoice, and be exceeding glad: for great is your reward in heaven: for so persecuted they the prophets which were before you.

—*Matthew* 5:3–12

Jesus Prays for His Followers

Before going with his disciples over the brook Cedron and into the Garden of Gethsemane where he was betrayed by Judas, Jesus delivered this prayer, which is a mandate not only for his disciples but for Christians for all time.

Father, the hour is come; glorify thy Son, that thy Son also may glorify thee:

As thou hast given him power over all flesh, that he should give eternal life to as many as thou hast given him.

And this is life eternal, that they might know thee the only true God, and Jesus Christ, whom thou hast sent.

I have glorified thee on the earth: I have finished the work which thou gavest me to do.

And now, O Father, glorify thou me with thine own self, with the glory which I had with thee before the world was.

I have manifested thy name unto the men which thou gavest me out of the world: thine they were, and thou gavest them me; and they have kept thy word.

Now they have known that all things whatsoever thou hast given me are of thee.

For I have given unto them the words which thou gavest me; and they have received them, and have known surely that I came out from thee, and they have believed that thou didst send me.

I pray for them: I pray not for the world, but for them which thou hast given me; for they are thine.

And all mine are thine, and thine are mine; and I am glorified in them.

And now I am no more in the world, but these are in the world, and I come to thee. Holy Father, keep through thine own name those whom thou hast given me, that they may be one, as we are.

While I was with them in the world, I kept them in thy name: those that thou gavest me I have kept, and none of them is lost, but the son of perdition; that the scripture might be fulfilled.

And now come I to thee; and these things I speak in the world, that they might have my joy fulfilled in themselves.

I have given them thy word; and the world hath hated them, because they are not of the world, even as I am not of the world.

I pray not that thou shouldest take them out of the world, but that thou shouldest keep them from the evil.

They are not of the world, even as I am not of the world.

Sanctify them through thy truth: thy word is truth.

As thou hast sent me into the world, even so have I also sent them into the world.

And for their sakes I sanctify myself, that they also might be sanctified through the truth.

Neither pray I for these alone, but for them also which shall believe on me through their word;

That they may all be one; as thou, Father, art in me, and I in thee, that they also may be one in us: that the world may believe that thou hast sent me.

And the glory which thou gavest me I have given them; that they may be one, even as we are one:

I in them, and thou in me, that they may be made perfect in one; and that the world may know that thou hast sent me, and hast loved them, as thou hast loved me.

Father, I will that they also, whom thou hast given me, be with me where I am; that they may behold my glory, which thou hast given me: for thou lovedst me before the foundations of the world.

O righteous Father, the world hath not known thee: but I have known thee, and these have known that thou hast sent me.

And I have declared unto them thy name, and will declare it: that the love wherewith thou hast loved me may be in them, and I in them.

—*John* 17:1–26

Jesus' Prayer in the Garden

Just before his betrayal Jesus went with Peter and the two sons of Zebedee to a quiet spot away from the other disciples. There he prayed while Peter and the others slept. The hour had come, and Jesus was ready to face his betrayer.

And he went a little further, and fell on his face, and prayed, saying, O my Father, if it be possible, let this cup pass from me: nevertheless, not as I will, but as thou wilt.

And he cometh unto the disciples, and findeth them asleep, and saith unto Peter, What! could ye not watch with me one hour?

Watch and pray, that ye enter not into temptation: the spirit indeed is willing, but the flesh is weak.

He went away again the second time, and prayed, saying, O my Father, if this cup may not pass away from me, except I drink it, thy will be done.

And he came and found them asleep again: for their eyes were heavy.

And he left them, and went away again, and prayed the third time, saying the same words.

Then cometh he to his disciples, and saith unto them, Sleep on now, and take your rest: behold, the hour is at hand, and the Son of man is betrayed into the hands of sinners.

Rise, let us be going: behold, he is at hand that doth betray me.
—*Matthew* 26:39–46

Jesus' Prayer on the Cross

The words from *Psalm* 31:5 were the last uttered by Jesus on the cross. They were also the last spoken by Stephen, Polycarp, Basil, Bernard, Huss, Luther, Columbus, John Knox, and Hannah More.

Father, forgive them; for they know not what they do. . . .
Father, into thy hands I commend my spirit.
—*Luke* 23:34, 46

St. Paul Prays for the Church

On Paul's third missionary journey he went to Ephesus; his two-and-a-half-year stay there was the most fruitful period of his life. Ephesus was to become a center of Christianity, and his epistle to the congregation there contains this great prayer. In it is to be found the Pauline analogy of the perfect union of Christians.

Wherefore I also, after I heard of your faith in the Lord Jesus, and love unto all the saints, cease not to give thanks for you, making mention of you in my prayers; that the God of our Lord Jesus Christ, the Father of glory, may give unto you the spirit of wisdom and revelation in the knowledge of him: the eyes of your understanding being enlightened; that ye may know what is the hope of his calling, and what the riches of the glory of his inheritance in the saints, and what is the exceeding greatness of his power to us-ward who believe, according to the working of his mighty power, which he wrought in Christ, when he raised him from the dead, and set him at his own right hand in the heavenly places, far above all principality, and power, and might, and dominion, and every name that is named, not only in this world, but also in that which is to come; and hath put all things under his feet, and gave him to be the head over all things to the church, which is his body, the fulness of him that filleth all in all. . . .

For this cause I bow my knees unto the Father of our Lord Jesus Christ, of whom the whole family in heaven and earth is named, that he would grant you, according to the riches of his glory, to be strengthened with might by his spirit in the inner man; that Christ may dwell in your hearts by faith; that ye, being rooted and grounded in love, may be able to comprehend with all the saints what is the breadth, and length, and depth and height; and to know the love of Christ, which passeth knowledge, that ye might be filled with all the fulness of God. Now unto him that is able to do exceeding abundantly above all that we ask or think, according to the power that worketh in us, unto him be glory in the church by Christ Jesus, throughout all ages, world without end. *Amen.*

—*Ephesians* 1:15–23; 3:14–21

Wait on the Lord

The *Book of Psalms* appears in the Old Testament and consists of 150 poetic pieces of great beauty. It has been the hymnal for both Jews and Christians, and practically all of the psalms may be considered prayers. Besides "Wait on the Lord," here quoted and attributed to David, Penitential Psalms and Psalms of Praise and Exaltation, including the so-called Hallelujah Psalms, are quoted.

One thing have I desired of the Lord, that will I seek after; that I may dwell in the house of the Lord all the days of my life, to behold the beauty of the Lord, and to inquire in his temple.

For in the time of trouble he shall hide me in his pavilion: in the secret of his tabernacle shall he hide me: he shall set me up upon a rock.

And now shall mine head be lifted up above my enemies round about me: therefore will I offer in his tabernacle sacrifices of joy; I will sing, yea, I will sing praises unto the Lord.

Hear, O Lord, when I cry with my voice: have mercy also upon me, and answer me.

When thou saidst, Seek ye my face; my heart said unto thee, Thy face, Lord, will I seek.

Hide not thy face far from me; put not thy servant away in anger: thou hast been my help; leave me not, neither forsake me, O God of my salvation.

When my father and my mother forsake me, then the Lord will take me up.

Teach me thy way, O Lord, and lead me in a plain path, because of mine enemies.

Deliver me not over unto the will of mine enemies; for false witnesses are risen up against me, and such as breathe out cruelty.

I had fainted, unless I had believed to see the goodness of the Lord in the land of the living.

Wait on the Lord: be of good courage, and he shall strengthen thine heart: wait, I say, on the Lord.

—Psalm 27:4–14

The Penitential Psalms

O Lord, rebuke me not in thine anger, neither chasten me in thy hot displeasure.

Have mercy upon me; O Lord, for I am weak: O Lord, heal me; for my bones are vexed.

My soul is also sore vexed: but thou, O Lord, how long?

Return, O Lord, deliver my soul: oh save me for thy mercies' sake.

For in death there is no remembrance of thee: in the grave who shall give thee thanks?

I am weary with my groaning; all the night make I my bed to swim; I water my couch with my tears.

Mine eye is consumed because of grief; it waxeth old because of all mine enemies.

Depart from me, all ye workers of iniquity: for the Lord hath heard the voice of my weeping.

The Lord hath heard my supplication; the Lord will receive my prayer.

—Psalm 6:1–10

Blessed is he whose transgression is forgiven, whose sin is covered.

Blessed is the man unto whom the Lord imputeth not iniquity, and in whose spirit there is no guile.

When I kept silence, my bones waxed old through my roaring all the day long.

For day and night thy hand was heavy upon me: my moisture is turned into the drought of summer.

I acknowledge my sin unto thee, and mine iniquity have I not hid. I said, I will confess my transgressions unto the Lord; and thou forgavest the iniquity of my sin.

For this shall every one that is godly pray unto thee in a time when thou mayest be found: surely in the floods of great waters they shall not come nigh unto him.

Thou art my hiding place; thou shalt preserve me from trouble; thou shalt compass me about with songs of deliverance.

I will instruct thee and teach thee in the way which thou shalt go: I will guide thee with mine eye.

Be ye not as the horse, or as the mule, which have no understanding; whose mouth must be held in with bit and bridle, lest they come near unto thee.

Many sorrows shall be to the wicked: but he that trusteth in the Lord, mercy shall compass him about.

Be glad in the Lord, and rejoice, ye righteous: and shout for joy, all ye that are upright in heart.

—Psalm 32

O Lord, rebuke me not in thy wrath; neither chasten me in thy hot displeasure.

For thine arrows stick fast in me, and thy hand presseth me sore.

There is no soundness in my flesh because of thine anger; neither is there any rest in my bones, because of my sin.

For my iniquities are gone over my head; as an heavy burden they are too heavy for me.

My wounds stink, and are corrupt, because of my foolishness.

I am troubled; I am bowed down greatly; I go mourning all the day long.

For my loins are filled with a loathsome disease; and there is no soundness in my flesh.

I am feeble and sore broken: I have roared by reason of the disquietness of my heart.

Lord, all my desire is before thee; and my groaning is not hid from thee.

My heart panteth, my strength faileth me: as for the light of mine eyes, it is also gone from me.

For I am ready to halt, and my sorrow is continually before me.

For I will declare mine iniquity; I will be sorry for my sin.

Forsake me not, O Lord: O my God, be not far from me.

Make haste to help me, O Lord my salvation.

—Psalm 38

Have mercy upon me, O God, according to thy loving kind-ness: according unto the multitude of thy tender mercies blot out my transgressions.

Wash me thoroughly from mine iniquity, and cleanse me from my sin.

For I acknowledge my transgressions: and my sin is ever be-fore me.

Against thee, thee only, have I sinned, and done this evil in thy sight: that thou mightest be justified when thou speakest, and be clear when thou judgest.

Behold, I was shapen in iniquity; and in sin did my mother conceive me.

Behold, thou desirest truth in the inward parts: and in the hidden part thou shalt make me to know wisdom.

Purge me with hyssop, and I shall be clean: wash me, and I shall be whiter than snow.

Make me to hear joy and gladness; that the bones which thou hast broken may rejoice.

Hide thy face from my sins, and blot out all mine iniquities.

Create in me a clean heart, O God; and renew a right spirit within me.

Cast me not away from thy presence; and take not thy holy spirit from me.

Restore unto me the joy of thy salvation; and uphold me with thy free spirit.

Then will I teach transgressors thy ways; and sinners shall be converted unto thee.

Deliver me from bloodguiltiness, O God, thou God of my salvation: and my tongue shall sing aloud of thy righteousness.

O Lord, open thou my lips; and my mouth shall shew forth thy praise.

For thou desirest not sacrifice; else would I give it: thou delightest not in burnt offering.

The sacrifices of God are a broken spirit: a broken and contrite heart, O God, thou wilt not despise.

—*Psalm* 51:1–17

Hear my prayer, O Lord, and let my cry come unto thee.

Hide not thy face from me in the day when I am in trouble; incline thine ear unto me: in the day when I call, answer me speedily.

For my days are consumed like smoke, and my bones are burned as an hearth.

My heart is smitten, and withered like grass; so that I forget to eat my bread.

By reason of the voice of my groaning, my bones cleave to my skin.

I am like a pelican of the wilderness: I am like an owl of the desert.

I watch, and am as a sparrow alone upon the housetop.

Mine enemies approach me all the day; and they that are mad against me are sworn against me.

For I have eaten ashes like bread, and mingled my drink with weeping,

Because of thine indignation and thy wrath: for thou hast lifted me up and cast me down.

My days are like a shadow that declineth; and I am withered like grass.

But thou, O Lord, shalt endure forever; and thy remembrance unto all generations.

Thou shalt arise, and have mercy upon Zion: for the time to favour her, yea, the set time, is come.

—*Psalm* 102:1–13

Out of the depths have I cried unto thee, O Lord.

Lord, hear my voice: let thine ears be attentive to the voice of my supplications.

If thou, Lord, shouldest mark iniquities, O Lord, who shall stand?

But there is forgiveness with thee, that thou mayest be feared.

I wait for the Lord, my soul doth wait, and in his word do I hope.

My soul waiteth for the Lord more than they that watch for the morning: I say, more than they that watch for the morning.

Let Israel hope in the Lord: for with the Lord there is mercy, and with him is plenteous redemption.

And he shall redeem Israel from all his iniquities.

—Psalm 130

Hear my prayer, O Lord; give ear to my supplications: in thy faithfulness answer me, and in thy righteousness.

And enter not into judgment with thy servant: for in thy sight shall no man living be justified.

For the enemy hath persecuted my soul; he hath smitten my life down to the ground; he hath made me to dwell in darkness, as those that have been long dead.

Therefore is my spirit overwhelmed within me; my heart within me is desolate.

I remember the days of old; I meditate on all thy works; I muse on the work of thy hands.

I stretch forth my hands unto thee: my soul thirsteth after thee, as a thirsty land.

Hear me speedily, O Lord: my spirit faileth: hide not thy face from me, lest I be like unto them that go down into the pit.

Cause me to hear thy lovingkindness in the morning; for in thee do I trust: cause me to know the way wherein I should walk; for I lift up my soul unto thee.

Deliver me, O Lord, from mine enemies: I flee unto thee to hide me.

Teach me to do thy will; for thou art my God: thy Spirit is good; lead me into the land of uprightness.

Quicken me, O Lord, for thy name's sake: for thy righteousness' sake bring my soul out of trouble.

—*Psalm* 143:1–11

Psalms of Praise and Exaltation

Make a joyful noise unto the Lord, all ye lands.

Serve the Lord with gladness: come before his presence with singing.

Know ye that the Lord he is God: it is he that hath made us, and not we ourselves; we are his people, and the sheep of his pasture.

Enter into his gates with thanksgiving, and into his courts with praise: be thankful unto him, and bless his name.

For the Lord is good; his mercy is everlasting; and his truth endureth to all generations.

—*Psalm* 100

Praise ye the Lord. Praise ye the name of the Lord; praise him, O ye servants of the Lord.

Ye that stand in the house of the Lord, in the courts of the house of our God.

Praise the Lord; for the Lord is good: sing praises unto his name; for it is pleasant.

For the Lord hath chosen Jacob unto himself, and Israel for his peculiar treasure.

For I know that the Lord is great, and that our Lord is above all gods.

Whatsoever the Lord pleased, that did he in heaven, and in earth, in the seas, and all deep places.

He causeth the vapours to ascend from the ends of the earth; he maketh lightnings for the rain; he bringeth the wind out of his treasuries.

Who smote the firstborn of Egypt, both of man and beast.

Who sent tokens and wonders into the midst of thee, O Egypt, upon Pharaoh, and upon all his servants.

Who smote great nations, and slew mighty kings;

Sihon king of the Amorites, and Og king of Bashan, and all the kingdoms of Canaan:

And gave their land for an heritage, an heritage unto Israel his people.

Thy name, O Lord, endureth for ever; and thy memorial, O Lord, throughout all generations.

For the Lord will judge his people, and he will repent himself concerning his servants.

The idols of the heathen are silver and gold, the work of men's hands.

They have mouths, but they speak not; eyes have they, but they see not;

They have ears, but they hear not; neither is there any breath in their mouths.

They that make them are like unto them: so is every one that trusteth in them.

Bless the Lord, O house of Israel: bless the Lord, O house of Aaron:

Bless the Lord, O house of Levi: ye that fear the Lord, bless the Lord.

Blessed be the Lord out of Zion, which dwelleth at Jerusalem. Praise ye the Lord.

—Psalm 135

O give thanks unto the Lord; for he is good: for his mercy endureth for ever.

O give thanks unto the God of gods: for his mercy endureth for ever.

O give thanks to the Lord of lords: for his mercy endureth for ever.

To him who alone doeth great wonders: for his mercy endureth for ever.

To him that by wisdom made the heavens: for his mercy endureth for ever.

To him that stretched out the earth above the waters: for his mercy endureth for ever.

To him that made great lights: for his mercy endureth for ever:

The sun to rule by day: for his mercy endureth forever:

The moon and stars to rule by night: for his mercy endureth for ever.

To him that smote Egypt in their firstborn: for his mercy endureth for ever.

And brought out Israel from among them: for his mercy endureth for ever:

With a strong hand and with a stretched out arm: for his mercy endureth for ever.

To him which divided the Red sea into parts: for his mercy endureth for ever:

And made Israel to pass through the midst of it: for his mercy endureth for ever:

But overthrew Pharaoh and his host in the Red sea: for his mercy endureth for ever.

To him which led his people through the wilderness: for his mercy endureth for ever.

To him which smote great kings: for his mercy endureth for ever:

And slew famous kings: for his mercy endureth for ever:

Sihon king of the Amorites: for his mercy endureth for ever:

And Og the king of Bashan: for his mercy endureth for ever:

And gave their land for an heritage: for his mercy endureth for ever:

Even an heritage unto Israel his servant: for his mercy endureth for ever.

Who remembered us in our low estate: for his mercy endureth for ever:

And hath redeemed us from our enemies: for his mercy endureth for ever.

Who giveth food to all flesh: for his mercy endureth for ever.

O give thanks unto the God of heaven: for his mercy endureth for ever.

—*Psalm* 136

Praise ye the Lord. Praise, O ye servants of the Lord, praise the name of the Lord.

Blessed be the name of the Lord, from this time forth and for evermore.

From the rising of the sun, unto the going down of the same the Lord's name is to be praised.

The Lord is high above all nations, and his glory above the heavens.

Who is like unto the Lord our God, who dwelleth on high;

Who humbleth himself to behold the things that are in heaven, and in the earth!

He raiseth up the poor out of the dust, and lifteth the needy out of the dunghill;

That he may set him with princes, even with the princes of his people.

He maketh the barren woman to keep house, and to be a joyful mother of children. Praise ye the Lord.

—*Psalm* 113

When Israel went out of Egypt, the house of Jacob from a people of strange language,

Judah was his sanctuary, and Israel his dominion.

The sea saw it, and fled: Jordan was driven back.

The mountains skipped like rams, and the little hills like lambs.

What ailed thee, O thou sea, that thou fleddest? thou Jordan, that thou wast driven back?

Ye mountains, that ye skipped like rams; and ye little hills, like lambs?

Tremble, thou earth, at the presence of the Lord, at the presence of the God of Jacob;

Which turned the rock into a standing water, the flint into a fountain of waters.

—*Psalm* 114

Not unto us, O Lord, not unto us, but unto thy name give glory, for thy mercy, and for thy truth's sake.

Wherefore should the heathen say, Where is now their God?

But our God is in the heavens; he hath done whatsoever he hath pleased.

Their idols are silver and gold, the work of men's hands.

They have mouths, but they speak not; eyes have they, but they see not;

They have ears, but they hear not; noses have they, but they smell not;

They have hands, but they handle not; feet have they, but they walk not; neither speak they through their throat.

They that make them are like unto them; so is every one that trusteth in them.

O Israel, trust thou in the Lord: he is their help and their shield.

O house of Aaron, trust in the Lord; he is their help and their shield.

Ye that fear the Lord, trust in the Lord: he is their help and their shield.

The Lord hath been mindful of us: he will bless us; he will bless the house of Israel; he will bless the house of Aaron.

He will bless them that fear the Lord, both small and great.

The Lord shall increase you more and more, you and your children.

Ye are blessed of the Lord which made heaven and earth.

The heaven, even the heavens, are the Lord's: but the earth hath he given to the children of men.

The dead praise not the Lord, neither any that go down into silence.

But we will bless the Lord from this time forth and for evermore. Praise the Lord.

—Psalm 115

I love the Lord, because he hath heard my voice and my supplications.

Because he hath inclined his ear unto me, therefore will I call upon him as long as I live.

The sorrows of death compassed me, and the pains of hell gat hold upon me: I found trouble and sorrow.

Then called I upon the name of the Lord: O Lord, I beseech thee, deliver my soul.

Gracious is the Lord, and righteous; yea, our God is merciful.

The Lord preserveth the simple: I was brought low, and he helped me.

Return unto thy rest, O my soul; for the Lord hath dealt bountifully with thee.

For thou hast delivered my soul from death, mine eyes from tears, and my feet from falling.

I will walk before the Lord in the land of the living.

I believed, therefore have I spoken: I was greatly afflicted.

I said in my haste, All men are liars.

What shall I render unto the Lord for all his benefits toward me?

I will take the cup of salvation, and call upon the name of the Lord.

I will pray my vows unto the Lord now in the presence of all his people.

Precious in the sight of the Lord is the death of his saints.

O Lord, truly I am thy servant; I am thy servant, and the son of thine handmaid: thou hast loosed my bonds.

I will offer to thee the sacrifice of thanksgiving, and will call upon the name of the Lord.

I will pay my vows unto the Lord now in the presence of all his people.

In the courts of the Lord's house, in the midst of thee, O Jerusalem. Praise ye the Lord.

—*Psalm* 116

O Praise the Lord, all ye nations: praise him, all ye people.

For his merciful kindness is great toward us: and the truth of the Lord endureth for ever. Praise ye the Lord.

—*Psalm* 117

O give thanks unto the Lord; for he is good; because his mercy endureth for ever.

Let Israel now say, that his mercy endureth for ever.

Let the house of Aaron now say, that his mercy endureth for ever.

Let them now that fear the Lord say, that his mercy endureth for ever.

I called upon the Lord in distress: the Lord answered me, and set me in a large place.

The Lord is on my side; I will not fear: what can man do unto me?

The Lord taketh my part with them that help me: therefore shall I see my desire upon them that hate me.

It is better to trust in the Lord, than to put confidence in man.

It is better to trust in the Lord, than to put confidence in princes.

All nations compassed me about: but in the name of the Lord will I destroy them.

They compassed me about; yea, they compassed me about: but in the name of the Lord will I destroy them.

They compassed me about like bees; they are quenched as the fire of thorns: for in the name of the Lord will I destroy them.

Thou hast thrust sore at me, that I might fall: but the Lord helped me.

The Lord is my strength and song, and is become my salvation.

The voice of rejoicing and salvation is in the tabernacles of the righteous; the right hand of the Lord doeth valiantly.

The right hand of the Lord is exalted; the right hand of the Lord doeth valiantly.

I shall not die, but live, and declare the works of the Lord.

The Lord hath chastened me sore: but he hath not given me over unto death.

Open to me the gates of righteousness: I will go into them, and I will praise the Lord:

This gate of the Lord, into which the righteous shall enter.

I will praise thee; for thou hast heard me, and art become my salvation.

The stone which the builders refused is become the head stone of the corner.

This is the Lord's doing; it is marvellous in our eyes.

This is the day which the Lord hath made; we will rejoice and be glad in it.

Save now, I beseech thee, O Lord: O Lord, I beseech thee, send now prosperity.

Blessed be he that cometh in the name of the Lord: we have blessed you out of the house of the Lord.

God is the Lord, which hath shewed us light: bind the sacrifice with cords, even unto the horns of the altar.

Thou art my God, and I will praise thee: thou art my God, I will exalt thee.

O give thanks unto the Lord; for he is good: for his mercy endureth for ever.

—*Psalm* 118

I will extol thee, my God, O King; and I will bless thy name for ever and ever.

Every day will I bless thee; and I will praise thy name for ever and ever.

Great is the Lord, and greatly to be praised; and his greatness is unsearchable.

One generation shall praise thy works to another, and shall declare thy mighty acts.

I will speak of the glorious honour of thy majesty, and of thy wondrous works.

And men shall speak of the might of thy terrible acts: and I will declare thy greatness.

They shall abundantly utter the memory of thy great goodness, and shall sing of thy righteousness.

The Lord is gracious, and full of compassion: slow to anger, and of great mercy.

The Lord is good to all; and his tender mercies are over all his works.

All thy works shall praise thee, O Lord; and thy saints shall bless thee.

They shall speak of the glory of thy kingdom, and talk of thy power;

To make known to the sons of men his mighty acts, and the glorious majesty of his kingdom.

Thy kingdom is an everlasting kingdom, and thy dominion endureth throughout all generations.

The Lord upholdeth all that fall, and raiseth up all those that be bowed down.

The eyes of all wait upon thee: and thou givest them their meat in due season.

Thou openest thine hand, and satisfiest the desire of every living thing.

The Lord is righteous in all his ways, and holy in all his works.

The Lord is nigh unto all them that call upon him, to all that call upon him in truth.

He will fulfil the desire of them that fear him: he also will hear their cry, and will save them.

The Lord preserveth all them that love him: but all the wicked he will destroy.

My mouth shall speak the praise of the Lord; and let all flesh bless his holy name for ever and ever.

—Psalm 145

Praise ye the Lord. Praise the Lord, O my soul.

While I live will I praise the Lord: I will sing praises unto my God while I have any being.

Put not your trust in princes, nor in the son of man, in whom there is no help.

His breath goeth forth, he returneth to his earth; in that very day his thoughts perish.

Happy is he that hath the God of Jacob for his help, whose hope is in the Lord his God:

Which made heaven, and earth, the sea, and all that therein is; which keepeth truth for ever;

Which executeth judgment for the oppressed: which giveth food to the hungry. The Lord looseth the prisoners.

The Lord openeth the eyes of the blind: the Lord raiseth them that are bowed down: the Lord loveth the righteous:

The Lord preserveth the strangers; he relieveth the fatherless and widow: but the way of the wicked he turneth upside down.

The Lord shall reign for ever, even thy God, O Zion, unto all generations. Praise ye the Lord.

—Psalm 146

Praise ye the Lord: for it is good to sing praise unto our God; for it is pleasant; and praise is comely.

The Lord doth build up Jerusalem: he gathereth together the outcasts of Israel.

He healeth the broken in heart, and bindeth up their wounds.

He telleth the number of the stars; he calleth them all by their names.

Great is our Lord, and of great power: his understanding is infinite.

The Lord lifteth up the meek: he casteth the wicked down to the ground.

Sing unto the Lord with thanksgiving; sing praise upon the harp unto our God;

Who covereth the heaven with clouds, who prepareth rain for the earth, who maketh grass to grow upon the mountains.

He giveth to the beast his food, and to the young ravens which cry.

He delighteth not in the strength of the horse: he taketh not pleasure in the legs of a man.

The Lord taketh pleasure in them that fear him, in those that hope in his mercy.

Praise the Lord, O Jerusalem; praise thy God, O Zion.

For he hath strengthened the bars of thy gates; he hath blessed thy children within thee.

He maketh peace in thy borders, and filleth thee with the finest of the wheat.

He sendeth forth his commandment upon earth: his word runneth very swiftly.

He giveth snow like wool: he scattereth the hoar frost like ashes.

He casteth forth his ice like morsels: who can stand before his cold?

He sendeth out his word, and melteth them: he causeth his wind to blow, and the waters flow.

He sheweth his word unto Jacob, his statutes and his judgments unto Israel.

He hath not dealt so with any nation; and as for his judgments, they have not known them. Praise ye the Lord.

—*Psalm* 147

Praise ye the Lord. Praise ye the Lord from the heavens: praise him in the heights.

Praise ye him, all his angels: praise ye him, all his hosts.

Praise ye him, sun and moon: praise him, all ye stars of light.

Praise him, ye heavens of heavens, and ye waters that be above the heavens.

Let them praise the name of the Lord: for he commanded, and they were created.

He hath also stablished them for ever and ever: he hath made a decree which shall not pass.

Praise the Lord from the earth, ye dragons, and all deeps.

Fire, and hail; snow, and vapours; stormy wind fulfilling his word:

Mountains, and all hills; fruitful trees, and all cedars:

Beasts, and all cattle; creeping things, and flying fowl:

Kings of the earth, and all people; princes, and all judges of the earth:

Both young men and maidens; old men and children:

Let them praise the name of the Lord: for his name alone is excellent; his glory is above the earth and heaven.

He also exalteth the horn of his people, the praise of all his saints, even of the children of Israel, a people near unto him. Praise ye the Lord.

—Psalm 148

Praise ye the Lord. Sing unto the Lord a new song, and his praise in the congregation of saints.

Let Israel rejoice in him that made him; let the children of Zion be joyful in their King.

Let them praise his name in the dance: let them sing praises unto him with the timbrel and harp.

For the Lord taketh pleasure in his people: he will beautify the meek with salvation.

Let the saints be joyful in glory: let them sing aloud upon their beds.

Let the high praises of God be in their mouth, and a two edged sword in their hand;

To execute vengeance upon the heathen, and punishments upon the people;

To bind their kings with chains, and their nobles with fetters of iron;

To execute upon them the judgment written: this honour have all his saints. Praise ye the Lord.

—Psalm 149

Praise ye the Lord. Praise God in his sanctuary: praise him in the firmament of his power.

Praise him for his mighty acts: praise him according to his excellent greatness.

Praise him with the sound of the trumpet: praise him with the psaltery and harp.

Praise him with the timbrel and dance: praise him with stringed instruments and organs.

Praise him upon the loud cymbals: praise him upon the high sounding cymbals.

Let every thing that hath breath praise the Lord. Praise ye the Lord.

—Psalm 150

GREAT PRAYERS FROM

LITERATURE

THE ARTISTS OF PROSE AND POETRY *have an advantage over the theologians of the world. The writers can marshal their thoughts and make them sing, in words, sweeter than men of any other calling. Words are their tools. That is why this section of the book seems to me like a many-colored floral arrangement on a black-and-white altar.*

These are my betters.

Would that I had thought of, much less been able to write, the words of Michelangelo:

> *Thou gavest me on earth this soul divine;*
> *And Thou within the body weak and frail*
> *Didst prison it—how sadly there to live!*
> *How can I make its lot less vile than mine?*

You will read Elizabeth Browning's "Prayer for a Baby" and perhaps, like me, you will not weep, but you will not speak either. Stephen Vincent Benét's prayer for brotherhood almost compels a reexamination of conscience. Tolstoi, Emerson, Dr. Johnson, Chesterton, Dickens, Oliver Wendell Holmes—these and many more are here.

I remember some of these from earlier years. One is Joyce Kilmer's "Prayer of a Soldier in France," which begins:

My shoulders ache beneath my pack;
(Lie easier, Cross, upon His back).
I march with feet that burn and smart;
(Tread, Holy Feet, upon my heart).

I will not forget it, ever.

Michelangelo's Prayer

Michelangelo Buonarrotti (1475–1564) was a gifted poet as well as sculptor, painter, and architect. From 1534 to 1541 this great figure of the Italian Renaissance worked on the "Last Judgment" in the Sistine Chapel in Rome. During this time he formed a great friendship with Vittoria Colonna, and to her he dedicated many religious sonnets. The deep moral conflicts that rose within his own spirit are reflected in this prayer-poem.

Oh, make me see Thee, Lord, where'er I go!
   If mortal beauty sets my soul on fire,
   That flame when near to thine must needs expire,
   And I with love of only Thee shall glow.
Dear Lord, thy help I seek against this woe,
   These torments that my spirit vex and tire;
   Thou only with new strength canst reinspire
   My will, my sense, my courage faint and low.
Thou gavest me on earth this soul divine;
   And Thou within the body weak and frail
   Didst prison it—how sadly there to live!
How can I make its lot less vile than mine?
   Without Thee, Lord, all goodness seems to fail.
   To alter fate is God's prerogative.
—from Sonnets of Michel A. B.

A Prayer to the Holy Trinity

Ben Jonson (1574–1637), great English dramatist and poet, was first
a bricklayer, soldier, and actor. In 1598 he was tried for killing another
actor in a duel but escaped execution. While in prison he was converted
to Roman Catholicism but returned to the Church of England twelve
years later. He was a friend of Shakespeare, of whom he said, "He was
not of an age, but for all time."

O Holy, blessed, glorious Trinitie
Of Persons, still one God in Unitie,
The faithful man's beleevéd mysterie,
           Helpe, helpe to lift
Myselfe up to Thee, harrow'd, torne, and bruised
By sinne and Sathan and my flesh misused;
As my heart lies in peeces, all confused,
           O take my gift.

All-gracious God, the sinner's sacrifice,
A broken heart Thou wert not wont despise;
But 'bove the fat of rammes and bulls, to prize—
           An offering meet
For Thy acceptance; O behold me right
And take compassion on my grievous plight!
What odour can be than a heart contrite
           To Thee more sweet?

Eternall Father, God, who didst create
This All of nothing, gav'st it form and fate
And breath'd into it life and light and state,
           To worship Thee!
Eternall God, the Sonne, who not denyd'st
To take our nature; becam'st man, and died'st
To pay our debts, upon Thy Crosse, and cryd'st
           All's done in Me!

Eternall Spirit, God from both proceeding,
Father and Sonne—the Comforter, imbreeding
Pure thoughts in man, with fiery zeale them feeding
    For acts of grace!
Increase those acts, O Glorious Unitie,
Of Persons, still one God in Trinitie
Till I attain the longed-for mysterie
    Of seeing your face,

Beholding One in Three, and Three in One,
A Trinitie to shine in Union;
The gladdest light darke man can thinke upon—
    O grant it me!
Father, and Sonne and Holy Ghost, you Three,
All co-eternall in your Majestie
Distinct in Persons, yet in Unitie—
    One God to see.

My Maker, Saviour and my Sanctifier!
To heare, to meditate, to sweeten my desire
With grace and love, with cherishing entire;
    Oh then how blest!
Among Thy saints elected to abide,
And with Thy angels placéd side by side,
But in Thy presence truly glorified,
    Shall I there rest.
     —Ben Jonson, from *The Underwoods*
      (Poems of Devotion)

A Hymn to God the Father

John Donne (1573–1631) was an English metaphysical poet, whose sermons were famous. He was reared a Roman Catholic, educated at Oxford, and became a court secretary. However, his secret marriage to his employer's niece ruined his court career. He later served in Parliament when James I acceded to the throne and was persuaded by the monarch to take holy orders in 1615, becoming Dean of St. Paul's in 1621. His profoundly religious and philosophical poetry is among the finest literature in the language.

> Wilt Thou forgive that sin where I begun,
>   Which is my sin, though it were done before?
> Wilt Thou forgive that sin, through which I run,
>   And do run still: though still I do deplore?
>   When Thou hast done, Thou hast not done,
>   For, I have more.
>
> Wilt Thou forgive that sin by which I have won
>   Others to sin? and made my sin their door?
> Wilt Thou forgive that sin by which I did shun
>   A year, or two: But wallowed in, a score?
>   When Thou hast done, Thou hast not done,
>   For, I have more.
>
> I have a sin of fear, that when I have spun
>   My last thread, I shall perish on the shore;
> Swear by Thyself, that at my death Thy Son
>   Shall shine as He shines now, and heretofore;
>   And, having done that, Thou hast done,
>   I fear no more.

—John Donne

The Shepherd Boy's Song

John Bunyan (1628–1688), English tinker and soldier, became a non-conformist lay preacher in 1653. Imprisoned for unlicensed preaching, he began the first of his great religious books. During a second imprisonment he is supposed to have written the first part of *The Pilgrim's Progress*, which was published in 1678. It is considered one of the world's great books and has been translated into many languages.

> He that is down needs fear no fall,
>   He that is low, no pride;
> He that is humble ever shall
>   Have God to be his guide.
>
> I am content with what I have,
>   Little be it or much:
> And, Lord, contentment still I crave,
>   Because Thou savest such.
>
> Fullness to such a burden is
>   That go on pilgrimage:
> Here little, and hereafter bliss,
>   Is best from age to age.
> —John Bunyan, from *The Pilgrim's Progress*

The Dwelling Place

Henry Vaughan, Welsh-born English poet (1622–1695), attended Oxford, studied law, then became a soldier and later a physician. Vaughan wrote secular poetry and prose, but his fame rests on his deeply mystical sacred poems.

> What happy secret fountain,
> Fair shade or mountain,
> Whose undiscovered virgin glory
> Boasts it this day, though not in story,

Was then thy dwelling? did some cloud
Fix'd to a tent, descend and shroud
My distrest Lord? or did a star,
Beckoned by thee, though high and far,
In sparkling smiles haste gladly down
To lodge light and increase her own?
My dear, dear God! I do not know
What lodged thee then, nor where, nor how;
But I am sure thou now dost come
Oft to a narrow, homely room,
Where thou too hast but the least part,
My God, I mean *my sinful heart.*

—Henry Vaughan

The Resignation

Thomas Chatterton, English romantic poet, began writing poetry at the age of twelve. He went to London in 1770 and tried without success to sell his poems to various publications. At the point of starvation and too proud to borrow or beg, he poisoned himself and died at the age of seventeen.

O God, whose thunder shakes the sky,
  Whose eye this atom globe surveys,
To Thee, my only rock, I fly,
  Thy mercy in Thy justice praise.

The mystic mazes of Thy will,
  The shadows of celestial light,
Are past the pow'r of human skill—
  But what th' Eternal acts, is right.

O teach me in this trying hour,
  When anguish swells the dewy tear,
To still my sorrows, own Thy pow'r,
  Thy goodness love, Thy justice fear.

If in this bosom ought but Thee,
 Encroaching sought a boundless sway,
Omniscience could the danger see,
 And Mercy took the cause away.

Then why, my soul, dost thou complain?
 Why, drooping, seek the dark recess?
Shake off the melancholy chain,
 For God created all to bless.

But ah! my breast is human still;
 The rising sigh, the falling tear,
My languid vitals' feeble rill
 The sickness of my soul declare.

But yet, with fortitude resign'd,
 I'll thank th' inflicter of the blow;
Forbid the sigh, compose my mind,
 Nor let the gush of mis'ry flow.

The gloomy mantle of the night,
 Which on my sinking spirit steals,
Will vanish at the morning light,
 Which God, my East, my Sun reveals.
      —Thomas Chatterton

Prayer against Perplexing Thoughts

Samuel Johnson (1709–1784) was born to the family of a poor English bookseller. A prodigious scholar and author, Johnson dictated London's literary tastes in the reign of George III. At the time of its publication, his *Dictionary* was the most complete in the language. A classic biography is Boswell's *Life of Johnson*. Deeply religious, Johnson wrote many notable prayers right until the eve of his death. Here are three of his most outstanding prayers.

O Lord, my maker and protector, who hast graciously sent me into this world to work out my salvation, enable me to drive from me all such unquiet and perplexing thoughts as may mislead or hinder me in the practice of those duties which Thou hast required. When I behold the works of Thy hands and consider the course of Thy providence, give me grace always to remember that Thy thoughts are not my thoughts nor Thy ways my ways. And while it shall please Thee to continue me in this world, where much is to be done and little to be known, teach me by Thy Holy Spirit to withdraw my mind from unprofitable and dangerous inquiries, from difficulties vainly curious, and doubts impossible to be solved. Let me rejoice in the light which Thou hast imparted; let me serve Thee with active zeal and humble confidence, and wait with patient expectation for the time in which the soul which Thou receivest, shall be satisfied with knowledge. Grant this, O Lord, for Jesus Christ's sake. *Amen.*   —Samuel Johnson

Prayer of Repentance

O merciful God, full of compassion, long-suffering, and of great pity, who sparest when we deserve punishment, and in thy wrath thinkest upon mercy; make me earnestly to repent, and heartily sorry for all my misdoings; make the remembrance so burdensome and painful, that I may flee to Thee with a troubled spirit and a contrite heart; and, O merciful Lord, visit, comfort and relieve me; cast me not out from thy presence, and take not thy Holy Spirit from me, but excite in me true repentance; give me in this world knowledge of thy truth, and confidence in thy mercy, and in the world to come life everlasting, for the sake of our Lord and Saviour, thy Son Jesus Christ. *Amen.*   —Samuel Johnson

Last Prayer

Almighty and most merciful Father, I am now, as to human eyes it seems, to commemorate for the last time, the death of thy Son Jesus Christ our Saviour and Redeemer. Grant, O Lord, that my whole hope and confidence may be in his merits, and his mercy; enforce and accept my imperfect repentance; make this commemoration available to the confirmation of my faith, the establishment of my hope, and the enlargement of my charity; and make the death of thy Son Jesus Christ effectual to my redemption. Have mercy upon me, and pardon the multitude of my offences. Bless my friends; have mercy upon all men. Support me, by the grace of thy Holy Spirit, in the days of weakness, and at the hour of death; and receive me, at my death, to everlasting happiness, for the sake of Jesus Christ. *Amen.*   —Samuel Johnson
                                    See biographical note above.

Father! Take My Hand

William Wordsworth (1770–1850) was graduated from Cambridge in 1791 and traveled to France, where he became imbued with the principles of Rousseau and republicanism. He later became Poet Laureate of England, succeeding his friend Robert Southey. Wordsworth was a profoundly serious thinker, yet his poetry also reflects his great love of nature and people.

> The way is dark, my Father! Cloud on cloud
> Is gathering thickly o'er my head, and loud
> The thunders roar above me. See I stand
> Like one bewildered! Father, take my hand
>   And through the gloom
>   Lead safely home
>   Thy child!
>
> The day goes fast, my Father! and the night
> Is drawing darkly down. My faithless sight
> Sees ghostly visions. Fears, a spectral band,
> Encompass me. O Father! take my hand,
>   And from the night
>   Lead up to light
>   Thy child!
>
> The way is long, my Father! and my soul
> Longs of the rest and quiet of the goal;
> While yet I journey through this weary land,
> Keep me from wandering, Father! take my hand;
>   Quickly and straight
>   Lead to heaven's gate
>   Thy child!
>
> The path is rough, my Father! Many a thorn
> Has pierced me; and my weary feet, all torn,

And bleeding, mark the way. Yet thy command
Bids me press forward. Father, take my hand;
    Then, safe and blest,
    Lead up to rest
    Thy child!

The throng is great, my Father! Many a doubt
And fear and danger encompass me about;
And foes oppress me sore; I cannot stand
Or go alone. O Father! take my hand,
    And through the throng
    Lead safe along
    Thy child!

—William Wordsworth

A Prayer in Prospect of Death

Robert Burns (1759–1796) was the son of a poor, hard-working Scottish farmer. He left the farm to become a writer of songs and verse, some of which are among the most familiar and best loved in the English language. These include "Auld Lang Syne," "Flow Gently, Sweet Afton," and "Comin' Thro' the Rye." Burns died at thirty-seven, leaving English poetry much the richer because of the humanitarianism, simplicity, genuine emotion, and spontaneity that characterized his work.

O thou unknown, Almighty Cause
    Of all my hope and fear!
In whose dread presence, ere an hour,
    Perhaps I must appear!

If I have wandered in those paths
    Of life I ought to shun;
As something, loudly in my breast
    Remonstrates I have done;

Thou know'st that thou hast formed me,
   With passions wild and strong;
And listening to their witching voice
   Has often led me wrong.

Where human weakness has come short,
   Or frailty stepped aside,
Do thou, All-Good! for such Thou art,
   In shades of darkness hide.

Where with intention I have erred,
   No other plea I have,
But, Thou art good; and Goodness still
   Delighteth to forgive.
                —Robert Burns

Last Lines

The Brontë sisters, Emily Jane (1818–1848), Anne (1820–1849), and
Charlotte (1816–1855), were the daughters of an Anglican clergyman of
Irish birth. The sisters first wrote poetry under pseudonyms, and their
identity as novelists also was unknown at first, even to their publishers,
until 1849, after the deaths of Emily and Anne. Charlotte was famous
for *Jane Eyre,* Emily for *Wuthering Heights,* and Anne for *Agnes Grey.*

No coward soul is mine,
   No trembler in the world's storm troubled sphere:
I see heaven's glories shine,
   And faith shine equal, arming me from fear.

O God within my breast,
   Almighty, ever-present Deity!
Life—that in me has rest,
   As I—undying life—have power in Thee!

Vain are the thousand creeds
    That move men's hearts:
Unutterably vain; worthless as withered reeds,
    Or idlest froth amid the boundless main,

To waken doubt in one
    Holding so fast by thine infinity;
So surely anchored on
    The steadfast rock of immortality.

With wide-embracing love
    Thy Spirit animates eternal years,
Pervades and broods above,
    Changes, sustains, dissolves, creates, and rears.

Though earth and man were gone,
    And suns and universes ceased to be,
And Thou wert left alone,
    Every existence would exist in Thee.

There is not room for Death,
    Nor atom that his might could render void:
Thou—*Thou* art Being and Breath,
    And what *Thou* art may never be destroyed.
                                    —Emily Brontë

The Doubter's Prayer

Eternal power, of earth and air!
    Unseen, yet seen in all around;
Remote, but dwelling everywhere;
    Though silent heard in every sound;

If e'er thine ear in Mercy lent,
   When wretched mortals cried to Thee,
And if indeed, Thy Son was sent,
   To save lost sinners such as me:

Then hear me now, while kneeling here,
   I lift to thee my heart and eye,
And all my soul ascends in prayer,
   Oh, give me—Give me Faith! I cry.

While Faith is with me, I am blest;
   It turns my darkest night to day;
But while I clasp it to my breast,
   I often feel it slide away.

Then, cold and dark, my spirit sinks,
   To see my light of life depart;
And every friend of Hell, methinks,
   Enjoys the anguish of my heart.

What shall I do if all my love,
   My hopes, my toil, are cast away,
And if there be no God above,
   To hear and bless me while I pray?

If this be vain delusion all,
   If death be an eternal sleep
And none can hear my secret call,
   Or see the silent tears I weep!

O help me God! for Thou alone
   Canst my distracted soul relieve;
Forsake it not, it is Thine own,
   Though weak, yet longing to believe.
                 —Anne Brontë

See biographical note on page 299.

Dinah's Prayer for Hetty

George Eliot (1819–1880), great English novelist, was the pen name of
a woman named Mary Ann Evans. Her best-known works, in addition to
Adam Bede, include *Silas Marner* and *The Mill on the Floss*. The following prayer is taken from *Adam Bede*. Hetty Sorrel was in prison on the
charge of murdering her baby. Dinah's prayer was effective, as we learn.
" 'Dinah,' Hetty sobbed out, throwing her arms round Dinah's neck, 'I
will speak . . . I will tell . . . I won't hide it any more.' "

Jesus, thou present Saviour! Thou hast known the depths of
all sorrow, thou hast entered that black darkness where God
is not, and has uttered the cry of the forsaken. Come, Lord,
and gather the fruits of the travail and thy pleading; stretch
forth thy hand, thou who art mighty to save to the uttermost,
and rescue this lost one. She is clothed round with thick darkness; the fetters of her sin are upon her, and she cannot stir to
come to thee: she can only feel her heart is hard, and she is
helpless. She cries to me, thy weak creature . . . Saviour! It is a
blind cry to thee. Hear it! Pierce the darkness! Look upon her
with thy face of love and sorrow, that thou didst turn on him
who denied thee, and melt her hard heart.

See, Lord,—I bring her, as they of old brought the sick and
helpless, and thou didst heal them; I bear her on my arms and
carry her before thee. Fear and trembling have taken hold on
her; but she trembles only at the pain and death of the body;
breathe upon her thy life-giving Spirit, and put a new fear
within her,—the fear of her sin. Make her dread to keep the
accursed thing within her soul: make her feel the presence of
the living God, who beholds all the past, to whom the darkness
is as noonday; who is waiting now, at the eleventh hour, for her
to turn to him and confess her sin, and cry for mercy, . . . now
before the night of death comes, and the moment of pardon is
forever fled, like yesterday that returneth not.

Saviour! It is yet time,—time to snatch this poor soul from
everlasting darkness. I believe in thy infinite love. What is *my*

love or *my* pleading? It is quenched in thine. I can only clasp her in my weak arms, and urge her with my weak pity. Thou— thou wilt breathe on the dead soul, and it shall arise from the unanswering sleep of death.

Yea, Lord, I see thee coming through the darkness, coming like the morning with healing on thy wings. The marks of thy agony are upon thee,—I see, I see thou art able and willing to save,—thou wilt not let her perish forever. Come, mighty Saviour! Let the dead hear thy voice; let the eyes of the blind be opened. Let her see that God encompasses her; let her tremble at nothing but at the sin that cuts her off from him. Melt the hard heart; unseal the closed lips. Make her cry with her whole soul, "Father, I have sinned—"

—George Eliot

Prayer of the Wiltshire Laborers

Charles Dickens (1812–1870) was famous for his many novels depicting life among the English lower and middle classes. His evocation of the sights, sounds, and smells of London is unmatched in English fiction, and his powerful, often satirical stories—some based on his own life— helped bring about much-needed social reform in England. His *A Christmas Carol* and his great novels are immortal. Among these are *David Copperfield*, *Pickwick Papers*, and *A Tale of Two Cities*.

O God, who by thy prophet's hand
    Didst smite the rocky brake,
Whence water came at thy command
    Thy people's thirst to slake;
Strike now upon this granite wall,
    Stern, obdurate and high;
And let some drops of pity fall
    For us who starve and die!

The God who took a little child,
   And set him in the midst,
And promised him his mercy mild,
   As by thy Son, thou didst;
Look down upon our children dear,
   So gaunt, so cold, so spare,
And let their images appear,
   Where lords and gentry are!

Oh God, teach them to feel how we,
   When our poor infants droop,
Are weakened in our trust in thee,
   And how our spirits stoop;
For in thy rest, so bright and fair,
   All tears and sorrows sleep;
And their young looks, so full of care,
   Would make their angels weep!

The God who with his finger drew
   The judgment coming on,
Write for these men, what must ensue,
   Ere many years be gone!
O God, whose bow is in the sky,
   Let them not brave and dare,
Until they look, too late, on high,
   And see an arrow there!

Oh God, remind them! In the bread
   They break upon the knee,
Those sacred words may yet be read
   "In Memory of Me!"
Oh God, remind them of his sweet
   Compassion for the poor,
And how he gave them bread to eat,
   And went from door to door!
             —Charles Dickens

A Child's Prayer

Hear my prayer, O Heavenly Father,
   Ere I lay me down to sleep;
Bid thy angels, pure and holy,
   Round my bed their vigils keep.

My sins are heavy but thy mercy
   Far outweighs them every one;
Down before thy cross I cast them,
   Trusting in thy help alone.

Keep me through this night of peril
   Underneath its boundless shade;
Take me to thy rest, I pray thee,
   When my pilgrimage is made.

None shall measure out thy patience
   By the span of human thought;
None shall bound thy tender mercies
   Which thy holy Son has bought.

Pardon all my past transgressions,
   Give me strength for days to come;
Guide and guard me with thy blessing
   Till thy angels bid me home.

                —Charles Dickens

See biographical note on page 303.

Prayer for a Baby

Elizabeth Barrett Browning (1806–1861) was the wife of the English poet Robert Browning and a noted poet in her own right. *Sonnets from the Portuguese* was inspired by her own love story, which has been immortalized in the play *The Barretts of Wimpole Street* by Rudolph Besier.

Dear Lord, Dear Lord!
Thou, who didst not erst deny
The mother-joy to Mary mild,
Blessèd in the blessèd child,
Which hearkened in meek babyhood
Her cradle-hymn, albeit used
To all that music interfused
In breasts of angels high and good!
Oh, take not, Lord, my babe away—
Oh, take not to thy songful heaven,
The pretty baby thou hast given,
Or ere that I have seen him play
Around his father's knees, and known
That he knew how my love has gone
From all the world to him.
Think, God among the cherubim,
How I shall shiver every day
In thy June sunshine, knowing where
The grave-grass keeps it from his fair
Still cheeks! and feel, at every tread,
His little body which is dead
And hidden in the turfy fold,
Doth make thy whole warm earth a-cold!
O God, I am so young, so young—
I am not used to tears at nights
Instead of slumber—not to prayer
With sobbing lips and hands outwrung!
Thou knowest all my prayings were
"I bless thee, God, for past delights—

Thank God!" I am not used to bear
Hard thoughts of death. The earth doth cover
No face from me of friend or lover;
And must the first who teaches me
The form of shrouds and funerals, be
Mine own first-born beloved? he
Who taught me first this mother-love?
Dear Lord, who spreadest out above
Thy loving, transpierced hands to meet
All lifted hearts with blessing sweet,—
Pierce not my heart, my tender heart
Thou madest tender! Thou who art
So happy in thy heaven alway,
Take not mine only bliss away!

I changed the cruel prayer I made,
And bowed my meekened face and prayed
That God would do His will! and thus
He did it, nurse; He parted us.
And His sun shows victorious
The dead, calm face;—and I am calm;
And heaven is hearkening a new psalm.
    —Elizabeth Barrett Browning, from *Isobel's Child*

The Prayer of Columbus

Walt Whitman (1819–1892), born in West Hills, Long Island, spent his boyhood in Brooklyn. He was for some time a newspaperman. His first volume of poetry, *Leaves of Grass*, was published at his own expense. It was ignored at first, but through the years the volume was enlarged and Whitman's reputation grew with it until he became recognized as one of America's great poets.

A batter'd wreck'd old man,
Thrown on this savage shore, far, far from home,
    Pent by the sea and dark rebellious brows, twelve dreary
       months,
    Sore, stiff with many toils, sicken'd and nigh to death,
    I take my way along the island's edge,
    Venting a heavy heart.

    I am too full of woe!
    Haply I may not live another day;
I cannot rest O God, I cannot eat or drink or sleep,
Till I put forth myself, my prayer, once more to Thee,
    Breathe, bathe myself once more in Thee, commune with
       Thee,
    Report myself once more to Thee.

Thou knowest my years entire, my life,
My long and crowded life of active work, not adoration merely;
    Thou knowest the prayers and vigils of my youth,
    Thou knowest my manhood's solemn and visionary medita-
       tions,
Thou knowest how, before I commenced, I devoted all to come
       to Thee,
    Thou knowest I have in age ratified all those vows and strictly
       kept them,
Thou knowest, I have not once lost—nor faith nor ecstasy in
       Thee,
    In shackles, prison'd, in disgrace, repining not,
    Accepting all from Thee, as duly come from Thee.

All my emprises have been fill'd with Thee,
My speculations, plans, begun and carried on in thoughts of
       Thee,
   Sailing the deep or journeying the land for Thee;
   Intentions, purports, aspirations mine, leaving results to
       Thee.

O I am sure they really came from Thee,
The urge, the ardor, the unconquerable will,
   The potent, felt interior command, stronger than words,
   A message from the Heavens whispering to me even in sleep,
   These sped me on.

By me and these the work so far accomplish'd,
By me earth's elder cloy'd and stifled lands uncloy'd, unloos'd,
   By me the hemispheres rounded and tied, the unknown to
       the known.
The end I know not, it is all in Thee,
Or small or great I know not—haply what broad fields, what
       lands,
   Haply the brutish measureless human undergrowth I know,
   Transplanted there—may rise to stature, knowledge worthy
       Thee,
Haply the swords I know may there indeed be turn'd to reaping
       tools,
   Haply the lifeless cross I know, Europe's dead cross, may bud
       and blossom there.

One effort more, my altar this bleak sand;
   That Thou O God my life hast lighted,
   With ray of light, steady, ineffable, vouchsafed of Thee,
Light rare untellable, lighting the very light,
Beyond all signs, descriptions, languages;
   For that O God, be it my latest word, here on my knees,
   Old, poor, and paralyzed, I thank Thee.

My terminus near,
The clouds already closing in upon me,

The voyage balk'd, the course disputed, lost,
I yield my ships to Thee.

My hands, my limbs grow nerveless,
My brain feels rack'd, bewilder'd,
    Let the old timbers part, I will not part,
I will cling fast to Thee, O God, though the waves buffet me,
    Thee, Thee at least I know.

Is it the prophet's thought I speak, or am I raving?
    What do I know of life? What of myself?
    I know not even my own work past or present,
Dim ever-shifting guesses of it spread before me,
Of newer, better worlds, their mighty parturition,
Mocking, perplexing me.

    And these things I see suddenly, what mean they?
    As if some miracle, some hand divine unseal'd my eyes,
Shadowy vast shapes smile through the air and sky,
And on the distant waves sail countless ships,
    And anthems in new tongues I hear saluting me.
                                        —Walt Whitman, from *Leaves of Grass*

Pied Beauty

Gerard Manley Hopkins was born an Anglo-Catholic in 1844 at Stratford, Essex. He attended Oxford, and studying the classics there he became the friend of Robert Bridges, who edited his poems posthumously. Striving to find "the one visible church," he joined the Catholic Church and finally became a Jesuit priest. A characteristic peculiar to his poetry was the intricate rhythm he used, which he termed "sprung rhythm." Many of his poems are concerned, as "Pied Beauty" is, with nature and religion.

Glory be to God for dappled things—
    For skies of couple-colour as a brinded cow;
        For rose-moles all in stipple upon trout
                that swim;

Fresh-firecoal chestnut-falls; finches' wings;
    Landscape plotted and pieced—fold,
        fallow, and plow;
    And all trades, their gear and tackle and trim.

All things counter, original, spare, strange;
    Whatever is fickle, freckled (who knows how?)
      With swift, slow; sweet, sour; adazzle, dim;
He fathers-forth whose beauty is past change: Praise him.
                  —Gerard Manley Hopkins

Leo Tolstoi's Daily Prayer

Leo Tolstoi (1828–1910), great Russian novelist and philosopher, was the author of *War and Peace*. Tolstoi was converted late in life to the doctrine of Christian love, and accepted also the principle of nonresistance to evil. Although he was excommunicated by the Russian Church, a Tolstoian cult grew up in Russia and abroad. For the rest of his life he dedicated himself to the practice and propagation of his new faith.

I have long ago contracted the habit of praying in solitude every morning, and this my daily prayer is as follows:—

Our Father who art in Heaven, hallowed be Thy name: And after this I add from the Gospel of John: Thy name is love, God is love. He who abides in love abides in God, and God in him. No man hath seen God anywhere, but if we love one another then He abides in us, and his love is fulfilled in us. If any man say "I love God" but hateth his brother, he is a liar, for he that loveth not his brother whom he sees, how can he love God whom he hath not seen? Brothers, let us love one another; love is from God, and every man that loveth is from God and knoweth God, because God is love.

Thy Kingdom come. And I add: Seek ye the kingdom of God and His righteousness and all the rest will be added unto you. The Kingdom of God is within you.

Thy will be done on earth as it is in Heaven. And here I ask myself whether I really believe that I am in God and God in me? And do I believe that my life consists in increasing love in myself? I ask, do I remember that today I am alive, and tomorrow dead? Is it true that I do not wish to live for personal desires and human glory, but only for the fulfillment of the will of God? And I add the words of Jesus from the three Gospels: Not my will, but Thine; and not what I desire but what thou desirest. And not as I desire but as Thou desirest.

Give us this day our daily bread. I add: My food consists in doing the will of Him that sent me, and completing it. Deny thyself, take up thy cross for each day, and follow me. Take my yoke upon you and learn of me, for I am meek and humble in my heart, and you will find peace for your soul. For my yoke is easy, and my burden is light.

And forgive us our sins as we forgive those who sin against us. I add: And your Father will not forgive you your sins unless each one of you forgive his brother who has sinned against him.

And lead us not into temptation. I add: Beware of the temptations of the flesh, of ambition, of ill-will, of gluttony, adultery, human glory. Do not give your alms before men, but so that your right hand does not know what your left is doing. And he is not meet for the kingdom of God who having taken the plow looks back. Rejoice when thou art abused and humiliated.

But deliver us from evil. I add: Beware of what issues from the heart: evil thoughts, murders (every ill-will toward men), thefts (profiting by what one has not earned), adultery (even in thought), false witness, slander.

I conclude the prayer again with the words of the Gospel of John: "And we know that we have passed from death into life if we love our brother. He that loveth not his brother has not eternal life abiding in him."

So do I daily pray, adapting the words of this prayer to my actions and my spiritual state.

—Leo Tolstoi, from *Personal Letters*

Father in Heaven, We Thank Thee

Ralph Waldo Emerson (1803–1882), born in Boston, was the son of a Unitarian minister and descended from a long line of New England clergymen. In 1829 he became pastor of the Old North Church (Unitarian) in Boston. He resigned in 1832 to travel, lecture, and write. He helped form the group known as Transcendentalists in Concord, where he settled. He traveled to Europe, where he met Coleridge, Carlyle, and Wordsworth. He also wrote poetry and his famous *Essays, Letters and Social Aims,* and *Journals.*

> For flowers that bloom about our feet;
> For tender grass, so fresh and sweet;
> For song of bird and hum of bee;
> For all things fair we hear or see—
>   Father in heaven, we thank Thee!

> For blue of stream, for blue of sky;
> For pleasant shade of branches high;
> For fragrant air and cooling breeze;
> For beauty of the blowing trees—
>   Father in heaven, we thank Thee!

> For mother-love, for father-care;
> For brothers strong and sisters fair;
> For love at home and school each day;
> For guidance lest we go astray—
>   Father in heaven, we thank Thee!

> For Thy dear, everlasting arms,
> That bear us o'er all ills and harms;
> For blessed words of long ago;
> That help us now Thy will to know—
>   Father in heaven, we thank Thee!
>   —Ralph Waldo Emerson

A Last Prayer

Helen Hunt Jackson (1830–1885) was a New Englander and a school friend of Emily Dickinson. She began to write after the death of her husband, and her *Verses, Sonnets and Lyrics* were the first to appear. She is also the author of *Ramona*, famous novel on the American Indian problem, as well as children's stories and travel sketches.

> Father, I scarcely dare to pray,
>   So clear I see, now it is done,
> That I have wasted half my day,
>   And left my work but just begun;
>
> So clear I see that things I thought
>   Were right or harmless were a sin;
> So clear I see that I have sought
>   Unconscious, selfish aims to win;
>
> So clear I see that I have hurt
>   The soul I might have helped to save;
> That I have slothful been, inert,
>   Deaf to the calls thy leaders gave.
>
> In outskirts of thy kingdoms vast,
>   Father, the humblest spot give me;
> Set me the lowliest task thou hast:
>   Let me repentant work for thee!
>   —Helen Hunt Jackson

Prayer from the "Living Temple"

Oliver Wendell Holmes (1809–1894), born in Cambridge, Massachusetts, became a distinguished physician in Boston but was also a contributor and editor of the *Atlantic Monthly*. His column in the *Atlantic* was the basis of his famous book *Autocrat of the Breakfast Table*.

> O Father! grant thy love divine
> To make these mystic temples thine!
> When wasting age and wearying strife
> Have sapped the leaning walls of life,
> When darkness gathers over all,
> And the last tottering pillars fall,
> Take the poor dust thy mercy warms,
> And mould it into heavenly forms!
> —Oliver Wendell Holmes

To a Dying Wife

James Russell Lowell (1819–1891) was born in Cambridge, Massachusetts, and educated at Harvard as a lawyer. He abandoned law for a long and fruitful career as editor and contributor to various periodicals, as well as professor of languages at Harvard. His *Poems* and *The Bigelow Papers* are among his outstanding contributions to American letters.

> God! do not let my loved one die,
>   But rather wait until the time
> That I am grown in purity
>   Enough to enter thy pure clime,
> Then take me I will gladly go,
>   So that my love remain below!
>
> O, let her stay! She is by birth
>   What I through death must learn to be;

We need her more on our poor earth
  Than thou canst need in heaven with thee;
She hath her wings already, I
  Must burst this earth shell ere I fly.

Then, God, take me! We shall be near,
  More near than ever, each to each;
Her angel ears will find more clear
  My heavenly than my earthly speech;
And still, as I draw nigh to thee,
  Her soul and mine shall closer be.
                                    —James Russell Lowell

An Affirmation of Faith

John Ruskin (1819–1900) was the son of wealthy English parents who were interested in evangelism and trained him for the ministry. Breaking with organized religion, he turned to art and letters and later became interested in political economy and social theory. Although he died insane, many of his social theories have become accepted doctrine.

I trust in the living God, Father Almighty, maker of heaven and earth and of all things and creatures visible and invisible. I trust in the kindness of his law and the goodness of his work. And I will strive to love him and keep his law and see his work while I live. I trust in the nobleness of human nature, in the majesty of its faculties, the fulness of its mercy, and the joy of its love. And I will strive to love my neighbor as myself, and even when I cannot, will act as if I did.

I will not kill nor hurt any living creature needlessly, nor destroy any beautiful thing, but will strive to save and comfort all gentle life, and guard and perfect all natural beauty upon the earth. I will strive to raise my own body and soul daily into all the higher powers of duty and happiness, not in rivalship or contention with others, but for the help, delight and honor of others, and for the joy and peace of my own life.
                                    —John Ruskin, from *Creed of St. George's Guild*

The Prayer

John Galsworthy (1867–1933), English novelist and dramatist, is famous for his *The Forsyte Saga* and his poems and plays dealing with social problems. In 1932 he received the Nobel Prize for Literature.

If on a Spring night I went by,
And God were standing there,
What is the prayer that I would cry
To Him? This is the prayer:
O Lord of Courage grave!
O Master of this night of Spring!
Make firm in me a heart too brave
To ask Thee anything!
—John Galsworthy

Prayer for Family Life

Lord, behold our family here assembled. We thank Thee for this place in which we dwell; for the love that unites us; for the peace accorded us this day; for the hope with which we expect the morrow; for the health, the work, the food and the bright skies that make our lives delightful; for our friends in all parts of the earth, and our friendly helpers in this foreign isle.

Let peace abound in our small company. Purge out of every heart the lurking grudge. Give us grace and strength to forbear and persevere. Offenders, give us the grace to accept and to forgive offenders. Forgetful ourselves, help us to bear cheerfully the forgetfulness of others.

Give us courage, gaiety and the quiet mind. Spare to us our friends, soften to us our enemies. Bless us, if it may be in all our innocent endeavours. If it may not, give us the strength to encounter that which is to come, that we brave it in peril, constant in tribulation, temperate in wrath, and in all changes of fortune and down to the gates of death, loyal and loving one to another.

As the clay to the potter, as the windmill to the wind, as children of their sire, we beseech of Thee this help and mercy for Christ's sake. *Amen.*

—Robert Louis Stevenson
See biographical note on page 126. This prayer was written in Samoa while he lay dangerously ill with tuberculosis.

Stevenson on the Night before Dying

We beseech Thee, Lord, to behold us with favor, folk of many families and nations gathered together in peace of this roof, weak men and women existing under the covert of Thy patience.

Be patient still; suffer us yet a little longer—with our broken purposes of good, with our idle endeavors against evil, suffer us awhile longer to endure, and (if it may be) help us to do better.

Bless to us our extraordinary mercies; if the day come when these must be taken, brace us to play the man under affliction.

Be with our friends, be with ourselves. Go with each of us to rest; if any awake, temper to them the dark hours of watching; and when the day returns, return to us, our sun and comforter, and call us up with morning faces and with morning hearts— eager to labor—eager to be happy, if happiness shall be our portion—and if the day is marked for sorrow, strong to endure it. *Amen.*

—Robert Louis Stevenson
See biographical note on page 126.

Milton's Prayer in Blindness

John Milton (1608–1674), author of *Paradise Lost,* is considered among the greatest poets of all time. While an official in the government of Oliver Cromwell he lost his eyesight and carried on his work thenceforth through secretaries. This prayer by a little-known poet, E. L. Howell, captures the spirit of Milton's life and thought.

O merciful One!
When men are farthest, then thou art most near;
When friends pass by me, and my weakness shun,
Thy chariot I hear.

Thy glorious face
Is leaning toward me; and its holy light
Shines in upon my lonely dwelling-place,—
And there is no more night.

On my bended knee
I recognize thy purpose clearly shown:
My vision thou hast dimmed, that I may see
Thyself,—thyself alone.

I have naught to fear;
This darkness is the shadow of thy wing;
Beneath it I am almost sacred; here
Can come no evil thing.

O, I seem to stand
Trembling, where foot of mortal ne'er hath been;
Wrapped in the radiance of thy sinless land,
Which eye hath never seen!

—E. L. Howell

O God of Earth and Altar

Gilbert Keith Chesterton (1874–1936), English essayist and novelist, was a convert to Roman Catholicism, becoming an outspoken champion of his new faith. He was also a clever artist and illustrated the books of Hilaire Belloc. He is widely known as the creator of the much-loved Father Brown the detective.

O God of earth and altar,
　　Bow down and hear our cry,
Our earthly rulers falter,
　　Our people drift and die;
The walls of gold entomb us,
　　The swords of scorn divide,
Take not Thy thunder from us,
　　But take away our pride.

From all that terror teaches,
　　From lies of tongue and pen,
From all the easy speeches
　　That comfort cruel men,
From sale and profanation
　　Of honor and the sword,
From sleep and from damnation,
　　Deliver us, good Lord!

Tie in a living tether
　　The priest and prince and thrall,
Bind all our lives together,
　　Smite and save us all;
In ire and exultation
　　Aflame with faith, and free,
Lift up a living nation,
　　A single sword to Thee.
　　　　　　　　—Gilbert K. Chesterton

For the Freedom of Mankind

Stephen Vincent Benét was born in Bethlehem, Pennsylvania, in 1898. He wrote poetry while still in college and in 1929 won the Pulitzer Prize for his long poem *John Brown's Body*. His short stories were some of the best of his time, and his unfinished American epic *Western Star* was published after his death in 1943, winning the Pulitzer Prize in 1944.

God of the free, we pledge our hearts and lives today to the cause of all free mankind.

Grant us victory over the tyrants who would enslave all free men and nations. Grant us faith and understanding to cherish all those who fight for freedom as if they were our brothers. Grant us brotherhood in hope and union, not only for the space of this bitter war, but for the days to come which shall and must unite all the children of earth.

Our earth is but a small star in the great universe. Yet of it we can make, if we choose, a planet unvexed by war, untroubled by hunger or fear, undivided by senseless distinctions of race, color or theory. Grant us that courage and foreseeing to begin this task today that our children's children may be proud of the name of man.

The spirit of man has awakened and the soul of man has gone forth. Grant us the wisdom and the vision to comprehend the greatness of man's spirit, that suffers and endures so hugely for a goal beyond his own brief span. Grant us honor for our dead who died in the faith, honor for our living who work and strive for the faith, redemption and security for all captive lands and peoples. Grant us patience with the deluded and pity for the betrayed. And grant us the skill and valor that shall cleanse the world of oppression and the old base doctrine that the strong must eat the weak because they are strong.

Yet most of all grant us brotherhood, not only for this day but for all our years—a brotherhood not of words but of acts and deeds. We are all of us children of earth—grant us that simple knowledge. If our brothers are oppressed, then we are oppressed. If they hunger we hunger. If their freedom is taken away our freedom is not secure. Grant us a common faith that man shall know bread and peace—that he shall know justice and righteousness, freedom and security, an equal opportunity and an equal chance to do his best, not only in our own lands, but throughout the world. And in that faith let us march toward the clean world our hands can make.

—from *Prayers of the Free Spirit*

Prayer for This House

Louis Untermeyer was born in New York City in 1885. He is best known for his many anthologies but is a poet in his own right as well as an erudite and clever parodist. He has also translated the poems of Heinrich Heine and written a biography of that great German poet.

> May nothing evil cross this door,
> And may ill fortune never pry
> About these windows; may the roar
>   And rain go by.
>
> Strengthened by faith, these rafters will
> Withstand the battering of the storm;
> This hearth, though all the world grow chill,
>   Will keep us warm.
> Peace shall walk softly through these rooms,
> Touching our lips with holy wine,
> Till ev'ry casual corner blooms
>   Into a shrine.
>
> Laughter shall drown the raucous shout;
> And, though these sheltering walls are thin,
> May they be strong to keep hate out
>   And hold love in.

—Louis Untermeyer, from *This Singing World*

Prayer of a Soldier in France

Joyce Kilmer (1886–1918), born in New Brunswick, New Jersey, was both a journalist and a poet. He was killed in France in World War I and is known chiefly as the author of the poem "Trees."

My shoulders ache beneath my pack;
(Lie easier, Cross, upon His back).

I march with feet that burn and smart;
(Tread, Holy Feet, upon my heart).

Men shout at me that may not speak;
(They scourged Thy back and smote Thy cheek).

I may not lift a hand to clear
My eyes of salty drops that sear.

(Then shall my guilty soul forget
Thy agony of Bloody Sweat?)

Lord, Thou didst suffer more for me
Than all the hosts of land and sea.
So let me render back again
This millionth of Thy gift. *Amen.*
    —Joyce Kilmer, from *The Golden Book of Prayer*

Chorus of Women of Canterbury

Thomas Stearns Eliot was born in St. Louis, Missouri, in 1888. He has lived most of his life in England and in 1927 became a British subject. He is one of the most influential modern poets, and he was awarded the Nobel Prize for Literature in 1948. His plays in verse, including *Murder in the Cathedral* and *The Cocktail Party*, have set a new trend in the modern theater.

We praise Thee, O God, for Thy glory displayed in all the creatures of the earth,

In the snow, in the rain, in the wind, in the storm; in all of Thy
creatures, both the hunters and the hunted.

For all things exist only as seen by Thee, only as known by
Thee, all things exist

Only in Thy light, and Thy glory is declared even in that which
denies Thee; the darkness declares the glory of light.

Those who deny Thee could not deny, if Thou didst not exist;
and their denial is never complete, for if it were so, they
would not exist.

They affirm Thee in living; all things affirm Thee in living; the
bird in the air, both the hawk and the finch; the beast on the
earth, both the wolf and the lamb; the worm in the soil and
the worm in the belly.

Therefore man, whom Thou hast made to be conscious of Thee,
must consciously praise Thee, in thought and in word and in
deed.

Even with the hand to the broom, the back bent in laying the
fire, the knee bent in cleaning the hearth, we, the scrubbers
and sweepers of Canterbury,

The back bent under toil, the knee bent under sin, the hands to
the face under fear, the head bent under grief,

Even in us the voices of seasons, the snuffle of winter, the song
of spring, the drone of summer, the voices of beasts and of
birds, praise Thee.

We thank Thee for Thy mercies of blood, for Thy redemption
by blood. For the blood of Thy martyrs and saints

Shall enrich the earth, shall create the holy places.

For wherever a saint has dwelt, wherever a martyr has given
  his blood for the blood of Christ,

There is holy ground, and the sanctity shall not depart from it

Though armies trample over it, though sightseers come with
  guide-books looking over it;

From where the western seas gnaw at the coast of Iona,

To the death in the desert, the prayer in forgotten places by the
  broken imperial column,

From such ground springs that which forever renews the earth

Though it is forever denied. Therefore, O God, we thank Thee

Who hast given such blessing to Canterbury.

Forgive us, O Lord, we acknowledge ourselves as type of the
  common man,

Of the men and women who shut the door and sit by the fire;

Who fear the blessing of God, the loneliness of the night of
  God, the surrender required, the deprivation inflicted;

Who fear the injustice of men less than the justice of God;

Who fear the hand at the window, the fire in the thatch, the fist
  in the tavern, the push into the canal,

Less than we fear the love of God.

We acknowledge our trespass, our weakness, our fault; we
  acknowledge

That the sin of the world is upon our heads; that the blood of
the martyrs and the agony of the saints

Is upon our heads.

Lord, have mercy upon us.

Christ, have mercy upon us.

Lord, have mercy upon us.

Blessed Thomas, pray for us.

—T. S. Eliot, from *Murder in the Cathedral* (Part II)

PRAYERS FROM
OTHER LANDS AND
PEOPLES

THIS GROUP OF PRAYERS *is not only from many countries of the world but from several faiths as well. There is a wonderful sameness in prayer: no matter what the language, no matter what the church, the appeal of the Children of God to their Maker remains essentially the same. The shadings of skin may vary, but the heartbeats are constant at seventy-eight to the minute and the aspirations are as unvarying.*

There is a prayer in here from the Rig Veda, a collection of Hindu hymns sung by the faithful 1,000 years before Christ was born. The prayer opens:

Where there is eternal light, in that immortal imperishable sphere, where life is free, where the worlds are radiant, there make me immortal....

Here, succinctly, is a prayer as modern as the airplane, and with stronger wings. Though it was sung with fervor almost 3,000 years ago, it is far from being the oldest known prayer. The antiquity of prayer, and its changeless plea for immortality, is its greatest strength.

In the field of communications between man and God there are no new fashions. This section of the book proves the point.

Nebuchadnezzar to Marduk

Nebuchadnezzar was king of Babylon (about 605–562 B.C.) at the time it was the greatest city in the world. He defeated the Egyptians and also put down a revolt of the Jewish King Jehoiakim of Judah. A new revolt took place, and Jerusalem was sacked and her king and many notables carried off to Babylon. Nebuchadnezzar figures in the *Book of Daniel*, which tells of his going mad and eating grass as was prophesied. Marduk is the legendary king of the gods of the Babylonian Empire.

I love thy sublime appearance as my own precious life—since I love the fear of thy divinity and I am zealous for thy rule, be gracious to my prayer for I am the king who adorns thy temple—the thoughtful governor who beautifies all thy settlements. At thy command, O merciful Marduk, may the house that I have built endure forever. May I be satiated with its splendor, attain old age therein with abundant offspring and receive therein tribute of the kings of all regions from all mankind.

—Nebuchadnezzar, from *The Civilization of Babylonia and Assyria*

Hymn to Osiris

This hymn comes from the Egyptian *Book of the Dead*. Osiris is the male god of the fecund earth, killed by the evil Set and buried by his wife Isis. But he rises again in the form of ripe grain, symbol of life after death.

Glory to Osiris, the Prince of Everlastingness,
Who traveleth through all the million years into Eternity,
Crowned with the North and South, the Lord of gods and men,
Bearing the crook and whip of mercy and of power.

O King of Kings, O Prince of Princes, Lord of Lords,
Through thee the world is green again by virtue of thy Passion;
Thou leadest in thy train what has been and what shall be,

My heart shall rest content upon the hidden Mountain.

Thy body is of shining metal, and thy head is azure;
The color of turquoise plays about thee where thou goest.
All-pervading is thy body, radiant thy countenance,
As the fields and river valleys of the world hereafter.
—from *An Anthology of World Poetry*

Zarathustra's Prayer

Zarathustra, or Zoroaster, was born in Persia about 660 B.C. and lived
until about 583 B.C. He was the founder of the religion which bears his
name, Zoroastrianism, which was a reform of the nature religion of ancient Persia. In time the King of Persia was converted, and the religion
grew to be the national religion of the Persian Empire, until Alexander's
conquest of Persia brought disruption of the state and overwhelming of
Zoroastrianism. It is still practiced in modern times by many in Iran and
in India.

I

This do I ask of Thee, O Lord; speak, and make me to know the
       truth!
   How may I (even I) in right humility worship one like thee
   Who knoweth all things? And, wilt thou teach not—one like
       me, thy friend?
   Vouchsafing in accord with thy law, the great joy of working
       with thee,
   Visiting us, likeminded to theeward, with thine own most
       holy mind?

II

This do I ask of Thee, O Lord: speak, and make me to know the
       truth!
   How I with gladness may verily come to the help of the Lord
       of heaven,

Who hath himself at our hearts and hands required such service of praise?

For thou, most gracious in holiness, by thy law of truth and right

Dost ward off destruction from body and soul—a faithful friend who knoweth our need.

III

This do I ask of Thee, O Lord: speak, and make me to know the truth!

Who in the beginning was father of the holy law revealed through order and beauty?

Who established their everlasting paths for the glorious sun and the stars?

Yea, who save thee determineth still how the moon shall wax and wane?

These truths, and others like them, would I hear from thyself, O thou who knowest all.

IV

This do I ask of Thee, O Lord: speak, and make me to know the truth!

Who upholdeth the earth, and the heaven above and beneath;

That they fall not? Who erst brought forth the waters and the tall trees?

Who yoked the two fleet steeds with the winds unto the storm clouds?

Who wrought the mighty will unto holiness, and made it abide in the heart of man?

V

This do I ask of Thee, O Lord: speak, and make me to know the truth!

Who with subtlety brought forth the light of heaven and the darkness of night?

Who fashioned well the eager will of the wakeful soul, and
  sleep?

Who the order unchanging whereby the dawn doth spread
  twixt midnight and noon

Showing forth to the man it floodeth with light what service
  is due unto thee?

VI

This do I ask of Thee, O Lord: speak, and make me to know the
  truth!

Make sure in faith the truth of the doctrine thou biddest me
  publish abroad:

Doth a ready will to serve thee increase by good deeds the
  sway of thy holy law?

Dost thou by thy holy spirit appoint thy kingdom unto them
  that do right?

For whose sake else hast thou made the mother-soul of thy
  faithful herd to multiply joy?

VII

This is my prayer unto Thee, O Lord: speak, and make me to
  know the truth!

Who hath established the blessed will ever zealous to serve
  in thy kingdom on earth?

Who by his deeply implanted will hath caused son to honor
  sire?

With these queries I urge thee, who knowest all things, that
  I may know all from thee,

O thou, by thy spirit gracious Creator and giver of all good
  things.

VIII

This is my prayer unto Thee, O Lord: speak, and make me to
  know the truth!

What is thy blessed doctrine that I may meditate thereon
  evermore?

What are the inspiring songs of praise wherefor, inspired of
    thee, I implored thee?
And what sure testimonies shall enable thy people to serve
    thee in quiet steadfastness?
Whereby may my soul press forward in goodness, speak,
    speak that compelling Word!

IX

This is my prayer unto Thee, O Lord: speak, and make me to
    know the truth!
How may I sanctify unto myself the vision of truth thou hast
    bestowed,
That as a master in the kingdom of loving-kindness, persua-
    sively I may impart it,
That possessing them both, indeed, I may with authority set
    thee forth
Who with the law dost dwell with thy people, and in the
    good will of every heart?

X

This do I ask of Thee, O Lord: speak, and make me to know the
    truth!
What doctrine of all revelations of faith is in thy sight the
    best?
Which shall cause our homes to see good days that go hand
    in hand with thy law?
Which ordereth our ways by justice and virtue to that will
    which ensueth the good?
May the prayers of my enlightened heart draw thee verily
    nigh unto me.

XI

This do I ask of Thee, O Lord: speak, and make me to know
    the truth!
Shall the mind that is swift unto goodness come from thee
    unto these thy servants

For whose sake, O all-knowing God, thy wisdom is published
  abroad?
For lo, am not I in these blessed gifts confessed of thy servants the foremost
Who all false gods, and them that worship the Lie, do cast
  out and abhor!

—Zarathustra, translated from Parsee Service

Chaldean Prayer to the Sun

Chaldea is that portion of the Tigris-Euphrates Valley which comprised
the Babylonian Empire (sixth century B.C.). Astrology was much developed in this period, and the term Chaldean came to mean astrologer.
The term is also used to mean Aramaean in the Bible.

The Lord has sent me; the great god Hea,
  has sent me.

Thou, in thy course thou directest the
  human race
Cast upon him a ray of peace, and let it
  cure his suffering.

The man, son of his god, has laid before him
  his shortcomings and transgressions; his
  feet and hands are in pain, grievously
  defiled by disease.

Sun, to the lifting up of my hands pay
  attention; eat his food, receive the victim,
  give his god, for a support, to his hand!

By his order let his shortcomings be pardoned! Let
  his transgressions be blotted out!

May his troubles leave him! May he recover from
  his disease!

Give back life to the King!

Then, on the day that he revives, may thy
  sublimity envelop him!

Direct the King who is in subjection to thee!

And me, the magician, thy humble servant, direct me!
                                    —from *Pagan Prayers*

Hymn to Zeus

Cleanthes, Stoic philosopher, lived from about 300–220 B.C. He was a
pupil of Zeno and differed from the other Stoics in that he regarded the
sun as the governing principle of the world. He died of voluntary starvation. His "Hymn to Zeus" is considered one of the great prayers of all
time. The passage from the *New Testament*, "As certain also of your own
poets have said, For we are also His offspring" (*Acts* 17:28) alludes to
line 4 of this hymn.

Mightiest of the Immortals, all-praised and all-powerful for-
  ever,
Zeus, the Creator, who rulest the world Thou hast fashioned
  with law,
Thine be the fruit of the lips, who permittest all flesh to address
  Thee.
For we are Thine offspring, made in Thine image, who dwell on
  the earth.
Therefore to Thee be my hymn, Thy strength be my song ever-
  more.
Lo! the high heavens are Thine, and the lights of the heavens,
  Thy servants,

Circle the earth at thy bidding: thou guidest their motions in
    order.

In Thine hand is the power: in Thy right hand are the light-
    nings,

Two-edged, terrible, fiery, swift, and from everlasting.

Thine is the frost, and Thine is the snow, Thou sovran Disposer,

Lord of the great lights, Lord of the small, and King above all
    things.

Neither is anything done on the earth without Thy command-
    ment,

Nor in the heavens above, nor in the waters below,

Save what the wicked do, by following after their folly.

But Thou hast understanding to set straight even the crooked,

Out of the void bringest form, and out of alien kinship,

So Thou hast fashioned in one the good and the evil together,

That Thy Word should be One-in-All through all generations.

Woe unto them who flee that Word, woe, woe to the wicked,

Ever pursuing desires of their heart, and a good which is not
    good,

Blind are their eyes to Thy light, and their ears are deaf to Thy
    precepts,

Blind and deaf to the signs which lead to victorious living;

They are a guide to themselves; each erreth alone and in dark-
    ness;

Vain is unbridled ambition, and vain is the counsel of fools,

Vain are the lusts of the flesh—and all who seek them shall
    perish.

But oh, bountiful Zeus! oh, Cloud-girt! clothed with the
    thunder,

Cleanse Thou man from his faults, scatter the seeds from his
    soul,

Plant Thy wisdom within, which ruleth all things rightly,

That we may give Thee glory, wherewith Thou hast glorified
    us! . . .

Thou art the Law and the Life: praised be Thy name ever-
    more!   —Cleanthes

Hymn to Brahman

Brahman, or Brahma, in Hinduism is the Absolute, or God entirely impersonal. However, he became endowed with personality and was thought of as Creator. The Brahmins of India, the highest caste in the system of Hinduism, claim Brahman as the founder of their religion.

O Brahman Supreme!
Formless art thou, and yet
(Though the reason none knows)
Thou bringest forth many forms;
Thou bringest them forth, and then
Withdrawest them to thyself.
Fill us with thoughts of thee!

Thou art the fire,
Thou art the sun,
Thou art the air,
Thou art the moon,
Thou art the starry firmament,
Thou art Brahman Supreme:
Thou art the waters—thou,
The creator of all!

Thou art woman, thou art man,
Thou art the youth, thou art the maiden,
Thou art the old man tottering with his staff;
Thou facest everywhere.

Thou art the dark butterfly,
Thou art the green parrot with red eyes,
Thou art the thunder cloud, the seasons, the seas.
Without beginning art thou,
Beyond time, beyond space,
Thou art he from whom sprang
The three worlds.

Thou art the Primal Being.
Thou appearest as this universe
Of illusion and dream.
Thou art beyond time.
Indivisible, infinite, the Adorable One—
Let a man meditate on thee
Within his heart,
Let him consecrate himself to thee,
And thou, infinite Lord,
Wilt make thyself known to him.

Thou, womb and tomb of the universe,
And its abode;
Thou, source of all virtue,
Destroyer of all sins—
Thou art seated in the heart.
When thou art seen,
Time and form disappear.
Let a man feel thy presence,
Let him behold thee within,
And to him shall come peace,
Eternal peace—
To none else, to none else!
Thou art the eternal among non-eternals,
The consciousness of the conscious;
Though one, thou fulfillest
The desires of many.

Let a man devote himself
To knowledge of thee,
Let him follow thy path,
And he shall know thee:
All his fetters shall be loosed.

Can a man roll up the sky
Like a piece of skin?
Can he end his misery
And not know thee?   —from *The Upanishads*

Hindu Prayer

This Indian prayer is from the *Rig Veda,* one of the four sacred books of the Brahmins and the oldest of the collections of Hindu hymns. The Vedic period is estimated to have begun about 1500 to 1000 B.C.

Where there is eternal Light, in that immortal imperishable sphere, where life is free, where the worlds are radiant, there make me immortal; where joys reside, where the desire of our desires is attained, there make me immortal. . . . May that soul of mine—which is a ray from out the inextinguishable light— be united, by Divine meditation, to the Spirit supremely blest, supremely intelligent.

—from the *Rig Veda*

Hindu Prayer to Buddha

Buddha was born about 563 B.C. in India near Nepal with the family name of Gautama. His family was wealthy, but he renounced a life of ease to become a hermit and wanderer. During this time he learned the principles on which Buddhism is based, became a teacher, with disciples who were the first Buddhist monks, and helped spread the new religion abroad. He died about 483 B.C., having won the title of Buddha (En- lightened One).

Thou in whom innumerable creatures believe!

Thou, Buddha, Victor over the hosts of evil!

Thou, all-wise Being, come down to our world!

Made perfect and glorified by innumerable by-gone revolutions; always pitiful, always gracious toward all creatures!

Look down upon us; for the time has come to pour
out blessings on all creatures.

Be gracious to us from thy throne built in thy
heavenly world.

Thou art the eternal redemption of all creatures,
therefore bow down to us with all thy unstained
heavenly societies.

—from the *Rig Veda*

As Cherry Blossoms Fall

Among the briefest but most descriptive and colorful prayers from other
lands are these four prayers of the Japanese.

*Just after the Cherry Blossom Festival a Japanese pastor was
heard to pray:*

As the cherry blossoms quickly fall and are forgotten, so in
thy bounteous mercy grant that our sins may be shed and remembered no more.

Like the Gallant Carp

*At the time of the Boys' Festival, when paper and cloth fish are
hung out on bamboo poles, a father prayed thus:*

Grant to my boy the high mettle, the dauntless courage, the
dashing boldness of the carp; and, when at last death summons
him, may he, like this gallant fish, remain fearless and unflinch-
ing to the end, meeting his fate in quiet resignation.

As Mt. Fuji

O Thou, whose glory reaches to the heavens, our Peerless One, grant that, as Fuji's pain-wrought crown is reflected in the muddy paddy fields near its base, we may each in his own place and in his own pattern catch a fragment of thy likeness and all together reveal the perfection of thy beauty.

Bedtime Prayer for a Japanese Girl

O God of infinite beauty and perfect love, at this hour of peace and calm, I open to thee the moon-window of my soul's chamber. Flood it, gracious Father, with the celestial light, fragrant with the winter plum of thy divine love and purity.

—from *The World at One in Prayer,* by Dr. Hachiroa Yuasa

To Shang-Ti

The Shang or Yin dynasty of China dates from about 1766 to 1122 B.C. The Shang had a complex agricultural civilization of peasants and city-dwelling craftsmen, with a priestly class, nobles, and a king or emperor.

I The Emperor, have respectfully prepared
    this paper to inform the spirit of the
    sun, the spirit of the moon, the spirits
    of the five planets, of the stars, of the
    clouds, of the four seas, of the great
    rivers, of the present year,

That on the first of next month we shall
    reverently lead our officers and people
    to honor the great name of Shang-Ti.

We inform you beforehand, O ye celestial
and terrestrial spirits, and will trouble
you on our behalf, to exert your spiritual
power, and display your vigorous efficacy,
communicating our poor desire to Shang-Ti,
praying him to accept our worship, and be
pleased with the new title which we shall
reverently present to him.

Thou, O Ti, didst open the way for the forces
of matter to operate;

Thou, O Spirit, didst produce the beautiful
light of the sun and moon, that all thy
creatures might be happy.

Thou hast vouchsafed to hear us, O Ti, for
thou regardest us as thy children.

I, thy child, dull and ignorant, can poorly
express my feelings.

Honorable is thy great name!
—from *Pagan Prayers*

Korean Thanksgiving at Harvest

This beautiful prayer of thanksgiving is translated from a Korean book of
prayers.

At this time, O Lord, we are especially thankful for the
golden ripe grain and for the hundred kinds of red fruits. Where
do these come from? The farmers who take them into their
barns think they are the result of their own labors. But, O

Lord, they are thine. To sustain our lives thou hast given us the needed sunshine and the proper rain; by these we sustain our lives and for this we are grateful. Just as the farmers, following the natural law, are diligent in time of sowing that they may reap, so may we follow the laws which thou hast established and sow righteousness day by day. *Amen.*

—from *The World at One in Prayer*

In Tune

Ceylonese of three denominations have cooperated in establishing the Christa Seva Ashram. The day of service in the community begins often with this Tamil lyric, at 4:30 A.M.

When all the strings of my life be tuned, O Master, then at every touch of thine shall come out the music of Love.

Gilbert Islands

This prayer is by a Samoan Christian pastor in the Gilbert Islands. These islands are low-lying coral reefs in the heart of the Pacific. There are no rivers or hills and little vegetation except the cocoanut palms.

As we hear the sound of the ocean waves by which we are surrounded, so may we at all times hear thy voice, O God. We thank thee for the refreshing wind which ever blows from the sea; may this experience remind us of thy Spirit blowing where it listeth. Thou hast given us the light and heat of the sun; O make our hearts warm like the sun at noon. Be a river of life to our thirsty islands and revive our souls that are parched with sin. As the great ocean about us never ceases to cleanse the rubbish from the beaches of our little homes, so may thy mighty Spirit cleanse our hearts that they may become places in which thou canst dwell forever. We thank thee that thou dost not hide thyself from us. Our ancestors worshiped fishes and stones as their gods; but thou hast found us, and we have found thee. *Amen.*

—from *The World at One in Prayer*

God

There are few single poems as widely known throughout the world as the Russian hymn or prayer of Derzhavin. It was translated into Japanese by Imperial order, embroidered in gold, and hung in the temple of Jeddo. It has been translated into Chinese and inscribed on silk. It has even been translated into the Tatar tongue. The author, Gavriil Romanavich Derzhavin, was born at Kazan, July, 1743. He became a military engineer and was advanced to the post of Secretary of State by Catherine II. After twenty years at court, he retired to write. The following poem is Russia's outstanding contribution to religious poetry; and its author is regarded as the greatest Russian poet before Pushkin.

"O Thou eternal One! whose presence bright
   All space doth occupy, all motion guide;
Unchanged through time's all devastating flight;
   Thou only God! there is no God beside!
Being above all beings! Mighty one!
   Whom none can comprehend and none explore,
Who fill'st existence with thyself alone;
   Embracing all, supporting, ruling o'er;
   Being whom we call God, and know no more!

"In its sublime research, Philosophy
   May measure out the ocean deep, may count
The sands or the sun's rays; but God! for Thee
   There is no weight nor measure; none can mount

Up to thy mysteries; Reason's brightest spark,
   Though kindled by thy light, in vain would try
To trace thy counsels, infinite and dark;
   And thought is lost ere thought can soar so high;
   Even like past moments in eternity.

"Thou from primeval nothingness didst call
   First chaos, then existence; Lord, on Thee
Eternity had its foundation; all
   Sprang forth from Thee—of light, joy, harmony
Sole origin; all life, all beauty, Thine.
   Thy word created all, and doth create;
Thy splendor fills all space with rays divine.
   Thou art, and wert, and shalt be, glorious, great,
   Life-giving, life-sustaining Potentate!

"Thy chains the unmeasured universe surround,
   Upheld by Thee, by Thee inspired with breath,
Thou the beginning with the end hast bound,
   And beautifully mingled life and death!
As sparks mount upward from the fiery blaze,
   So suns are born, so worlds spring forth from Thee;
And as the spangles in the sunny rays
   Shine round the silver snow, the pageantry
Of heaven's bright army glitters in thy praise.

"A million torches, lighted by thy hand,
   Wander unwearied through the blue abyss;
They own thy power, accomplish thy command,
   All gay with life, all eloquent with bliss.
What shall we call them?—piles of crystal light?
   A glorious company of golden streams?
Lamps of celestial ether burning bright?
   Suns lighting systems with their joyous beams?
But Thou to these art as the noon to night.

"Yes! as a drop of water in the sea,
    All this magnificence in Thee is lost;
What are ten thousand worlds compared to Thee?
    And what am I, then?—Heaven's unnumbered host
Though multiplied by myriads, and arrayed
    In all the glory of sublimest thought,
Is but an atom in the balance weighed
    Against thy greatness—is a cipher brought
    Against infinity! O what am I, then?—Naught.

"Naught! But the effluence of thy light divine,
    Pervading worlds, hath reached my bosom, too;
Yes! in my spirit doth thy Spirit shine,
    As shines the sunbeam in a drop of dew.
Naught!—but I live, and on hope's pinions fly
    Eager towards thy presence; for in Thee
I live, and breathe, and dwell; aspiring high,
    Even to the throne of thy divinity.
    I am, O God, and surely Thou must be!

"Thou art! directing, guiding all. Thou art!
    Direct my understanding, then, to Thee;
Control my spirit, guide my wandering heart;
    Though but an atom 'mid immensity,
Still I am something fashioned by thy hand;
    I hold a middle rank 'twixt heaven and earth,
On the last verge of mortal being stand,
    Close to the realms where angels have their birth;
Just on the boundary of the spirit-land!

"The chain of being is complete in me;
    In me is matter's last gradation lost;
And the next step is spirit—Deity!
    I can command the lightning, and am dust!
A monarch, and a slave! a worm, a god!

Whence came I here, and how? so marvellously
Constructed and conceived! Unknown! This clod
   Lives surely through some higher energy!
   For from itself alone it could not be!

"Creator, yes! thy wisdom and thy word
   Created me! Thou Source of life and good!
Thou Spirit of my spirit, and my Lord!
   Thy light, thy love, in their bright plenitude,
Filled me with an immortal soul, to spring
   O'er the abyss of death, and bade it wear
The garments of eternal day, and wing
   Its heavenly flight beyond this little sphere,
   Even to its source—to Thee—its Author, there.

"O, thoughts ineffable! O vision blest!
   Though worthless our conceptions all of Thee,
Yet shall thy shadowed image fill our breast,
   And waft its homage to thy Deity.
God! thus alone my lowly thoughts can soar;
   Thus seek thy presence, Being wise and good!
'Midst thy vast work admire, obey, adore!
And, when the tongue is eloquent no more,
   The soul shall speak in tears of gratitude."
                    —Gavriil Romanavich Derzhavin

Apache Prayer

Stenatlihan is the supreme sky goddess of the Apache Indians of the
Southwestern United States.

Stenatlihan, You are good!
I pray for a long life.
I pray for your good looks.

I pray for good breath.
I pray for good speech.
I pray for feet like yours to carry me through
    a long life.
I pray for a life like yours.
I walk with people, ahead of me all is well.
I pray for people to smile as long as I live.
I pray to live long.
I pray, I say, for a long life to live with you
    where the good people are.
I live in poverty.
I wish the people there to speak of goodness and to
    talk to me.
I wish you to divide your good things with me,
    as a brother.
Ahead of me is goodness, lead me on.
                  —from *Pagan Prayers*

Hymn to the All-Mother

This Mexican goddess is Teteo-Inan, the "Mother of Gods," also known
by another name meaning "Heart of the Earth." Her chief temple was
on the spot where the "Lady of Guadalupe" made her appearance, and
the native shrine was torn down.

Hail to our Mother who makes the yellow flowers to bloom—
who scatters the seeds of the maguey as she comes from the
Land Divine!

Hail to our Mother who casts forth white flowers in abundance!

Hail to our Mother who shines in the thorn bush as a bright
butterfly!

Ho! She is our Mother—the woman god of the earth. In the desert she feeds the wild beasts, and gives them to live.

Thus—thus you see her ever abundant gifts to all flesh.

And as you see the goddess of earth give to the beasts, so also she is giving to the green herbs and the fishes.

Hail to our Mother who casts forth yellow flowers to the sun from the Land Divine!

—from *Pagan Prayers*

Prayer of the Sower

This prayer by a Finnish farmer dates back hundreds of years.

Blessing to the seed I scatter,
Where it falls upon the meadow,
By the grace of Ukko mighty,
Through the open finger spaces
Of the hand that all things fashioned.
Queen of meadow-land and pasture!
Bid the earth unlock her treasures.
Bid the soil the young seed nourish,
Never shall their teeming forces
Never shall their strength prolific
Fail to nourish and sustain us
If the Daughters of Creation,
They, the free and bounteous givers
Still extend their gracious favor
Offer still their strong protection.
Rise, O Earth! from out thy slumbers
Bid the soil unlock her treasures!

—from *Pagan Prayers*

For the Rising of the Nile

This Egyptian prayer is from the Coptic Liturgy of St. Mark, where it is part of the service of the Mass.

Vouchsafe, O Lord, to bless the waters of the river; bring them up after their due measure, according to thy grace. Gladden the face of the earth; may her furrows be watered, her fruits multiplied; prepare it for seed and for harvest; provide for our life as may be most expedient according to thy holy and blessed will. Bless the crown of the year with thy goodness for the sake of the poor of the people, for the sake of the widow and the orphan and the stranger and the sojourner and for the sake of us all who hope in thee and supplicate thy holy name; for the eyes of all wait upon thee, O Lord, for thou givest them their meat in due season. Deal with us after thy goodness, who givest food to all flesh; fill our hearts with joy and gladness that we also always having sufficiency in all things may abound in every good work. Vouchsafe, O Lord, to bless the fulness of the rivers of water; bring them up. *Amen.*

—from *The World at One in Prayer*

To the Good and Great Doctor

Bolumbu Sala, from Africa's Belgian Congo, can neither read nor write, but her prayer reveals her keen spiritual awareness.

O great and good Father whose home is above, we who have our home here below praise thee and pray to thee. The birds and fowl lifted their voices in adoration to thee and announced to us who slept as dead people thy gift of a new day, and we would not be behind them in praising thee for light and life on this thy day.

As a new mother cares for her babe, wash thou us and cleanse us for we have desire to paint ourselves with the things of the world. Make us clean and becoming in thy sight.

As our white teacher leads us here and there over plain and hill, through forest and swamp, go thou before and fix the path; free it from stumbling things, thorns, stinging insects and snakes. Bring us at last safely to our home at Ntondo and to a happy reunion with our friends.

The word sown in each country, they have but sown it. You, our Father, water it and bring it to full fruition. Open the eyes of our hearts that we may know thy will. Open our ears and hearts to hear whatsoever word shall be spoken in this place today.

You who are the good and great Doctor, heal the many sick in their houses. We have a sickness of sin. Thou Healer of sins, heal us. Forgive us for all our sins and mistakes. Throw them all into the pit of forgetting, because we pray in the name of Jesus Christ, our Saviour, thy Son. *Amen.*

—Bolumbu Sala, from *The World at One in Prayer*

Traditional Irish Prayer

Three things are of the Evil One:
>   An evil eye;
>   An evil tongue;
>   An evil mind.

Three things are of God, and these three are
what Mary told to her Son, for she heard them in Heaven:
>   The merciful word,
>   The singing word,
>   And the good word.

May the power of these three holy things be on all men and women of Erin for evermore, *Amen.*

Abraham's Prayer

Mohammedans deem Abraham ancestor, through Ishmael, of the Arabs. They, like the Hebrews of the Bible, use his titles, Father of the Faithful and Friend of God.

My Lord! Make this a region of security and bestow upon its people fruits, such of them as believe in Allah and the Last Day....

And when Abraham and Ishmael were raising the foundations of the House (Abraham prayed): Our Lord! Accept from us (this duty). Lo! Thou, only Thou, art the Hearer, the Knower.

Our Lord! And make us submissive unto Thee, and show us our ways of worship, and relent toward us. Lo! Thou, only Thou, art the Hearer, the Knower.

Our Lord! And make us submissive unto Thee and of our seed a nation submissive unto Thee, and show us our ways of worship, and relent toward us. Lo! Thou, only Thou, art the Relenting, the Merciful.

Our Lord! And raise up in their midst a messenger from among them who shall recite unto them Thy revelations, and shall instruct them in the Scripture and in wisdom and shall make them grow. Lo! Thou, only Thou, art the Mighty, Wise.

—from *The Koran*

Peruvian Hymn to the Unknown God

O Ruler! Lord of the universe,
Whether thou art male,
Whether thou art female,
Lord of reproduction
Wherever thou mayest be!

O Lord of divination
Where art thou?
Thou mayest be above,
Thou mayest be below,
Or perhaps around
Thy splendid throne and sceptre.
O hear me!
From the sky above,
In which thou mayest be.
Creator of the world,
Maker of all men;
Lord of all Lords
My eyes fail me for longing to see thee
For the sole desire to know thee.

O Look down upon me
For thou knowest me.
The sun—the moon—
The day—the night—
Spring—winter,
Are not ordained in vain
By thee, O Deity!
They all travel
To the assigned place;
They all arrive
At their destined ends
Whithersoever thou pleasest.
Thy royal sceptre
Thou holdest.
O hear me!
O choose me!
Let it not be
That I should tire,
That I should die!
                    —from *Pagan Prayers*

Praise Be to God

Mahomet or Mohammed, the Prophet of Islam and founder of Moham-
medanism, is one of the great figures of history. He was born in 570 and
at forty felt himself selected by God to be a prophet of true religion. His
revelations are recorded in *The Koran,* which is the Bible of Islam. The
following prayers represent a large part of the peoples of the Middle
East.

Praise be to God, the Lord of all creatures, the most merciful. Thee do we worship, and of Thee do we beg assistance.
Direct us in the right way, in the way of those to whom Thou
hast been gracious, and not of those who go astray.

—from *The Koran*

Mohammedan Call to Prayer

God is great! God is great! There is no God but God. Mahomet is the apostle of God. Come to prayers! Come to prayers!
God is great! God is great! There is no God but God.

—from *Life of Mahomet* (Irving)

Prayer of Mohammed

God! There is no God but He, the living, the ever living; he
sleepeth not, neither doth he slumber. To him belongeth the
heavens, and the earth, and all that they contain. Who shall intercede with him unless by his permission? He knoweth the
past and the future, but no one can comprehend anything of
his knowledge but that which he revealeth. His sway extendeth
over the heavens and the earth, and to sustain them both is
no burden to him. He is the High, the Mighty!

—from *Life of Mahomet* (Irving)

The Prayer of Abraham

"The Prayer of Abraham," according to Moslem tradition, was uttered by the patriarch Abraham from the top of the Hill of Kubeis near Mecca when he preached the true faith to the whole human race.

Here am I in Thy service, O God! Here am I in Thy service! Thou hast no companion. To Thee alone belongeth worship. From Thee cometh all good. Thine alone is the kingdom. There is none to share it with Thee.

—from *Life of Mahomet* (Irving)

The Sea of Thy Love

This prayer from Syria is quoted from Bright's translation of the Syrian Clementine Liturgy.

O God, who art the unsearchable abyss of peace, the ineffable sea of love, the fountain of blessings and the bestower of affection, who sendest peace to those that receive it; open to us this day the sea of thy love, and water us with plenteous streams from the riches of thy grace and from the most sweet springs of thy benignity. Make us children of quietness and heirs of peace. Enkindle in us the fire of thy love; sow in us thy fear; strengthen our weakness by thy power; bind us closely to thee and to each other in one firm and indissoluble bond of unity. *Amen.*

—from the *Clementine Liturgy*

PRAYERS FOR
SPECIAL INTENTIONS

Most of us *need guidance when we are hurt. At those times we ask beseechingly and repeatedly. Perhaps all too often God hears a cry from a man or woman or child who couples his adoration with an itemized plea.*

Archbishop Fénelon is one of the few whose personal prayer is almost entirely selfless. His diocese was in Cambrai, France, and he wrote a prayer called "Teach Me" sometime around the year 1710.

Lord, I know not what I ought to ask of Thee; Thou only knowest what I need; Thou lovest me better than I know how to love myself. . . . Smite or heal; depress me or raise me up; I adore all Thy purposes without knowing them.

It is an exquisite sentiment. Still, God admonished man to ask and he shall receive. This means, as I see it, that the petitioner should be specific in his prayers. He must ask for the home, or the job, or the health that he feels he needs.

Some whose prayers are not answered affirmatively feel that

*God has not listened. This, as any cleric of any church can
explain, is wrong. God listens to all pleas, and, being omnipotent, He is able to listen to millions of prayers in a day and to
heed all of them. He grants those which He is disposed to grant.*

*A most tragic situation is to hear a mother praying for the
recovery of a sick child and to know the child will die. It almost never occurs to the grief-stricken mother that God, in His
infinite wisdom, sees deeper, more protracted pain ahead for
the child if he is permitted to live.*

*Or it may be that He desires, for His own reasons, to bring
that particular child closer to Himself.*

A Prayer of Dedication

Dwight Lyman Moody, author of this prayer, was born in Northfield,
Massachusetts, in 1837 and died in 1899. Successful in business in Chicago, he turned to evangelism and, together with Ira D. Sankey, toured
the United States and Britain. He founded the Moody Bible Institute in
Chicago and the Northfield Seminary for Girls in Northfield, Massachusetts, as well as the Mount Hermon School for Boys.

Use me then, my savior, for whatever purpose, and in whatever way, Thou mayest require. Here is my poor heart, an
empty vessel; fill it with Thy grace. Here is my sinful and troubled soul; quicken it and refresh it with Thy love. Take my
heart for Thine abode; my mouth to spread abroad the glory
of Thy name; my love and all my powers for the advancement
of Thy believing people; and never suffer the steadfastness and
confidence of my faith to abate—so that at all times I may be
enabled from the heart to say, "Jesus needs me, and I Him."

—Dwight Lyman Moody

To Be Brought Near to God

Phillips Brooks (1835–1893) was born in Boston and educated at Harvard and in the theological seminary at Alexandria, Virginia. After a memorable ministry at Trinity Church in Boston he was consecrated Bishop of Massachusetts in 1891. He was the author of the Christmas hymn "O Little Town of Bethlehem."

O Lord, by all thy dealings with us, whether of joy or pain, of light or darkness, let us be brought to thee. Let us value no treatment of thy grace simply because it makes us happy or because it makes us sad, because it gives us or denies us what we want; but may all that thou sendest us bring us to thee; that knowing thy perfectness we may be sure in every disappointment that thou art still loving us, and in every darkness that thou art still enlightening us, and in every enforced idleness thou art still using us; yea, in every death thou art giving us life, as in his death thou didst give life to thy Son, our Saviour Jesus Christ. *Amen.*

—Phillips Brooks

The Cross the Inspiration

Samuel McComb was born in Londonderry, Ireland, in 1864. He began his professional life as a Presbyterian clergyman and came to America, where he became canon of the Cathedral of the Incarnation in Baltimore in 1916. He is the author of a number of important religious books, including *Religion and Medicine* and *The Making of the English Bible,* as well as books on prayer.

O God, our Refuge and our Strength! Thou art so high that the very Heaven of Heavens cannot contain Thee, yet dost Thou dwell with him that is of a contrite and humble spirit. Thou livest in eternity, we are the creatures of a moment. Yet Thou hast committed to us the solemn tasks of love and duty.

Though we fail and forget, Thou remainest faithful. Thou dost
not despair when Thou findest us degraded and miserable in
our sin, but bringest us forgiveness and hope. We are overwhelmed, O Lord, with wonder, to think that Thou dost believe in us, and wilt not let us go. From the pleasures of sin,
from the torment of guilt, from poverty and blighted hopes and
ill-requited love, we turn to Thee, our Father, for comfort and
satisfaction. Make clear to us how the evils of the soul war
against our happiness and health, how we are so fearfully
and wonderfully made that not a wrong thought, or base desire, or strained emotion, but leaves its mark upon our bodies.
Take possession of us, and so inspire us with great thoughts
and noble aspirations and unselfish feelings, that our bodies
may become fit temples for the habitation of Thy good Spirit.
So occupy us with self-forgetting service for Thee that no
time or strength may remain for our besetting sins. Lay upon
us the burdens of the weak, the crosses of other lives. Are any
sick? Let us bring to them help and good cheer, and, if it may
be, some gift of healing. Are there any naked and hungry? Let
us clothe and feed them. Are there any sad and depressed?
Give to us the insight and sympathy, in the presence of which
the burdened heart will be eased and the darkened mind il-
lumined. Are there any remorseful and despairing? Speak to
them through us, as Thy messengers, and say, "I am thy salvation." Thus may the fires of a Christlike charity burn with a
steady flame within us, and thus may our souls be kept pure
and fresh and strong. O true and holy Light, that lightenest
every man, shine into these hearts of ours that we may hold
converse with the sinful, yet contract no stain; that we may
share the pleasures and mingle in the noise and dust of life, yet
keep our garments unspotted from the world. Forgive us that
we have sinned so often against those around us, by failing to
draw near to them and to understand them, by want of pity
for their trials and sorrows, by passing on our heedless way,
with no ear for the still, sad voices of weary and laden souls.
Henceforth let us be at one with the mind that was in Christ

Jesus, who came not to be ministered unto, but to minister, and to give His life a ransom for many. Let the glory of His Cross be the inspiration of all our thought and service, that suffering with him here, we may reign with Him hereafter.

Hear us and answer us, for His sake. *Amen.*

—Samuel McComb, from *A Book of Prayers*

The Higher Good

Theodore Parker (1810–1860), American Unitarian clergyman and transcendentalist, was the son of a New England farmer and was educated at Harvard. He agitated against war and slavery and was the author of a number of books.

Father, I will not ask for wealth or fame,
Though once they would have joyed my carnal sense;
I shudder not to bear a hated name,
Wanting all wealth, myself my sole defence,
But give me, Lord, eyes to behold the truth,
A seeing sense that knows the eternal right;
A heart with pity filled and gentlest ruth;
A manly faith that makes all darkness light;
Give me the power to labor for mankind;
Make me the mouth of such as cannot speak;
Eyes let me be to groping men, and blind;
A conscience to the base; and to the weak
Let me be hands and feet; and to the foolish, mind;
And lead still further on such as thy kingdom seek.

—Theodore Parker

Teach Me

François Fénelon (1651–1715) was a French prelate, orator, and author. He was Archbishop of Cambrai and the author of searching tender prayers, of which the following is an example.

Lord, I know not what I ought to ask of Thee; Thou only knowest what I need; Thou lovest me better than I know how to love myself. O Father; give to Thy child that which he himself knows not how how to ask. I dare not ask either for crosses or consolations; I simply present myself before Thee, I open my heart to Thee. Behold my needs which I know not myself; see and do according to Thy tender mercy. Smite or heal; depress me, or raise me up; I adore all Thy purposes without knowing them; I am silent; I offer myself in sacrifice; I yield myself to Thee; I would have no other desire than to accomplish Thy will. Teach me to pray. Pray Thyself in me.

—François Fénelon

That Our Lives May Be an Inspiration

Lord, these things we would do: suceed, live well, laugh often, love much, gain the respect of intelligent men, and the love of little children, and leave the world a bit better than we found it. May we never lack appreciation of the beauty about us or fail to express it; and always to look for the best in others, and give to others the best we have in us: that thus, in some sense, our lives may be an inspiration and our memory a benediction. *Amen.*

—James Martineau
See biographical note on page 163.

O God, Animate Us to Cheerfulness

William Ellery Channing (1780–1842), American transcendentalist, was born in Newport, Rhode Island, and educated at Harvard. He was ordained minister of the Federal Street Congregational Church in Boston at the age of twenty-three and served until his death. He was a lucid writer as well as a great preacher and exercised a great influence on Emerson, Holmes, and Bryant.

O GOD, animate us to cheerfulness. May we have a joyful sense of our blessings, learn to look on the bright circumstances of our lot, and maintain a perpetual contentedness under Thy allotments. Fortify our minds against disappointment and calamity. Preserve us from despondency, from yielding to dejection. Teach us that no evil is intolerable but a guilty conscience, and that nothing can hurt us, if, with true loyalty of affection, we keep Thy commandments and take refuge in Thee; through Jesus Christ our Lord. *Amen.*

—William Ellery Channing

God Give Me Strength

Sir Rabindranath Tagore (1861–1941) was born in Calcutta of a wealthy Indian family. He studied law in England but soon abandoned it for a life of writing, teaching, and working in the Indian nationalist movement. He was a prolific author, and in 1913 was awarded the Nobel Prize for Literature.

This is my prayer to Thee, my lord—strike, strike at the root of penury in my heart.
Give me the strength lightly to bear my joys and sorrows.
Give me the strength to make my love fruitful in service.
Give me the strength to raise my mind high above daily trifles.
And give me the strength to surrender my strength to Thy will with love.   —Sir Rabindranath Tagore, from *Gitanjali*

For Purity and Inward Help

Walter Rauschenbusch (1861–1918) was born in Rochester, New York, and was ordained in the Baptist ministry in 1886. He was an influential leader in the social interpretation of Christianity and wrote a number of important books on this subject which have been widely translated. This prayer is from his famous book *Prayers of the Social Awakening*.

O Thou whose light is about me and within me and to whom all things are present, help me this day to keep my life pure in Thy sight. Suffer me not by any lawless act of mine to befoul any innocent life or add to the shame and hopelessness of any erring one that struggles faintly against sin. Grant me a steadfast scorn for pleasure bought by human degradation. May no reckless word or wanton look from me kindle the slow fires of wayward passion that will char and consume the divine beauties of any soul. Give me grace to watch over the imaginations of my heart, lest in the unknown hour of my weakness my secret thoughts leap into action and my honor be turned into shame. If any dear heart has staked its life and hopes on my love and loyalty, I beseech Thee that its joy and strength may never wither through my forgetfulness or guilt. O God, make me pure and a helper to the weak. Grant that even the sins of my past may yield me added wisdom and tenderness to help those who are tempted. Through Christ our Lord. *Amen.*

—Walter Rauschenbusch

Builders of Thy Spiritual Temple

Grant, Almighty God, that as we must carry on a wafare in this world, and as it is thy will to try us with many contests,—O grant that we may never faint, however extreme may be the trials which we may have to endure; and as thou hast favored us with so great an honor as to make us framers and builders of thy spiritual temple, may every one of us present and consecrate himself wholly to thee; and inasmuch as each of us has received some peculiar gift, may we strive to employ it in building this temple, so that thou mayest be worshiped among us perpetually; and especially may each of us offer himself wholly as a spiritual sacrifice to thee, until we shall at length be renewed in thine image, and be received into a full participation of that glory which has been attained for us by the blood of thine only begotten Son. *Amen.*

—John Calvin, from *Prayers and Devotions*
See biographical note on page 171.

For Fulfilment of God's Purpose

John S. Hoyland was born in England in 1887. He spent many years in India teaching and lecturing and is the author of many books. He was greatly influenced by Rabindranath Tagore in his devotional writing.

Master divine,
We bring to thee the tasks of this day—
Above all, the great task of being the men thou
wouldst have us to be,
Of fulfilling thy ambitions for us.

Grant into us a zeal to work with thee,
To co-operate in thy purpose for our lives.

We know that, for each one of us,
Thou hast a great and glorious future in store
If only we will permit thee freedom
To work out that future in us.

Help us therefore to give thee full scope in our lives,
That in serving thee and in serving our fellow men,
We may fulfill thy ambitions for us.

—J. S. Hoyland

For the Transforming of Everyday Life

Father, in these quiet moments we have caught a glimpse of Thy glory. Inspire us, our Father, to carry into the everyday-ness of our lives all to which we aspire at such a moment as this. May our faith have feet and hands, a voice and a heart, that it may minister to others, that the gospel we profess may shine in our faces and be seen in our lives.

May we return to face the grind of the monotonous and the humdrum routine of duty with a new vision. Wilt Thou transform for us our common tasks and glorify them with a new light, that we may this week apply ourselves to them with fidelity and devotion.

Bless the homemakers, the mothers, and the servants who minister in the home, who maintain the sanctuaries to which tired men return.

Bless that noble company in white, the doctors and nurses. May their ministrations interpret the love and the pity of God.

Bless the teachers, often unheralded and unappreciated.

Bless all who are responsible for our transportation, who move us across this lovely land; all who in silence, and sometimes in darkness, toil while others sleep, that we may enjoy life and enjoy it more abundantly.

May Thy blessing rest upon all men who minister to their fellows. May each of us in our daily round come to know the joy of partnership with Thee, our Father in Heaven. In the name of Him who came "not to be ministered unto but to minister," we join these, our prayers. *Amen.*

—Peter Marshall, from *The Prayers of Peter Marshall*

See biographical note on page 117.

Confidence in God

George Dawson (1821–1876) was born in London and in 1843 became pastor of a Baptist chapel, although he declined ordination. He became one of the most famous preachers and lecturers of his day and took an active part in English and foreign politics. He championed the cause of Polish freedom and was the friend of Mazzini, Kossuth, and other Polish exiles.

Almighty God, Lord of the storm and of the calm, the vexed sea and quiet haven, of day and night, of life and of death; grant unto us so to have our hearts stayed upon Thy faithfulness, Thine unchangingness and love, that, whatsoever betide us, however black the cloud or dark the night, with quiet faith trusting in Thee with untroubled eye, and walking in lowliness towards Thee, and in lovingness towards one another, abide all storms and troubles of this mortal life, beseeching Thee that they may turn to the soul's true good; we ask it for Thy mercy's sake, shown in Jesus Christ our Lord. *Amen.*

—George Dawson

For Forgiveness

O Thou who art of purer eyes than to behold iniquity, canst Thou bear to look on us conscious of our great transgression? Yet hide not Thy face from us, for in Thy light alone shall we see light.

Forgive us for the sins which crowd into the mind as we realize Thy presence; our ungovernable tempers, our shuffling insincerities, the craven fear of our hearts, the pettiness of our spirits, the foul lusts and fatal leanings of our souls. Not for pardon only, but for cleansing, Lord, we pray.

Forgive us, we beseech Thee, our unconscious sins; things which must be awful to thy sight, of which we yet know nothing. Forgive by giving us in fuller measure the awakening of Thy presence, that we may know ourselves, and lose all love of sin in the knowledge of what Thou art.

Forgive us for the things for which we can never forgive ourselves; those sad turned pages of our life which some chance wind of memory blows back again with shame; for the moment of cruel passion, the hour beyond recall, the word that went forth to poison and defame, the carelessness that lost our opportunity, the unheeded fading of bright ideals.

Forgive us for the things that others can never forgive; the idle tale, the cruel wrong, the uncharitable condemnation, the unfair judgment, the careless criticism, the irresponsible conduct.

Forgive us for the sins of our holy things; that we have turned the sacred page without a sigh, read the confessions of holy men and women and never joined therein, lived in Thy light and never prayed to be forgiven or rendered Thee thanksgiving; professed to believe in Thee and love Thee, yet dared to injure and hate.

Naught save being born again, nothing but a miracle of grace, can ever be to us forgiveness. Cleanse our hearts, renew our minds, and take not Thy Holy Spirit from us. *Amen.*

—William E. Orchard, from *The Temple*
See biographical note on page 127.

For Christ-Imitation

Johann Arndt (1555–1621) was a German Lutheran theologian and religious writer who contributed much to the spiritual literature of Lutheranism. His *True Christianity*, published in 1609, is a classic of Protestant writing.

O Thou blessed, friendly love-worthy Lord Jesus Christ, thou meek, humble, obedient heart, what a loving and virtuous example of holy living hast thou bequeathed to us so that we should walk in thy footsteps. Thou art an unsullied mirror of all virtue, a perfected example of holiness, a blameless rule of piety, a perfect rule of righteousness. How unlike my sinful life is unto thy holy life! I should live in thee as a new creation, but I live more in the old Adam than in thee, my dear Lord, Jesus Christ! I should live in the Spirit, but I live in the flesh! O thou friendly, patient, long-suffering heart, forgive my sin, cover up my offences, ignore my misdeeds. Close thy holy and tender eyes from my impurity, cast me not from thy countenance, and put me not out of thy house! Purge from my heart all pride, the devilish weed, and plant in me thy humility, the root of all virtue. Cast down all vanity and grant me thy noble meekness. O thou great ornament of all virtue, adorn my heart with pure faith, fervent love, living hope, and holy devotion—with childlike fear! O thou my one consolation, my love, my hope, my honor, my adornment! Thy life is nothing else than love, meekness, and humility! Therefore let such also be thy noble life within me; let thy virtuous life also be my life. Let me be one spirit, body and soul with thee so that I am in thee and thou within me. Dwell thou in me; let me live unto thee and not unto myself. Let me so confess and acknowledge thee that I walk as thou wouldst have me walk; if thou art my light, illuminate me; if thou art my life, abide in me; if thou art my glory, adorn me; if thou art my joy, gladden me; if I be thy temple, then possess me; let me be wholly thy instrument so that I am thine in body, soul and spirit. Guide me, thou eternal truth, refresh me, thou eternal life! Let me not be the evil spirit's tool; let him not work his evil lies, pride, greed, wrath, uncleanness in and through me—for this is the Satanic image from which thou dost wish to redeem me! Daily renew my body, soul, and spirit in thy image until it is perfect, so that I may enter with thee into thy glory. *Amen.*

—Johann Arndt, from *Private Devotions
for Home and Church*

The Strains of Life

Father, many among us are tired, wearied with the strains that life imposes upon us, the pressures under which we are forced to live. We remember the days that are gone and how harassed we were. We remember under what tension we have lived, and we know that Thou didst not design us to live like that. We remember the fears and anxieties that brooded over us like a fog, and we know that no child of Thine should ever be frightened by such specters.

We thank Thee, our Father, for a moment like this, when we may forget the sounds that have beat upon our eardrums with relentless monotony. We thank Thee for a moment in which we can no longer hear the chattering of typewriters, the jingling of bells, the jangling of money on counters, the whining of cash registers, the ringing of telephones, the noise of traffic.

And now, we forget these—and think only of Thee. Make within our hearts a quiet place. We release to Thee our demand to see what the future holds. We rest in Thee, content to know only Thy love and care in this present hour.

We release to Thee our struggle to cram too many activities and accomplishments into every hour. We rest in the knowledge that all of eternity, an infinitude of time, is Thy great gift to us.

We release to Thee the greed and overambition that has made us try to grasp too much of life too quickly. Help us to be content with simple tasks directed by Thee, done heartily and joyously as unto the Lord.

We release to Thee our impatience with other people and with circumstances. We ask Thee for the grace of patience and for the ability to relax when we must wait.

And now as we go back into the thick of life, may a quiet heart and mind attend us, to make straight our path, to open all doors ahead of us, to smooth the way in every human relationship. In Thy name, who art ever the Prince of Peace. *Amen.*

—Peter Marshall, *The Prayers of Peter Marshall*
See biographical note on page 117.

Hope of the Hopeless

Bishop Lancelot Andrewes (1555–1626) was one of the most learned men of his time and was among the first to be selected to make a new version of the Bible. He was royal chaplain to Elizabeth, James I, and Charles I, being the theologian of the High Church Party of the seventeenth century.

We beseech Thee, O Lord, remember all for good; have mercy upon all, O God. Remember every soul who, being in any trouble, stands in need of Thy mercy and help; all who are in need or distress; all who love or hate us.

Thou, O Lord, art the Helper of the helpless, the Hope of the hopeless, the Saviour of them who are tossed with tempests, the Haven of them who sail. Be Thou All to all . . . prosper Thou the work of our hands upon us; Oh, prosper Thou our handy-work.

Lord, be Thou within me, to strengthen me;

Without me, to keep me;

Above me, to protect me;

Beneath me, to uphold me;

Before me, to direct me;

Behind me, to keep me from straying;

Round about me, to defend me.

Blessed be Thou, O Lord, our Father, for ever and ever.

—Bishop Lancelot Andrewes

For Strength in Solitude

Francis Greenwood Peabody (1847–1936), American Unitarian theologian, was born in Boston, Massachusetts, and was pastor of the First Parish Church in Cambridge for many years. He taught at Harvard and was professor of theology and of Christian morals. He wrote numerous books, including *The Social Teaching of Jesus Christ*.

Our prayer is for those who by reason of hard experience find themselves in spiritual solitude, of mind or heart or will;

for the explorers of the truth, whose way leads them apart
from their fellows into the solitude of research; for the dreamers
of a better world, whose hope seems frustrated by selfish ambitions and sordid indifference, and who are tempted to cry, with
the ancient prophet: I, even I only, am a prophet of God; but
the prophets of Baal are four hundred and fifty men; and for
the bereaved and forsaken in the solitude of their sorrow, crav-
ing the solace of beloved companionship, but called to bear
their crosses alone.

Sustain such isolated souls by a strength which is not their
own, but which is drawn from the infinite resources of the
Eternal Will. Disclose to the truth-seeker some glimpse of
the light, to direct and reassure his solitary way. Reenforce
the hope of a better world by the vision of that divine event
towards which the whole creation moves. Comfort the uncom-
panioned heart by sanctifying memories and confident hopes,
that as these lonely lives recall the self-surrender of Jesus
Christ, his strength attained in solitude may not seem a vision-
ary dream, and his majestic words may find an echo in their
hearts: Behold, the hour cometh, yea, is now come, that ye
shall be scattered every man to his own, and shall leave Me
alone: and yet I am not alone, because the Father is with me.
In experiences like these, when the solitary soul must grope
its way toward the light, give the assurance of Divine companionship, that the path, even if it must be hard and steep,
may be safeguarded from despondency and despair, and the
faltering steps be steadied along their way.

And, from the abundance of Thy mercies, add the further
blessing, which is often denied to prosperous and contented
lives and is reserved for those who have felt the discipline of
solitude,—the blessing of helping other lives along their difficult and disheartening paths; that solitude may become the instrument of sympathy, and lives tempted to lose heart may be
sustained by the strength of other solitary souls. Restore the
confidence of those who must thus walk alone, as they discover

that through their own fortitude and fidelity other wayfarers upon the same dark road have found courage in their solitude and light upon their way.

—Francis Greenwood Peabody, from *Prayers*

For the Workers of the World

O God, who hatest nothing that thou hast made, carest for thy creation more than men care for their property, and lovest every soul of man more than a mother her only child; may this same care and love displace man's inhumanity and selfishness, until, in a new sense of the beauty of man's body and the eternal value of his soul, cruelty and neglect, pain and sorrow pass away.

We pray for the coming of the commonwealth where those who toil shall be honoured and rewarded, where a man's worth shall be reckoned higher than the price of things he fashions with hand or brain, where science shall serve, not destruction or private gain, but preservation and the common good.

We remember those who labor continually under the danger of death, that others may be protected, warmed and comforted. We are conscious of the sacrifice that others are called upon to make on our behalf. We remember those who are ready to lay down their lives for the preservation of our peace and the provision of our needs. May we so live that such sacrifice shall not have been in vain. May the whole community be stirred to wonder whether men need suffer as they do.

Give inspiration to those who labour at the perfecting of protective science, and who seek the redemption of the workers. Make a new tie of blood sacrifice between us all. Since thou didst, to our confusion and amazement, declare thy nature most of all in the Craftsman of Nazareth, so once again may redemption spring from the ranks of those who toil.

We do not ask to pass beyond the things of sense and time but to see in them thy presence; in the crises of our times, thy judgments; in the rising demand for righteousness, the coming of thy kingdom. *Amen.*

—William E. Orchard, from *The Temple*
See biographical note on page 127.

A Teacher's Prayer

Gabriela Mistral, Chilean poetess and Roman Catholic who was born in Vicuña in 1889, in 1945 was winner of the Nobel Prize for Literature for her poetry. She began life as a country primary-school teacher, and this prayer is an echo of those early days. Dr. John A. Mackay, who translated this prayer into English in *The Other Spanish Christ,* says that it "forms one of the choicest passages in modern Spanish literature.... A sense of vocation, a passion for even the humblest human beings, loyalty to truth, disregard for popular opinion, a life spent under the guiding eye of the Divine Friend."

Lord, Thou who didst teach, forgive me for teaching, for bearing the name of teacher which thou didst bear upon earth. Give me supreme love for my school.

Grant, Master, that my fervor may be enduring and my disappointment transient. Take from me this improper desire for justice which still disturbs me, this base suggestion of protest which rises within me when I am hurt. May I not be pained by the lack of understanding nor saddened by the forgetfulness of those whom I have taught. . . .

Make me more a mother than mothers are, that I may be able to love and defend as they do that which is not flesh of my flesh. May I succeed in making of one of my girls my perfect stanza, and in her bequeath thee my most enduring melody against the days when my lips shall sing no more. . . .

Show me the possibility of thy Gospel in my time that I may not give up the daily, hourly battle in its defense. . . .

Friend, come with me; sustain me; many a time I shall have

no one but thee at my side. When my doctrine is purer and the truth I teach more scorching, the worldly will abandon me, but thou wilt then press me against thy heart, thy heart which knew so well the meaning of loneliness and abandonment. Only in thy look shall I see the sweetest of approbation. *Amen.*
—Gabriela Mistral, from *The World at One in Prayer*

For All Mothers

O God, we offer Thee praise and benediction for the sweet ministries of motherhood in human life.

We bless Thee for our own dear mothers who built up our lives by theirs; who bore us in travail and loved us the more for the pain we gave; who nourished us at their breast and hushed us to sleep in the warm security of their arms.

We thank Thee for their tireless love, for their voiceless prayers, for the agony with which they followed us through our sins, and won us back, for the Christly power of sacrifice and redemption in mother-love.

We pray Thee to forgive us if in thoughtless selfishness we have taken their love as our due without giving the tenderness which they craved as their sole reward. And if the great treasure of a mother's love is still spared to us, may we do for her feebleness what she did for ours.
—Walter Rauschenbusch, from *Prayers of the Social Awakening*
See biographical note on page 362.

For Children

Almighty Father, we bless Thee for the children Thou hast given us, and for all the joys they have brought us. Truly children are a heritage from Thee. We would consecrate them anew to Thy service; we would train them in the knowledge and love of Thy commands. Reveal to them the glory and the beauty of life. Enable them to rise to their supreme opportunities; to cast aside all frivolity and carelessness; and to make ready body and mind for the work that awaits them. Inspire them with a spirit of truth and courage and self-control. Arm them against the temptations of their own hearts and of the world around. Let no evil passion have dominion over them. Write the law of Kindness in their hearts, that they may hate all cruelty with a perfect hatred and love all goodness and mercy with a perfect love. May the Child Christ lead them and teach them, so that as they grow in age they may grow in grace, and at the last may behold Thy face without fear or shame. Grant an answer to our prayer, through Jesus Christ. *Amen.* —Samuel McComb, from *A Book of Prayers*

See biographical note on page 357.

For Family Love

Father,

Grant unto us true family love,

That we may belong more entirely to those whom Thou hast given us,

Understanding each other, day by day, more instinctively,

Forbearing each other, day by day, more patiently,

Growing, day by day, more closely into oneness with each other.

Father,

Thou too art love:
Thou knowest the depth of pain and the height of glory

Which abide continually in love:

Make us perfect in love for these our dear ones,

As knowing that without them we can never be made perfect
in Thee.

Father,

Bring to full fruit in us Thine own nature,

That nature of humble redemptive devotion,

Which out of two responsive souls,

Can create a new heaven and a new earth,

One eternal glory of divine self-sharing.

—Anonymous

Consecration of a Home

Henry Hallam Saunderson was born in Ontario, Canada, in 1871 and
ordained a Unitarian minister in 1898, serving churches in Toronto and
in and around Boston, Massachusetts, for many years. He has been an official of the American Unitarian Association and is the author of a number of books, as well as editor of Responsive Readings of the *Methodist
Hymnal* and the Worship section of the *Pilgrim Hymnal*.

Almighty God, our Father, the refuge and home of thy children in every generation, we lift our hearts and voices in praise
and thanksgiving for the gifts of thy love and providence, for
thy fatherly care and protection, and we ask the benediction
of thy presence upon this household and thy regard for this
home. Bless this house in its foundation; may its walls stand
against storm and wind and all that walks in darkness; bless
thou this house in its sheltering roof, in its light and warmth
and cheer, in its hospitality and fellowship; bless it and this
household in bread and in store, this family with good health
of body, mind, and spirit. Here may Christ be a guest beside
its fire and at its table, and may God's peace that the world
cannot give nor take away here abide continually, for thy
love's sake in Christ. *Amen.*
        —Henry Hallam Saunderson, from *Pulpit and Parish Manual*

Child Ballad

Charles Kingsley (1819–1875), English clergyman and novelist, is best known for his novels *Westward Ho* and *Hereward the Wake,* as well as his children's book *The Water Babies.* He was one of the initiators of the Broad-Church Movement in England and started the controversy which led John Henry Newman to write his *Apologia pro vita sua.*

Jesus, He loves one and all,
Jesus, He loves children small,
Their souls are waiting round His feet,
On high, before His mercy-seat.

While He wandered here below
Children small to Him did go.
At His feet they knelt and prayed,
On their heads His hands He laid.

Came a Spirit on them then,
Better than of mighty men,
A Spirit faithful, pure and mild,
A Spirit fit for king and child.

Oh! that Spirit give to me,
Jesu, Lord, where'er I be!
—Charles Kingsley

My Example

Charles Wesley (1707–1788) was the brother of John Wesley and a famous writer of hymns as well as a Methodist preacher. Some 6,500 hymns came from his pen, many of which are still sung in Protestant churches. Among these are "Hark, the Herald Angels Sing" and "Jesus, Lover of My Soul."

Lamb of God, I look to Thee;
Thou shalt my example be;
Thou art gentle, meek, and mild;
Thou wast once a little child.

Thou didst live to God alone;
Thou didst never seek Thine own;
Thou Thyself didst never please;
God was all Thy happiness.

Loving Jesu, gentle Lamb,
In Thy gracious hands I am;
Make me, Saviour, what Thou art!
Live Thyself within my heart!

I shall then show forth Thy praise;
Serve Thee all my happy days;
Then the world shall always see
Christ, the Holy Child, in me.
                            —Charles Wesley

Bedtime Prayer

Lucy W. Peabody was born in 1861 in West Medford, Massachusetts, where she was a teacher and writer of books for children.

We thank Thee for the happy day,
For our pleasant work and play.
Now as we lie down to sleep
We ask that Thou wilt safely keep
All children round the world so wide,
Ev'ry one is near Thy side,
Thou dost see us, each and all,
And Thou wilt hear us when we call. *Amen.*
        —Lucy W. Peabody, from *Prayers for Little Children*

Prayer for Protection in Sleep

O Merciful God! Eternal Light shining in darkness. Thou Who dispellest the night of sin and all blindness of heart, since Thou hast appointed the night for rest and the day for labor, we beseech Thee grant that our bodies may rest in peace and quietness, that afterward they may be able to endure the labor they must bear. Temper our sleep that it be not disorderly, that we may remain spotless both in body and soul, yea, that even our sleep itself may be to Thy glory. Enlighten the eyes of our understanding that we may not sleep in death but always look for deliverance from this misery. Defend us against all assaults of the devil and take us into Thy holy protection. And although we have not passed this day without greatly sinning against Thee, we beseech Thee to hide our sins with Thy mercy as Thou hidest all things on earth with the darkness of the night, that we may not be cast out from Thy presence. Relieve and comfort all those who are afflicted in mind, body, or estate. Through Jesus Christ, our Lord. *Amen.*

—John Calvin
See biographical note on page 171.

Morning Prayer

In the name of God, the Father, Son, and Holy Ghost: I thank thee, my heavenly Father, through Jesus Christ, thy dear Son, that thou hast kept me this night from all harm and danger; and I pray thee that thou wouldst keep me this day also from sin and every evil, that all my doings and life may please thee. For into thy hands I commend myself, my body and soul, and all things. Let thy holy angel be with me that the wicked foe may have no power over me. *Amen.*

—Martin Luther, from *Small Catechism*
See biographical note on page 98.

For Love

Elisabeth Robinson Scovil is a Philadelphian and has written hymns as well as prayers for young people.

O God, Whose love sent Thy Son into this world to be our pattern of perfect love, grant me the best of Thy gifts, the power to win love. Fill my heart with love for others, that it may draw love to itself. Set me free from selfish cares, that I may have time and thought for others, and so deserve love by the loving service that I give to them. Grant me the kindly disposition, the graces of both mind and body, that win love. Let me not forget that self-seeking drives love away, and keep me from the jealousy that kills it. For Jesus' sake. *Amen.*

—Elisabeth Robinson Scovil, from *Prayers for Girls*

A Young Person's Prayer

John Underwood Stephens was born in Brooklyn, New York, in 1901 and was educated at Princeton. After teaching in China for several years, he returned to this country and was ordained in the Presbyterian ministry in 1929. He was active as a pastor until ill health in 1952 caused his retirement to Maine, where he devotes his time to writing.

My God and Father, who hast given *me* whatsoever *I* am and have: Hear *my* thanksgiving, and attend *my* prayer.

I thank Thee for the wonder of *my* body. Help *me* to keep *my* body clean and vigorous, in disciplined obedience to *my* mind and spirit; that it may be a fit temple for Thine indwelling.

I thank Thee for the wonder of *my* mind. Help *me* to use *my* mind for good, and not for evil; to train it according to *my* best ability; and to fill it with the highest wisdom which school and home, and Church, and diligence can furnish; that *I* may be equipped to be used of Thee, as the spirit of Christ directeth.

I thank Thee for the wonder of *my* soul, and of Thy Word in Christ, and of Thine ever present Spirit, whereby *I* know myself Thy child, and find, in time of sin, forgiveness, and, in time of aspiration, power. Help *me* never to neglect *my* soul; but rather to nurture it by living in Thy light and love, by feeding upon Jesus' mind and Spirit, by often praying, and by obeying all Christlike intuitions; that *I* may grow in the stature of Christ, and in understanding of Thy will.

I thank Thee for the wonder of Thy goodness, manifest in countless ways, O God. Strengthen *my* mind and heart to trust Thy loving-kindness, even when it shall seem that Thou hast failed *me*, and that faith is vain. Keep *me* Thine forever; *for Jesus' sake. Amen.*

    —John Underwood Stephens, from *Prayers of the Christian Life*

For Those of Middle Age

We who have reached the difficult years of middle age, when the self-confidence of youth has slackened and the serenity of old age has not arrived, pray for guidance through the problems and perplexities which now beset us. We have outgrown the expectancy and illusion of earlier years; the demands of life have become monotonous and wearisome; the poetry of experience has turned to prose; and we are threatened by tedious pleasures and irksome routine.

Summon us, we pray, by Thy call from this surrender to the temptations of middle age,—its sense of futility, its approach to dejection, its loss of joy; and lead us from the flatness of depression and self-contempt to the high places of opportunity which Thou hast reserved for those who stand between youth and age. May self-centred ambitions and passionate desires be no longer our masters; may the fever of life be calmed; may we be free to ascend to the fresher air of the True, the Beautiful, and the Good. Rescue us from the hypocrisies of social life, and from the indifference of cynicism; and let serenity and candor rule our hearts and tongues. Teach us, we pray, that loyalty to truth is obedience to Thee; that unperturbed veracity is rational worship; and through the many truths which invite our minds lead us to that truth which makes and keeps men free.

Reveal to us, also, a fresh sense of beauty in nature, in art, and in human life; and enrich our experience with the responsive and ennobling love of beautiful things and beautiful characters, the fine art of living, the beauty of holiness.

Nor can we fail to hear Thy special call to those of middle age for generous and self-effacing service. The competitions and ambitions of the world are no longer appealing. The obligations of our homes, and the self-interest of our undertakings are either satisfied or subordinated; and the right to lead, with the courage to act, displaces timidity and self-distrust. Direct us, we pray, in this search for the efficient life, by Thy wisdom from above, and teach us how to sanctify ourselves for others' sakes. Through the doing of Thy will may we learn more of Thy teaching, until at last the True and Beautiful and Good, which are the witnesses of Thy control, sustain our lives, and the Middle Ages become, not the Dark Ages, but bright with a joy and peace unattained by youth and treasured for old age.

—Francis Greenwood Peabody, from *Prayers*
See biographical note on page 369.

For Those Who Have Grown Old

Lord Jesus, bless us in the eventide of life.

We have grown old. We have lost the fire of youth and the urgency and anxiety of mid-life. And now, with so much that is treasured in the past, help us, Lord, to know beyond a shadow of doubt, that the best is yet to be.

So illumine the storehouse of memory, we pray, that as we look back we may with gratitude recall only the riches of our yesterdays, our little triumphs in Thy name, Thy great mercies toward us. For all the fellowship we have enjoyed with others and with Thee, and for all the sunshine Thy Presence has shed upon our varied path, we thank Thee, Lord. We love to remember how often the worst has turned best; how the joy of witnessing for Thee has swallowed up all reproach; how manifold have been Thy blessings; how constant has been Thy love. We have faltered, but Thy hand was there to save us from falling. We have been weak, but Thou hast been strong. We have lost sight of Thee for a little while, but Thou hast sought us day and night, following even when we tried to run away from Thee.

Lord, Lord, how great has been Thy love of us, sure it will not fail us now. Grant us light at eventide, and peace, a shining peace in our heart. We have done so little and have served so imperfectly and witnessed so timidly; but now, Lord, in Thy mercy, draw nearer than ever so that we may hear Thy still, small voice, and feel the very touch of Thy hand (nail-pierced for us) and know that it has still its ancient power.

So bless us as the shadows lengthen and the daylight fades; shine through the gloom, and not only point us to the skies, but let us lean upon Thine arm, dear Lord, and thus, with unfaltering step, walk gladly from earth's shadows into the eternal radiance of heaven. *Amen.*

—from *In This Manner Pray Ye*

In Sickness

Lord Jesus, Thou art the Lord of Lords, the King of Kings. Thou art still the ruler of this universe. Thou art its Great Architect.

In the beginning, Thou didst design every part of it—from the twinkling of the great stars to the molding of the petals of the wayside flowers; from the coloring of the heavens to the tint of the butterflies' wings, even to this body of mine which is the Temple of Thy Spirit. Hear me now as I pray for Thy healing touch.

I confess that in my desperation and my need, I have wondered about the Providence of God. Forgive, I pray, this lack of trust in His power and in His love.

I acknowledge my unworthiness to ask Thee for any good gift. Yet I ask not on any merit of mine but because of the claim purchased for me on the Cross.

Thou who didst Thyself explore all the vast treasures of pain on that Cross, bestow upon me Thy grace.

I have known Thee as the Saviour of my soul; now I would know Thee as the Saviour of my body. I would find in Thee this day the Great Physician.

I pray simply and humbly, with a deep conviction that Thou canst still heal and that Thou dost want to heal me. As I discover Thy strength in this time of weakness, may I never forget Thy mercy nor cease to give Thee thanks as health returns. In Thy lovely name, I pray. *Amen.*

—Peter Marshall, from *The Prayers of Peter Marshall*
See biographical note on page 117.

Before a Surgical Operation

Almighty God, whose love from birth enfoldeth us, and under whose protection all our days are spent: Lend unto Thy servant who shall perform this operation both wisdom and skill; bestir with a spirit of vigilance and carefulness those who shall assist him; banish from *my* mind all anxious thought;

and enable *me* with utter confidence to cast *myself* upon Thy care; that, if Thou wilt heal *me, I* may rejoice to be healed; and, if Thou wilt receive *me* into Thy nearer presence, *I* may exult to see Thy face; *through Jesus Christ our Lord. Amen.*
—John Underwood Stephens, from *Prayers of the Christian Life*
See biographical note on page 379.

For Those in Peril on the Sea

William H. Whiting (1824–1865) was born in Mississippi of New England stock. He was graduated from West Point in 1845 and fought with the Confederates in the Civil War, attaining the rank of Major General. He died of battle injuries, honored by North and South alike for his courage, courtesy, and brilliance. This prayer by William H. Whiting is sung at all formal church services of the United States Navy.

> Eternal Father! strong to save,
> Whose arm hath bound the restless wave,
> Who bidd'st the mighty ocean deep
> Its own appointed limits keep:
> O hear us when we cry to thee
> For those in peril on the sea.
>
> O Christ! whose voice the waters heard
> And hushed their raging at thy word,
> Who walkedst on the foaming deep,
> And calm amidst its rage didst sleep;
> O hear us when we cry to thee
> For those in peril on the sea!
>
> O Trinity of love and power!
> Our brethren shield in danger's hour;
> From rock and tempest, fire and foe,
> Protect them wheresoe'er they go;
> Thus evermore shall rise to thee
> Glad hymns of praise from land and sea....

Amen.   —William H. Whiting

Prisoners' Prayer

O God, we men and women in prison make our prayer to thee. We too claim thee as the Father of our spirit and the great friend of our better self.

Men have passed judgment on us by our outward acts, but thou alone knowest all things. Thou knowest how some of us were burdened by the sins of our ancestors, and some were tainted with vice in our youth before we understood, and some made a brave fight but the powers of evil were strong, and some thought they were doing right when they broke the law. We would hide nothing from thee, O thou Searcher of hearts, but we pray thee to pardon the frailties and mistakes of the past, and in the years still left to us do thou build up our lives to noble manhood and womanhood.

Give us back our freedom in due time. Protect our dear ones while we are away, and grant that soon we may once more hold them in our arms and read their love and forgiveness in their sweet faces.

Make a place for us where we can do honest and wholesome work among our fellow men. Give us strength to maintain our honor and never again to give needless sorrow to those who love us.

We pray thee for patience and hopefulness in these long and lonely days. May no unclean or hateful thoughts gain the mastery over our souls. May we be friends with all men of good will, and if any wrong us, may we have the spirit of Jesus Christ, who also was a prisoner and who prayed for those that hurt him.

May all the great world of men be filled more and more with thy saving love, so that fewer men and women may be snared in temptation and those who go wrong may be turned back to the right without the need of prisons. Grant that our own experience may in some way help others, that so our life may not be lived in vain, but may add a little to the common good and joy of mankind in the better days to come.....

Amen. —Walter Rauschenbusch, from *Prayers of the Social Awakening*

See biographical note on page 362.

In the First Hours of My Grief

This prayer is used by Jewish people for consolation in time of grief. It is a contribution peculiar to a people who have suffered as a group as well as individuals.

O God, help me to think of Thee in this bitter trial. Thou knowest how my heart is rent with grief. In my weakness, tested so severely in soul by this visitation, I cry unto Thee, Father of all life: give me fortitude to say with Thy servant Job: "The Lord hath given; the Lord hath taken away; blessed be the name of the Lord."

Forgive the thoughts of my rebellious soul. Pardon me in these first hours of my grief, if I question Thy wisdom and exercise myself in things too high for me. Grant me strength to rise above this trial, to bear with humility life's sorrows and disappointments. Be nigh unto me, O God. Bring consolation and peace to my soul.

Praised art Thou, O God, who comfortest the mourners. *Amen.*

In Adversity

Almighty God, who art full of compassion and tender mercy, hear us as we pray for those who are passing through hard times; those who have lost the health and strength that once was theirs; and those who are facing illness and suffering.

For all who are handicapped in the race of life through no fault of their own; for the defective and delicate and the permanently injured.

For those who lie in pain, for any who have to undergo operations, for the blind, the deaf and the dumb; and for all who have to watch their loved ones suffer.

For those whose livelihood is insecure, those who cannot find work, for the hungry, the homeless and the destitute.

For those who cannot bear their burdens alone, and for all those who have lost those whom they love.

For those who are in doubt or in anguish of soul, for those who are victims of depression, nerves and fear; and for those whose suffering is unrelieved by the knowledge of Thy love.

Oh, Lord, comfort all who are in trouble, sorrow, need, sickness or any other adversity, that by Thy blessing upon them and those who try to help them, they may find encouragement and peace; through Jesus Christ our Lord. *Amen.*

—from *In This Manner Pray Ye*

In Time of New Bereavement

Father, eyes blinded by the symbols of sorrow cannot see the stars. Even so, I, at this moment, can see nothing beyond my own grief.

I have been face to face with misery and loneliness in these days; with the strangeness of life and death that takes away a loved one and gives no explanation; with the mystery of a Providence I have tried to understand and cannot understand.

Thou, O Holy Spirit, Thou visitor in sorrow, Thou who art acquainted with human tears and broken hearts, sorely I need Thy help now.

Because my heart is sore, I have shut the door of my heart to my fellows, even to Thee. But I sense that withdrawal and the effort to dull my feelings is not the way toward healing. Help me now to dare to open my being wide to the balm of Thy loving Spirit, unafraid of any depth or height or intensity of overflowing emotion.

Thou hast promised to wipe away all tears from our eyes.
   I ask Thee to fulfill that promise now.

Thou hast promised to bind up our wounded spirits.
   I ask Thee to fulfill that promise now.

Thou hast promised to give us peace, not as the world
   gives but in the midst of our trouble.
   I ask Thee to fulfill that promise now.

Thou hast promised to be with us alway.
   I therefore thank Thee that Thou art walking
   beside me every step of the way.

I put my hand in Thine, and walk on into the future, knowing that it will be a good future because Thou art in it. *Amen.*
                    —Peter Marshall, from *The Prayers of Peter Marshall*
                                    See biographical note on page 117.

Thou Hearest Our Cry

Father in Heaven! Great is Thine infinite kingdom. Thou
who bearest the weight of the stars and who governest the
forces of the world through immense spaces; numberless as
the sands are those who have life and being through Thee.
And yet, Thou hearest the cry of all the creatures, and the cry
of man whom Thou hast specially formed. Thou hearest the
cry of all men without confusing their mixed voices and without distinguishing one from another in such a way as to play
favorites. Thou hearest not only the voice of one who is responsible for many others and so prays to Thee in their name,
as if his high function could bring him nearer to Thee; Thou
hearest not only the voice of one who prays for dear ones, as
if he could thereby attract Thine attention, he who is privileged

in having the dear ones; no, Thou hearest also the most miserable, the most abandoned, and most solitary man—in the desert, in the multitude. And if the forgotten one has separated himself from all others; and if in the crowd he has become unknown—having ceased to be a man except as a number on a list—Thou knowest him. Thou hast not forgotten him. Thou rememberest his name; Thou knowest him where he is, retired, hidden in the desert, unperceived in the crowd, in the multitude. And if in the thick shadows of dread, in the prey of terrible thoughts, he was abandoned by men, abandoned almost by the language men speak, still Thou wouldst not have forgotten him. Thou wouldst understand his language. Thou knowest also how quickly to find a way which leads to him, quick as sound, prompt as light; and if Thou shouldst wait it is not slowness but wisdom; and if Thou dost wait, it is not slowness, but because Thou only knowest the speed of Thy help; if Thou dost wait, it is not stingy parsimony, but paternal economy which keepest the best things reserved for the child, in a secure place, for a favorable moment. Lord our Father! Man cries to Thee in the day of distress and he gives thanks to Thee in the day of joy. Oh how wonderful to give thanks when man understands so easily that Thou art the giver of good and perfect gifts, when even the earthly heart is at once ready to understand and when even earthly prudence speedily consents. More blessed though it is to give thanks when life becomes a darkened story; more blessed though to give thanks when the heart is oppressed and the soul darkened, when reason is a traitor in its ambiguity and memory is mistaken in its forgetting, when egoism recoils in fright, when human wisdom resists, if not in rebellion then in discouragement—more blessed then to thank God, for the one who thus is thankful truly loves God. He dares to say to Thee, Thou all knowing God: Lord, Thou knowest all things, Thou knowest I love Thee.

—Søren Kierkegaard, from *The Sickness Unto Death*
See biographical note on page 123.

Cooperation among Races

Everett Ross Clinchy was born in New York in 1896 and ordained a minister in the Presbyterian Church, in 1921. He has been President of the National Conference of Christians and Jews since 1928 and recently became head of the World Interfaith Movement, to which he is devoting most of his time.

Our Father in Heaven, Creator and Sustainer of all that lives, we seek Thy presence in a world distraught, Thy love and healing in a world of enmity and hatred. Thou hast made of one blood all the peoples of mankind to dwell together as a family upon the face of the earth. We come to Thee for strength to break down the barriers that hold men apart, and to fashion unity amidst the diversity of creed and race and nation. Make us conscious of our common humanity. May those who are strong withhold no opportunity from the weak, those who are powerful keep none in subjection. Make us quick to recognize the talents of those of other races than our own and to give to all the honor that is their due. Forbid that we should belie the faith we proclaim that all men are equal by denying to those of other religious convictions and racial ties the rights which we claim for ourselves. Crown all our good with brotherhood. To Thee be the honor and the glory.

And now may the search for that which is true, the love of that which is beautiful, the enjoyment of that which is just and good, possess our hearts and minds as they have ennobled and enriched the lives of the great of every age. *Amen.*

—Everett R. Clinchy, from *A Symphony of Prayer*

For Our Enemies

Henry van Dyke (1852–1933), clergyman, educator, and author, was born in Germantown, Pennsylvania, and educated at Princeton, where he later taught. He was pastor of the Brick Presbyterian Church in New York City and United States Minister to the Netherlands and Luxemburg, 1913–1916. Among his popular inspirational works is the Christmas story *The Story of the Other Wise Man.*

Thou Father of all men, revealed in him who hast commanded us not to return evil for evil but to pray for those who hate us: Enable us by his blessed example and his loving Spirit to pray sincerely for our enemies. When we have offended, forgive us and help us to find a way of reconciliation. Let not anger burn between us but deliver them and us from the power of hatred, that we may be as ready to grant forgiveness as to ask it, and grant that thy peace may rule in all our hearts, both now and evermore. *Amen.*

—Henry van Dyke, from *Presbyterian Book of Common Worship*

Social Justice

John Haynes Holmes was born in Philadelphia, Pennsylvania, in 1879 and educated at Harvard. He is pastor emeritus of the Community Church of New York. He is a founder of the National Association for the Advancement of the Colored People and of the American Civil Liberties Union.

Our Father, who art in heaven, we are Thy children on this earth. Rich and poor, black and white, Jew and Gentile, native and alien, friend and enemy—we are all alike the heirs of Thy providence and the recipients of Thy love. As Thou hast done for us, so we should do for one another. But we have been selfish and cruel, and unrighteously have sought to serve not Thy will but our own.

We confess before Thee O God, the sins of which we have

been guilty. We have corrupted government, exploited labor, oppressed women and little children, preyed upon the weak and helpless, ground the faces of the poor, done public injustice for private gain. These are our hands, stained with the evil of our deeds! Behold our hearts, impure with sordid desires for place and profit! The world, which Thou hast made so fair, we have defaced. Our country, which Thou hast so richly blessed, we have defamed. Woe be unto us, that wickedness has so prevailed among us.

But Thou art patient, O God, and strong to save. Thy righteousness is mighty upon us, and cannot fail. Thou art building Thy kingdom in the hearts of men as from the beginning of the world, and seeking our aid as fellow-laborers with Thee. So would we turn to Thee, to plead Thy forgiveness as we cleanse the dark places of our lust and pride.

Help us to strive to do justice, to love mercy, and to walk humbly with Thee the way of righteousness. We would rid this nation's life of its abominations. Throughout the world we would deliver men from inequality, indignity and oppression. We would end poverty and war, establish freedom and security, and drive fear from every heart. We would reward the labor of men's hands with prosperity, and the love of men's souls with peace. So would we bring in that commonwealth of man which shall be Thy kingdom come at last upon the earth.

In Thy name, and for Thy sake, we ask it. *Amen.*
                    —John Haynes Holmes, from *A Symphony of Prayer*

That All May Be One

O God, who hast made of one blood all the nations of mankind, so that all are children and members one of another, how is it that we are so slow to trace the family likeness, so reluctant to claim our common kinship? We pray Thee, O our God, to make all the peoples one.

We pray for the Church of Christ so broken, scattered and dismembered, that none would think we followed all one Lord and held a common faith. Purge away the vanity, intolerance, and unforgiving spirit which keep us far apart. May the seamless robe not be utterly rent, nor the body any longer broken.

We pray that since man's need is one, we all may find the one way to Thee, the one God. Forbid that in our highest things we should find fellowship impossible. May the spirit of Christ break down all barriers and answer the desire of all nations.

We pray for a union so deep and universal that it shall gather all within one fold: those who pray and those who cannot; those whose faith is firm, and those whose doubt is slow to clear. May we never be content with aught that excludes another from the fulness of Thy grace, a single soul from the welcome of Thy heart. *Amen.*

—William E. Orchard, from *The Temple*
See biographical note on page 127.

For America

Charles Wolcott Merriam was born in Rochester, New York, in 1876 and ordained a Congregational minister in 1901. He has served in many churches and was associated with Deerfield Academy for some years, also having been active in civic and church work in nearby Greenfield, Massachusetts.

O Lord, make us more worthy heritage of that Pilgrim band, self-exiled from a land of beauty and security to go out and find a better country, they knew not whither, where their souls might feel at home. We have entered into the fruitage of their labors. Thou hast vouchsafed to us, through them, broader horizons, greater power and knowledge, and kindlier creeds. But, good Lord, preserve us from deserting the rock of faith upon which they builded with devotion to duty and exaltation of the sovereignty of God, Jesus Christ himself being the chief corner-stone. Forgive us for surrendering to the temporal things which were so secondary to them. Help us to follow the gleam, to launch our Mayflower, that we may win triumphs for thee and help open new worlds of power and freedom for all mankind. *Amen.*

—Charles Wolcott Merriam, from *Church Worship Book*

For World Peace

Pope Benedict XV (1854–1922) was born near Genoa and was the successor of Pius X and predecessor of Pius XI. He was made Archbishop of Bologna in 1907 and a cardinal in 1914, two months before his election as Pope. In World War I he founded the Vatican service for prisoners of war. France and England resumed diplomatic relations with the Holy See during his pontificate.

Dismayed by the strife and jealousy which are bringing ruin to peoples and nations, we turn, O Jesus, to Thy most loving Heart as our only hope. O God of mercy, with tears we invoke Thee to end wars and the horror of war. O King of Peace, we humbly implore the peace for which we long. . . .

Inspire rulers and peoples with counsels of meekness. Heal the discords that tear nations asunder. Thou Who didst shed Thy precious blood that they may live as brothers, bring men together once more in loving harmony. To the cry of the Apostle Peter: "Save us, Lord, we perish," Thou didst answer words of mercy and didst still the raging waves. Deign now to hear our trustful prayers and give back to the world order and peace.

And do thou, O most Holy Virgin, as in other times of distress, be our help, our protection, and our safeguard. *Amen.*

—Pope Benedict XV

For All Men

George Arthur Buttrick was born in Seaham Harbour, England, in 1892 and ordained a minister in the Congregational Church in 1915. He succeeded Henry Sloane Coffin as pastor of the Madison Avenue Presbyterian Church in 1927.

Almighty God, whose voice is best heard not in earthquake or wind or fire but in the stillness of our prayers, speak now in silence; and so grant us the gift of thy Spirit that our restless spirits may find peace—and then share thy peace.

We come burdened by failure. Yet the burden proves that we are made of thee for better things. We have been sharp tongued when we should have been patient and falsely patient when we should have spoken a brave word. We have been swift to blame our world and all too slow and blind to our own faults. We have been content while the heavenly vision has faded into the light of common day. We have lived as though Christ had never lived or died or broken the bonds of death. Now we come home to thee because we are tired of ourselves. Receive us, we pray, despite all our undeserving, and cleanse us, and give us a new heart.

We come with praises on our lips. How little we can do or earn; how much thou hast given! We cannot make seedtime and harvest, or grace of simple friendship, or the prophet's word, or the coming of Christ, or the life everlasting! Yet these thou dost give, good measure, pressed down, running over! Keep us from the shabbiness of our complaints, deepen our gratitude, and teach us to live among our fellows with glad love.

We come with prayers in behalf of all men. We pray thee to guide and guard this nation and all peoples, to bless men in their toil and to sustain thy Church. We pray for the sick and for the untroubled, for friend and for foe, for strangers and for those we love. Thus praying, we claim thy promise that as our days so shall our strength be—until we reach thy shining country where beyond these voices there is peace. For we pray in Christ's name. *Amen.*

—George A. Buttrick

For the Kingdom of God

O Christ, thou hast bidden us pray for the coming of thy Father's Kingdom, in which his righteous will shall be done on earth. We have treasured thy words, but have forgotten their meaning, and thy great hope has grown dim in thy Church. We bless thee for the inspired souls of all ages who saw afar the shining city of God, and by faith left the profit of the present to follow their vision. We rejoice that today their hope is becoming the clear faith of millions. Help us, O Lord, in the courage of faith to seize what has now come so near, that the glad day of God may dawn at last. As we have mastered nature that we might gain wealth, help us now to master the social relations of mankind that we may gain justice and a world of brothers.

Make us determined to live by truth and not by lies, to found our common life on the eternal foundations of righteousness and love, and no longer to prop the tottering house of wrong by legalized cruelty and force. Help us to make the welfare of all the supreme law of our land, that so our commonwealth may be built strong and secure on the love of all its citizens. Our Master, once more we make thy faith our prayer: "Thy Kingdom come. Thy will be done on earth." *Amen.*

—Walter Rauschenbusch, from *Prayers of the Social Awakening*
See biographical note on page 362.

An Act of Thanksgiving

It would rather behoove me, O Lord,
a sinner, and impenitent, and so wholly unworthy,
to lie prostrate before Thee,
and with tears and groanings to entreat
the pardon of my sins,
than to praise Thee with polluted mouth;
yet trusting in Thine innate goodness, I will
      adore Thee;
oh, receive Thou the praises that it is in my
      heart to sing.
I praise Thee, I bless Thee, I worship Thee,
      I glorify Thee;
Thou art worthy, O Lord, to receive the
      praises and the thanks,
Whom I, a sinner, am unworthy to invoke,
and to name, and even to conceive in my heart.
Blessed art Thou, O Lord,
   Who hast created and brought me forth into
      this life,
   and hast ordered that I should be a living soul
   and not senseless matter:
   a man, not a brute; civilized, not barbarous;
   free, not a slave; legitimate, not spurious;
   of good parentage; not sprung from vile
   extraction, and as vile myself;
   endued with sense, not an idiot;
   sound in senses, not blind nor deaf;
   sound in limbs, not halt nor maimed;
   educated, not exposed;
   brought up to literature, not to a mechanical trade;
   a Christian, not a pagan;
   preserved from dangers and infamy, not
   overwhelmed thereby;
   in the days of peace, not tossed in tempestuous
      struggles;

of competent fortune, so that I need neither to
    flatter nor to borrow;
set free from many sins;
endued with the gifts of grace, in redemption
    and calling;
with the gifts of nature and fortune.
Who according to Thy great mercy, hast
    begotten us again unto a lively hope,
    by the resurrection of Jesus Christ:
    unto an inheritance incorruptible and
    undefiled, and that fadeth not away;
    reserved in heaven for us:
Who hast blessed me with all spiritual blessings
    in heavenly things in Christ;
Who comfortest me in all my tribulation,
    that as the passions of Christ abound in me,
    so also my consolation should abound
    through Christ.
To Thee, O God of my fathers, I give thanks;
    Thee I praise, who hast in some measure
    endued me with wisdom and courage;
    and hast shewed me that which I requested of
    Thee,
and hast opened my mouth:
    and hast caused me to be the work of Thine
    hands, and the price of Thy Blood;
and the image of Thy countenance, and the
    servant of Thy purchase;
and the seal of Thy Name, and the child of
    Thine adoption;
and the temple of Thy Spirit, and a
    member of Thy Church.
—Bishop Lancelot Andrewes, from *The Private Devotions*
See biographical note on page 369.

From Glory to Glory

O God, we thank Thee for the world in which Thou hast placed us, for the universe whose vastness is revealed in the blue depths of the sky, whose immensities are lit by shining stars beyond the strength of mind to follow. We thank Thee for every sacrament of beauty; for the sweetness of flowers, the solemnity of the stars, the sound of streams and swelling seas; for far-stretching lands and mighty mountains which rest and satisfy the soul, the purity of dawn which calls to holy dedication, the peace of evening, which speaks of everlasting rest. May we not fear to make this world for a little while our home, since it is Thy creation and we ourselves are part of it. Help us humbly to learn its laws and trust its mighty powers.

We thank Thee for the world within, deeper than we dare to look, higher than we care to climb; for the great kingdom of the mind and the silent spaces of the soul. Help us not to be afraid of ourselves, since we were made in Thine image, loved by Thee before the worlds began, and fashioned for Thine eternal habitation. May we be brave enough to bear the truth, strong enough to live in the light, glad to yield ourselves to Thee.

We thank Thee for that world brighter and better than all, opened for us in the broken heart of the Saviour; for the universe of love and purity in Him, for the golden sunshine of His smile, the tender grace of His forgiveness, the red renewing rain and crimson flood of His great sacrifice. May we not shrink from its searching and surpassing glory, nor, when this world fades away, fear to commit ourselves to that world which shall be out everlasting home. *Amen.*

—William E. Orchard, from *The Temple*
See biographical comment on page 127.

INDEX

401

ABOUT THE AUTHOR

Jim Bishop, author of eight books, including the two famous hour-by-hour reconstructions *The Day Christ Died* and *The Day Lincoln Was Shot*, is not only a professional writer of experience and versatility but a man of deep religious interests as well. Among his early books, *Parish Priest*, published in 1953, and *The Making of a Priest* (1954) reflected this strong interest. In his long and distinguished career in American journalism, he has been a reporter and feature writer, editor on *Collier's* magazine, executive editor on *Liberty* magazine, and the director of the literary department at the Music Corporation of America. He was also founding editor of Gold Medal Books, worked for a time as executive editor of the *Catholic Digest*, and was founding editor of the *Catholic Digest* Book Club. Mr. Bishop is now a syndicated columnist for the King Features Syndicate.